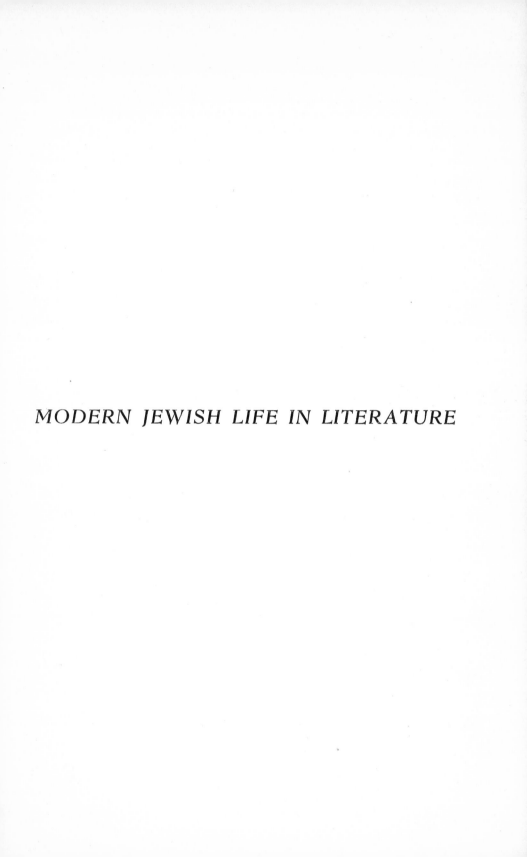

MODERN JEWISH LIFE IN LITERATURE

Modern Jewish Life

UNITED SYNAGOGUE COMMISSION

AZRIEL EISENBERG

Executive Vice-President, Jewish Education Committee of New York

In Literature

ON JEWISH EDUCATION · New York, 5712·1952

Revised Edition, 1952

PRINTED IN THE UNITED STATES OF AMERICA BY
THE STRATHMORE PRESS, NEW YORK

For My Wife

רחל

CONTENTS

PREFACE

THIS BOOK IS neither a literary anthology nor a source book in the commonly accepted meaning of these terms. It is a combination of both. It represents an earnest effort to integrate modern Jewish history with literature through the presentation of dramatic selections which are meant to give students a vivid insight into, and a warm appreciation of, the story of our people in the last fifty years. Many books, pamphlets, and periodicals were culled with a view to selecting those writings which reflect significant and varied aspects of Jewish life of the recent past and of the present. After a careful sifting, I included only those selections which tell vividly of the momentous changes and developments that have taken place in Jewish life during the past five decades—a period than which there has been none more critical since the Dispersion in 70 C.E. I have added a final section in order to stimulate and direct the thinking of the adolescent student who, in time, will be entrusted with the shaping of the community of tomorrow.

Like all anthologies, this work is, of course, subjective. Frankly, my aims were to impart to the students an emotional bias, to foster in them a deep sense of pride and identification with their people, and to strengthen their desire to carry on the tasks of this, the most momentous period of Jewish history.

From the very first page, the student reader is received and welcomed as a member of an historic people. This explains the frequent use of the personal pronoun. Throughout, I have used the term "Eretz Yisrael" (often abbreviated as "Eretz"), rather than Palestine, although the compilation of this book began long before November 29th, 1947. My reason for this usage is too obvious to belabor.

Generally speaking, only the works of our acknowledged men of letters in Hebrew, Yiddish and English (and a few in German) were included. Many of these men are comparatively new and unknown to the present generation of American Jewish youth. The study of their biographies should therefore be integrated with the study of the literary selections both as motivation and informational material. The book will thus introduce our young readers to a galaxy of some 50 men and women who have played leading roles in molding Jewish life and thought in our times.

It is my hope that our young readers will acquire a taste for Jewish literature and will form lifelong friendships with some of the authors. To satisfy the individuals whose interests have been aroused, a suggested partial bibliography of supplementary readings has been listed at the end of each section.

In order to make the book more readable, I have occasionally taken the liberty of substituting a simpler for a more difficult word. For the same reason, I have broken up long paragraphs into smaller units whenever necessary. Questions and topics for discussion have been provided so as to stimulate reflection and discussion, as well as further reading. Events, concepts and personalities outside the reader's range of knowledge are explained at the end of the book.

I am indebted to several friends and colleagues who have helped in the preparation of this work. First and foremost, I am deeply grateful to my lifelong friend and colleague, Dr. Abraham E. Millgram, Director of the United Synagogue Commission on Jewish Education, who gave very cheerfully and generously of his advice, assistance, time and effort at every stage of the work, from manuscript to printed book. My sincere thanks to the competent committee of readers, Dr. Ira Eisenstein, Dr. Jacob S. Golub, and Rabbi Jacob Kabakoff, for valuable critical suggestions. I am also indebted to my fellow educators, Rabbi Samuel Glasner and Mr. Abraham Segal, who gave me the benefit of their long experience as teachers of high school youth. Miss Freda Hauptman assisted in various phases of preparing the text. My daughter, Sora, often served as a criterion for determining the inclusion or exclusion of certain selections, while Miss Mollie Stern helped in compiling the bibliographical materials and Mr. William H. Riback read proof. Mr. and Mrs. Abraham J. Sossner extended many helpful services during the several summers when this book was taking shape. To all these friends, to the authors and publishers who granted me permission to use their copyright materials, and to many others who were of help, I am deeply obliged.

And a final word of appreciation to my wife, who read the manuscript and the proof and who coöperated in many ways to bring this work to successful completion.

Philadelphia, May 1948   AZRIEL EISENBERG

ACKNOWLEDGMENTS

THE AUTHOR AND PUBLISHER are grateful to the following authors and publishers for permission to use the selections indicated:

Adler, Mrs. Cyrus—for "The Seminary Aims to Preserve the Knowledge and Practice of Historical Judaism" by Cyrus Adler quoted in *What Is Conservative Judaism* by Theodore Friedman, n.d.

Alfred A. Knopf, Inc. — for "A Strike Meeting in the Synagogue" and "The Return Home," from *The Brothers Ashkenazi* by I. J. Singer, 1936; "Greens for *Shavuot*" by Sholom Aleichem, from *Jewish Children.*

Ark Publishing Co. — for "American Israel, a Community Such as the Prophet of the Exile Saw in His Vision," from *Past and Present* by Israel Friedlaender, 1919.

Behrman's Jewish Book House, New York — for *"Seder* Night in London" by Israel Zangwill, from *Anthology of Modern Jewish Poetry* by Philip M. Raskin, 1927; "Song to Be Sung at Dawn" and "Gift" from *Hath Not the Jew by* Abraham M. Klein, 1940; "The Jewish Community Must Enable the Jew to Experience the Reality of Jewish Fellowship," from *Judaism in Transition* by Mordecai M. Kaplan, 1941; "Credo" by Saul Tchernikhowsky, from *The Jewish Anthology* by Edmond Fleg, 1925.

Berman, Hannah—for "The Immortal Orange" by Zalman Schneour, from *Yisroel,* edited by Joseph Leftwich, 1945.

Bloch Publishing Company — for "Sabbath in Merhaviah" from *The Emek* by Jessie Sampter, 1927.

Brandeis Avukah Annual — for "The Hebrew University" by Chaim Weizmann, 1932; "Labor Alone Will Heal Us" from *On Labor* by A. D. Gordon, 1932.

Brentano's, New York — for "A Letter From America," from *A Lithuanian Village* by Leon Kobrin, 1920.

East and West Library, Oxford — for "The Jews and America" by Solomon Schechter, from *Solomon Schechter* by Norman Bentwich, 1947.

Ferber, Edna — for "Anti-Semitism in Ottumwa," from *A Peculiar Treasure* by Edna Ferber, 1939.

Fineman, Irving — for "In the Russian Army Barracks," from *Hear Ye Sons* by Irving Fineman, 1939.

Harcourt, Brace & Co. — for "I Go to *Heder*," from *Childhood in Exile* by Shmarya Levin, 1929.

Harper & Bros. — for "The Greenhorn's First Day in America," from *The Rise of David Levinsky* by Abraham Cahan, 1917; "Arthur Realizes His Mistake," from *The Island Within* by Ludwig Lewisohn, 1928; "We Alone Survived," from *Crisis and Decision* by Solomon Goldman, 1938.

Hashomer Hatzair — for "We Are Brothers" by Joseph Hayim Brenner, 1940; "A Prayer for Masadah," from *Gevurat Yisrael* by Itzhak Lamdan, n.d.

Horace Liveright — for "First Steps in the New Language," from *Aaron Traum* by Hyman and Lester Cohen, 1930.

Jewish Frontier — for "Confessions of a Survivor" by Mark Dworzecki, 1945; "Continue the Peaceful Work" by Albert Einstein, 1939; "Poems by Children in the Warsaw Ghetto," 1942; "Landing in Palestine," 1947.

Jewish Publication Society — for "The Three Who Ate," from *Yiddish Tales* by David Frishman, 1938; "Simon, the Shoemaker, First Citizen," from *Worlds That Passed* by A. S. Sachs, 1928; "Ud," "The Parachutists From Eretz Yisrael," "To the Captain of the Hannah Senesch," and "Song of the Haganah Blockade Runners," from *Blessed Is the Match* by Marie Syrkin, 1947.

Levin, Meyer — for "Fishkin Persuades Mr. Paley to Stay in the *Kibbutz*," from *Yehuda* by Meyer Levin, 1931.

Methuen and Co., London — for "Latifa," from *Palestine Caravan* by Moshe Smilansky, 1943.

Rabbinical Assembly and United Synagogue of America — for "Mourn Not!" by David Shimonowitz, and "I Live in You, in Each of You, in All of You" by Abraham Isaac Kook, from *Sabbath and Festival Prayer Book,* 1946.

The Reconstructionist — for "Shabbat" by E. Grindell, 1942; "The Letter of the Ninety-Three Maidens," 1943; "There Are Times," by Zalman Schneour, 1946; "Amos on Times Square" by Jacob J. Weinstein, 1942.

Roth, Henry — for "An East Side *Heder*," from *Call It Sleep* by Henry Roth, 1934.

Schwartz, Delmore — for "Shenandoah," from *Poetic Drama* by Alfred Kreymborg, 1941.

Schwartz, I. J. — for "Among Kentucky Neighbors," from *Kentucky* by I. J. Schwartz, 1925.

Sci-Art — for "My Son" by Morris Rosenfeld, from *The Golden Peacock* by Joseph Leftwich, 1939.

Sharon Books — for "The Power and the Charm of Eretz," from *Letters from the Desert* by Moshe Mosenson, 1945.

Silver, Abba Hillel — for poem "America."

Silverman, Morris — for "The Old Prayer Book," from *High Holiday Prayer-Book,* 1939.

Stanley Paul and Co., London — for "The Bookseller as Matchmaker," from *Fishke the Lame* by Mendele Mokher Sefarim, 1928.

The Viking Press — for "German Public School, 1920," from *No. 21 Castle Street,* by H. W. Katz, 1940; "Boycott Day in Nazi Germany, April 1, 1933," from *The Oppermans* by Lion Feuchtwanger, 1934; "A Common Responsibility," from *Henrietta Szold, Life and Letters* by Marvin Lowenthal, 1942.

Zionist Organization of America — for "Auto-Emancipation" by Leo Pinsker, 1944; "The *Matmid*" by Hayim Nahman Bialik, in *New Palestine,* 1926; "Excerpts From Diaries" by Theodor Herzl, in *New Palestine,* 1929; "The Full-Statured Jew," from *Pinsker and His Brochure* by Ahad Ha-Am, 1911; "The *Shomer*" from *Hashomer, the First Jewish Watch in Palestine* by Lotta Levensohn, 1939; "Every Jew Must Feel That He Is the Trustee of What Is Best in Jewish History," from *Brandeis on Zionism, a Collection of Addresses and Statements* by Louis D. Brandeis, 1942.

MODERN JEWISH LIFE IN LITERATURE

PART ONE

The Old World

"This book is a sort of pilgrimage among the
cities and inhabitants of a world which only
yesterday—as history goes—harbored the grandfathers and grandmothers of some millions of
American citizens. As a pilgrimage it is an act
of piety; on the other hand it is an exercise in
necromancy, or calling up of the dead. . . . For
that world is no more."

MAURICE SAMUEL

Introduction: THE OLD WORLD

LIFE IN THE "Pale" (the zone where the Jews of Russia were permitted to live) for the most part centered in and around the synagogue. The synagogue served as the *bet tefilah* (house of prayer), the *bet ha-midrash* (house of study), and the *bet ha-keneset* (house of assembly). Every day, morning and evening, it hummed with worshippers. Night and day it was filled with the chant and sing-song of the Talmudical students. It housed the young and the old. People came to it to right their wrongs. By the simple expedient of stopping the reading of the Torah until justice was done they compelled immediate action. In the synagogue, too, workers gathered to discuss the calling of a strike or the terms for its settlement.

The ideal which molded and shaped the ambitions and plans of the many was spiritual not material. To be a scholar, a learned man, was the aim of a large number of young people. Study, the cultivation of the mind, not money-making, was their primary goal. The scholar was an object of envy and emulation. He often enjoyed prestige and distinction as much as, if not more than, the man of wealth.

Most of his waking hours the child spent in *heder* or Hebrew school. In the short winter days he was cooped up within its narrow confines, not only the live-long day, but a good part of the night as well. Nevertheless, the world in which the young lived was not drab. On the contrary it was warm and rich. Fed on the fanciful tales of the Bible and the *Agadah,* the pupil's imagination rose above his surroundings. With Joseph he wandered through the tropical lands of the East. With young David he fought against the giant Goliath. With the rabbis of old he walked the streets of ancient, colorful, oriental cities.

The Sabbath and the festivals were central in the lives of adults and children. The Sabbath was a day of rest, prayer, study and social visits. It helped father and mother to forget their weekly grinding toil. Indeed, from sundown to sunset the Sabbath and festival were lived to the full. Every holiday had its special charm. Hanukah was a holiday of lights, gifts and festivity. Purim was anticipated eagerly for it was a rare day of play acting and exchange of presents. Especially memorable were the solemn days preceding the High Holy Days. They were fraught with

23

ominous significance for they prepared the Jew spiritually for the "fearful days" of penitence which culminated in *Yom Kippur.*

The world of the Jew was narrow, hemmed in, confined. Because of the lack of communication facilities, travel was infrequent. The occasional visits of preachers and emissaries from the outside world (especially from Eretz Yisrael) were hailed with great delight. Few, if any, newspapers, magazines or books (except, of course, prayer books, Talmudical and Biblical books) ever reached the Jewish town. Almost all of the available books were heavy, unattractive, without a picture to break the monotony of closely packed, unvoweled print. Books in Russian, worldly books in Yiddish, were regarded with suspicion and fear. They were prohibited because they opened dangerous new worlds to the imagination of the youth and boded ill for the authority of tradition as interpreted by the elders.

Although the life of the Jew was rich from within, externally it was oppressive and difficult. In the small towns and hamlets the Jews were petty storekeepers and itinerant peddlers. In the larger cities, many were factory workers. With rare exceptions, all were poor.

Always there lurked in the background the tyrannical government of the Czar. Military service lasting a period of four years was universal. Life in the Russian army was a veritable hell for the young Jew because of anti-semitism and the harsh treatment by the military. The cruelty of the government was alleviated only by the almost universal tendency of its officials to take bribes. "Crossing the palm" was in many cases almost a condition of earning a livelihood. No wonder that many young people joined the underground revolutionary movements to free the oppressed and the persecuted.

Living amidst rather primitive conditions and lacking the elementary facilities for sewage disposal, it was inevitable that occasional epidemics should strike the inhabitants of the town. When a fire broke out it would often spread unhindered from one straw thatched roof to another, sometimes razing an entire city. These calamities were viewed as acts of God which could be turned away by prayer, penitence and the practice of *mitzvot* (good deeds).

Suddenly into this settled and tranquil life of the villages, hamlets and townships of the Pale, there burst the exciting call of America. America, the land of limitless opportunities; the land where life was free and unbounded, where the policeman was a friend (even a Jew might be a policeman!) and where "gold covered the streets!" America meant chiefly freedom from the hated military service, from the fear of pogroms. America beckoned with its wealth and prosperity, its unbelievable wonders of water "flowing from the wall" (spigots), of "railroads

running above the roof tops." America, "land of Columbus" . . . land of
the free . . . land of wonder! . . . America spelled the doom of the Pale,
the end of its idyllic Jewish life.

But getting to America was not easy. One needed an emigration
passport which the government did not readily grant. Especially was it
difficult for those who most desired to go—the young men who faced
military duty. To get out of hated Czarist Russia one had to steal across
the border in the dead of night. Some were caught and sent back in
chains. But that did not discourage the Russian Jews from emigrating.
From 1882[1] to 1914 almost two million Jews entered the longed-for, the
blessed gates of America.

EVEN HIGHER
by I. L. Peretz

EVERY MORNING during the Days of Penitence, the *Rebbi*[2] of Nemirov would disappear. The members of his family would arise early for *Selihot*[3], go to synagogue and leave the doors open. Undoubtedly he left the house after them. But no one ever saw him, either in the street, or in the main synagogue, or in the *Bet Ha-Midrash,* or in any of the small congregations. As for his house which was left wide open, no one worried about it. Thieves would not dare trespass the *Rebbi's* home. One touch of the doorknob and the thief's hand would wither.

But where did the *Rebbi* vanish? all asked. The answer could be but one: Where else could he be but in heaven? Certainly he has many urgent matters to take care of. The High Holy Day season is here. The needs of Israel are many. Jews need to earn a living. They need peace and health. The Day of Judgment is at hand. Satan with his myriad eyes is on the alert as ever, diligently looking for sins. He looks into the heart, into the innermost recesses of the soul. He is busy enticing and seducing people to sin. And when he succeeds, he ascends immediately to high heaven and accuses them before the Supreme Judge. Who is there to plead their case if not the holy one of Nemirov? Undoubtedly he ascends in order to intercede with the Heavenly Throne on behalf of his people Israel.

One day there came a *Mitnaged*[4] to Nemirov, a *Litvak*[5] from Vilna, the Jerusalem of Lithuania, no less. He jeered at the belief of the town-folk. As is well known the strength of the Lithuanians lies in their logic. They are dry, matter-of-fact. They have no imagination, no faith in the supernatural powers of the *Rebbi.* Our *Litvak* scoffed at the townspeople and cited chapter and verse from the Talmud to prove that even Moses did not ascend to heaven proper but remained at a certain distance below. And if this was so in the case of Moses how much more so in the case of the *Rebbi* of Nemirov?

"Very well, smartie," retorted the townsmen. "Where then is the *Rebbi* during the *Selihot?*"

The Lithuanian replied drily that he had a list of more significant queries that begged for answers. Nevertheless he made up his mind to investigate and to get to the bottom of this matter.

That very day at twilight between the *Minhah* and *Maariv* services, the Lithuanian stole into the *Rebbi's* bedroom and crept under his bed. Being a *Litvak* he naturally had supreme confidence in his ability to stay awake through the long hours. To keep awake he selected some portion of the Talmud and reviewed it from memory.

An hour before the *Shamash*[6] called for *Selihot* the Lithuanian heard that the *Rebbi* was stirring. He heard him sigh and groan. Now it is well known that the *Rebbi's* sighs were saturated with sorrow, pain and anguish. All who heard them melted with grief. But not our Lithuanian. He did not pause even a moment from his silent study.

And when the *Shamash* rapped for *Selihot* the Lithuanian heard the commotion in the other rooms. People got out of bed, lit candles, washed their hands, dressed, walked about, opened doors. Finally quiet was restored and the light from under the doors of the nearby rooms soon disappeared. The two remained alone.

Later the Lithuanian confessed unabashed that when he was left alone with the *Rebbi* a great fear seized him. To be alone with the *Rebbi* during *Selihot* time is not a thing to be made light of. But the Lithuanian was persistent. He was all atremble, but he lay there.

Soon the *Rebbi* arose. He got out of bed and went over to the wardrobe and took out a bundle of clothing. The clothes were those of a peasant—wide short linen trousers, high boots smeared with pitch, a knee length heavy coat, a high fur cap and a leather belt set with brass studs. These the *Rebbi* put on. From the pocket of his coat dangled the end of a thick rope.

The Lithuanian could not believe his eyes. He pinched himself to make sure he was not dreaming. The *Rebbi* went out of his room with the Lithuanian following stealthily behind him. The *Rebbi* came to the kitchen, and from under the cook's bed took out an ax. He stuck it under his belt and left the house. The Lithuanian followed him. Truth to tell, for a moment the incredible thought occurred to him that the *Rebbi* led a double life, a *tzadik*[7] by day and a robber by night.

Outside the solemn spirit of the High Holy Days season prevailed. Every now and then were heard the moan of a sick person or the mournful chant of *Selihot*. The *Rebbi* glided along silently hugging the shadows of the houses. He seemed to dissolve in the dark and reappear suddenly in the light of the moon. The Lithuanian kept after him, his heart pounding as if it were echoing the footsteps of the *Rebbi*.

Soon the *Rebbi* passed the outskirts of the town. Near the town was a dense wood. The *Rebbi* entered the wood, approached a young oak tree, pulled the ax from his belt, and proceeded to chop it down.

The Lithuanian stood at a distance and watched the *Rebbi* chop

the tree into logs and the logs into kindling wood. Then he saw him take
out the rope from his coat pocket, tie it around a bundle of kindling
wood, heave the bundle over his shoulders and retrace his steps. Bowed
under his load the *Rebbi* walked back to the town. The Lithuanian
followed wondering whether the *Rebbi* was in his right mind.

The *Rebbi* kept a straight course. Soon he came to a dark alley and
stopped before a broken-down old hut. He approached the window and
knocked gently on the pane. From inside the house came the weak voice
of a sick woman.

"Who is there?"

"I," answered the *Rebbi* in Russian.

The woman continued: "Who is I?"

The *Rebbi* replied, "Vassil."

"Vassil? Which Vassil? And what do you want?"

The *Rebbi* replied in Russian, as before, that he has a bundle of
kindling wood for sale and that he would sell it cheaply. He did not wait
for an answer but opened the door and entered the house. The Lithuanian stole in behind him.

In the pale light of the silvery moon the Lithuanian saw a tiny low-
ceilinged room, containing a few rickety pieces of furniture. A sick
woman covered with rags lay on a bed. With a sigh she asked: "How
can I pay you? I am a penniless widow."

The *Rebbi* replied, "I trust you. It costs only six cents."

"I can't afford it even if you trust me. I don't see where I can get
the money to pay you later. I am helpless."

Meanwhile the *Rebbi* had already put down the bundle on the floor.
Pretending anger he retorted: "Foolish woman. I trust you with six cents
of kindling wood. You have a great, mighty and eternal God and yet you
have not enough faith in Him that some day He will provide you with
six cents to pay your loan."

"And who will light the oven for me? Who knows when my son will
return from work?"

"I'll do it for you," answered the *Rebbi*.

He suited action to word. When he put the wood into the oven he
chanted quietly the first part of the *Selihot*. When he kindled the wood
he chanted the second part, and when he closed the oven on the crackling
fire he chanted merrily the concluding portions.

*   *   *

This incident caused a change in the Lithuanian. He became an
ardent admirer and a devoted follower of the *Rebbi*. He would visit him
twice annually, and whenever he heard the *Hasidim* tell of the *Rebbi's*

miraculous ascent to heaven during *Selihot* he would not scoff but would say reverently: "Who knows, maybe even higher."[8]

QUESTIONS AND TOPICS FOR DISCUSSION

1. *Tell about the conflict between the* Hasidim *and* Mitnagdim.
2. *Inquire from people you know about the reputation that Lithuanians enjoy in Jewish life.*
3. *When is* Selihot *time? Describe your experience at* Selihot *services.*
4. *Why is the title, "Even Higher," suitable for the story?*

THE THREE WHO ATE
by David Frishman

EVEN IF I LIVE many years and grow old, I shall never forget the day and what was done on it; nor shall I ever forget the men, for they were no ordinary men, but great heroes.

Those were bitter times, such as had not been for long, and such as will not soon return.

A great calamity had fallen upon us from Heaven, and had spread abroad through town and country. The cholera had broken out.

The calamity had reached us from a distant land, and had entered our little town, and clutched at young and old.

By day and by night men died like flies, and those who were left hung between life and death. . . .

The summer came to an end and then came the Penitential Days, and finally the most solemn day of all—the Day of Atonement.

I shall remember that day as long as I live.

The eve of the Day of Atonement—the reciting of *Kol Nidre!*

At the desk before the ark there stand not, as usual, the cantor and two householders, but the Rabbi and his two *Dayanim*[9]. . . .

Hush! The Rabbi has begun to say something, and so have the *Dayanim,* and a groan rises from the congregation.

"With the consent of the All-Present and with the consent of this congregation, we give leave to pray with them that have sinned."

And a great fear fell upon me and upon all the people, young and old. In that same moment I saw the Rabbi mount the platform. Is he going to preach? Is he going to lecture the people at a time when they are falling dead like flies? But the Rabbi neither preached nor lectured. He only called to remembrance the souls of those who had died in the course of the last few days. But how long it lasted! How many names he mentioned! Will the list of souls never come to an end? Never? And it seems to me the Rabbi had better call out the names of those who are left alive, because they are few, instead of the names of the dead, who are without number and without end.

I shall never forget that night and the praying, because it was not really praying but one long, loud groan rising from the depth of the human heart, cleaving the sky and reaching to heaven. Never since the world began have Jews prayed in greater anguish of soul, never have hotter tears fallen from human eyes.

That night no one left the *Shul*.

After the prayers they recited the "Hymn of Unity,"[10] and after that, the Psalms, and then chapters from the *Mishnah*, and then selections from ethical books. . . .

That night no one left the *Shul*, but early in the morning there were some missing. Two of the congregation had fallen during the night and died before our eyes, and lay wrapped in their prayer shawls and white robes.

They kept on bringing messages into the *Shul* from the *Gass*,[11] but nobody wanted to listen or to ask questions lest he should hear what had happened in his own house. No matter how long I live, I shall remember that night, and all I saw and heard.

But the Day of Atonement, the day that followed, was more awful still.

And even now, when I shut my eyes, I see the whole picture, and I think I am standing once more among the people in the *Shul*.

It is *Yom Kippur* in the afternoon.

The Rabbi stands on the platform in the center of the *Shul*, tall and venerable, and there is a fascination in his noble features. . . . In truth, I never saw a nobler figure.

The Rabbi is old, seventy or perhaps eighty years, but tall and straight as a fir tree. His long beard is white like silver, but the thick, long hair of his head is whiter still, and his face is blanched, and his lips are pale, and only his large black eyes shine and sparkle like the eyes of a young lion.

I stood in awe of him when I was a little child. I knew he was a man of God, one of the greatest authorities in the Law, whose advice was sought by people throughout the world.

I knew also that he inclined to leniency in all his decisions, and that none dared oppose him.

The sight I saw that day in *Shul* is before my eyes now.

The Rabbi stands on the platform, and his black eyes gleam and shine out of the pale face and white beard.

The *Musaf*[12] Service is over, and the people are waiting to hear what the Rabbi will say, and one is afraid to draw one's breath.

And the Rabbi begins to speak.

His weak voice grows stronger every minute, and at last it is quite loud.

He speaks of the sanctity of the Day of Atonement and of the holy Torah, of repentance and of prayer, of the living and of the dead, and of the pestilence that has broken out and is destroying without pity and without pause—for how long? For how much longer?

And by degrees his pale cheeks redden, and I hear him say: "And when trouble comes to a man, he must look to his deeds, and not only to those which concern him and the Almighty, but to those which concern himself, his body, his flesh, his own health."

I was a child then, but I remember how I began to tremble when I heard these words, because I understood.

The Rabbi goes on speaking. He speaks of cleanliness and wholesome air, of dirt which is dangerous to man, and of hunger and thirst which are man's bad angels when there is a pestilence, devouring without pity

And the Rabbi goes on to say: " 'And men shall live by my commandments, and not die by them.' There are times when one must turn aside from the Law, if by so doing a whole community may be saved."

I stand shaking with fear. What does the Rabbi want? What does he mean by these words? What does he wish to accomplish? And suddenly I see that he is weeping, and my heart beats louder and louder. What has happened? Why does he weep? And there I stand in the corner, in silence, and I, too, begin to cry.

And to this day, if I shut my eyes, I see him standing on the platform. He makes a sign with his hand to the two *Dayanim* to the left and to the right of him. He and they whisper together. What has happened? Why does his cheek flame, and why are they as white as chalk?

And suddenly I hear them talking, but I cannot understand them, because the words do not enter my brain. And yet all three are speaking so sharply and clearly!

And all the people utter a groan, and after the groan I hear the words: "With the consent of the All-Present and with the consent of this congregation, we give leave to eat and drink on this Day of Atonement."

Silence. Not a sound is heard in the *Shul,* not an eyelid quivers, not a breath is drawn.

And I stand in my corner and hear my heart beating: one—two—one—two. A terror comes over me, and everything becomes dark before my eyes. The shadows move to and fro on the wall, and amongst the shadows I see the dead who died yesterday and the day before yesterday and the day before the day before yesterday—a whole people, a great assembly.

And suddenly I grasp what it is the Rabbi asks of us. The Rabbi calls on us to eat! The Rabbi calls on Jews not to fast but to eat on the Day of Atonement, because of the cholera—because of the cholera—because of the cholera—and I begin to cry loudly. And it is not only I—the whole congregation stands weeping, and the *Dayanim* on the platform weep, and the greatest of all stands there sobbing like a child.

And he implores like a child, and his words are soft and gentle, and every now and then he weeps so that his voice cannot be heard.

"Eat, Jews, eat! Today we must eat. This is a time to turn aside from the Law. We are to live by the commandments, and not die because of them!"

But no one in the *Shul* stirs from his place. The Rabbi stands and begs of them, weeping, and declares that he takes the whole responsibility upon himself, that the people shall be innocent. But no one stirs. And presently he begins again in a changed voice. He does not beg, he commands: "I give you leave to eat. I — I — I!"

And his words are like arrows shot from the bow.

But the people are deaf, and no one stirs.

Then he begins again with his former voice, and implores like a child: "What would you have of me? Why will you torment me till my strength fails? Think you I have not struggled with myself from early this morning till now?"

And the *Dayanim* also plead with the people.

And of a sudden the Rabbi grows as white as chalk, and lets his head fall on his breast. There is a groan from one end of the *Shul* to the other, and after the groan the people are heard to murmur among themselves.

Then the Rabbi, like one speaking to himself, says: "It is God's will. I am eighty years old, and have never yet broken a religious commandment. But this is also a commandment, it is a divine precept. Doubtless the Almighty wills it so! *Shamash!*"

The *Shamash* comes, and the Rabbi whispers a few words into his ear.

He also confers with the *Dayanim,* and they nod their heads in agreement.

And the *Shamash* brings out of the Rabbi's room cups of wine for

Kiddush and little rolls of bread. And though I should live many years and grow very old, I shall never forget what I saw then; and even now, when I shut my eyes, I see the whole thing: three rabbis standing on the pulpit in *Shul* and eating in the presence of the whole congregation, on the Day of Atonement.[13]

QUESTIONS AND TOPICS FOR DISCUSSION

1. *According to Jewish tradition, when may the laws of Sabbath and holidays, even such as* Yom Kippur, *be broken?*
2. *What were the functions of the* Dayan *in the European Jewish community?*
3. *Compare the scene on* Yom Kippur *described in the story with that in your synagogue on that sacred day.*
4. *During the Middle Ages Jews were often spared from epidemics. What specific Jewish ceremonies helped the Jew keep clean? How has modern hygiene proved the value of these ritual practices?*
5. *Read the essay "Rabbi Israel Salanter" in* Students, Scholars and Saints *by Louis Ginzberg, pp. 184-186, and compare its contents with the story, "The Three Who Ate."*

THE BOOKSELLER AS MATCHMAKER
by Mendele Mokher Sefarim

[*It happened on the fast-day of the Seventeenth of Tamuz that the author-narrator, Mendele the Bookseller, falls asleep on his wagon and awakes to find the wheels of his cart entangled in the cart of another. A quarrel ensues between the two drivers, when suddenly Mendele discovers that the "other" is his old friend, taciturn and sulky Alter Yaknahaz. Menedele proceeds to draw him out until Alter is persuaded to unburden his heart:*]

I AM AT THE fair, standing by the side of my cart and looking about. I see a vast crowd of Jews, all in a great hurry, doing business, and all very much alive. Jews at a fair are like fish in water, that is to say, in their own element. In their case the blessing of our Patriarch Jacob, "They shall multiply like fishes in the water," is fully realized. . . .

I see Jews running hither and thither, doing business, buying and selling. Among them I perceive Berl Teletze. In olden times he was a teacher's assistant, then clerk, and now he is a well-to-do merchant owning a big shop. I see Jews running about singly and in pairs, gesticulating, pointing with the index finger, chewing the points of their beards, every one in a hurry, greatly excited, too busy to say a word. I look at them and envy creeps into my heart. They are all running after fortune and evidently on the point of making money, whilst I am standing here like an automaton, a clumsy fool by the side of my cart, exhibiting my wares. What wares? Old prayer books and hymn books, hymns composed by the Pious Sarah[14], which are worth threepence. You can imagine the profit they will yield. And from these earnings I am supposed to marry my daughter! In my innermost heart I am cursing my cart, cursing my lean hag, wishing that they had never existed. Enough, I say, enough! I, too, must try my luck, do some big business like others. But what? I push back my cap, and both my brain and my hands begin to work. A straw from a neighboring wagon finds its way into my mouth. I chew it, whilst my brain and hands are busy. "I got it," I exclaim, "a splendid idea, a marriage between two merchants, well-to-do people, owning shops at the fair." You understand, Reb Mendele, I had made up my mind to turn matchmaker and to bring about a marriage between two well-to-do merchants, one of them being Reb Elyakim Sharogroder, and the other Reb Getzel Greidinger.

No sooner has the idea entered my head than I consign my cart and my hag, together with the printer, to the devil, and assiduously devote myself to my new business. There is hope and there are prospects. I run from Reb Getzel to Reb Elyakim and from Reb Elyakim to Reb Getzel. I run hither and thither, thank God, like other business men, very busy, no worse than other Jews. I work hard, for the business must succeed, and at once, that is to say, right here at the fair. There is no better opportunity for a marriage than a fair. Well then, quickly, in a hurry, the business is arranged. The fathers of the young people have seen each other and both are very willing. Well, what more do you want? I swell with pride and joy, counting my profits which I look upon as if I had them already in my pocket. I am already calculating how much dowry I will be able to give my daughter.

On the strength of my profits I buy feathers for bedding and am on the point of bargaining with a second-hand clothes dealer for a velvet overcoat. As for shirts, that is of course of minor importance, the last worry; it will be as luck will have it. Well, never mind; but listen what happened. I tell you, Reb Mendele, if you have no luck it is better you had never been born. I had no luck, for when we were already on the point of settling the business and breaking plates[15], and were incidentally thinking of bride and bridegroom—well, guess what happened! It is a shame and a heartache to relate. Nothing came of it. No, worse than nothing. It turned out topsy-turvy. Listen to my misfortune. . . . It turned out that both fathers had—what do you think they had?— They both had sons!"[16]

Questions and Topics for Discussion

1. *What was the role of the fair in European life?*
2. *What impression do you get from this selection as to how Jews made a living in the Eastern European town?*
3. *What kind of person do you envision the narrator of this episode to be?*
4. *What was the role of the* shadkhan *in Jewish life? Is he still in existence?*
5. *Do you know any "day dreamers" of the type portrayed here? Describe them.*

THE *MATMID*[17]
by Hayim Nahman Bialik
(ABRIDGED)

There are abandoned corners of our Exile
Remote, forgotten cities of Dispersion,
Where still in secret burns our ancient light,
Where God has saved a remnant from disaster.
There, brands that glimmer in a ruin of ashes,
Pent and unhappy souls maintain the vigil—
Spirits grown old beyond the reckoning of days.
And when thou goest forth alone, at nightfall,
Wandering in one of these, the sacred cities,
When heaven above is quick with breaking stars,
And earth beneath with whispering spirit-winds—
Thine ear will catch the murmur of a voice
Thine eye will catch the twinkle of a light
Set in a window, and a human form—
A shadow, like the shadow of death—beyond,
A shadow trembling, swaying back and forth,
A voice, in agony, that lifts and falls,
And comes toward thee upon the waves of silence.
Mark well the swaying shadow and the voice:
It is a *Matmid* in his prison-house,
A prisoner, self-guarded, self-condemned,
Self-sacrificed to study of the Law. . . .

Within these walls, within this prison-house,
Six years have passed above his swaying form:
Within these walls the child became the youth,
The youth became the man, fore-ripened swift,
And swift as these went, swifter yet were gone
The cheek's bloom and the lustre of his eyes.
Six years have passed since first he set his face

To the dark corner of the inner walls;
Six years since he has seen, for joyous sunlight,
Grey limestone, lizards and the webs of spiders;
Six years of wasting flesh and falling cheeks—
And all to him, as if it had not been.
He knows that Jews have studied thus of old,
He knows the fame and glory they have won. . . .

In the *Yeshivah* reigns a sacred silence
Which he, the sacred youth, is first to break;
For there, in the dark corner, wait for him—
Faithful companions since the day he came—
Three friends: his stand, his candle and his Talmud.
As if the moments could not move too swiftly,
That lie between him and his trusted friends,
He hastens to his place and takes his stand,
And like a pillar stands from morn till night.
Still standing he will eat his midday crust,
Still standing he will half outwatch the night.
Granite is yielding clay compared with him—
A Jewish boy unto the Torah vowed.
"*Oi, amar Rabba, tanu rabanan*[18],
Thus Rabbi speaks, and thus our teachers taught,"
Backward and forward swaying he repeats,
With ceaseless singsong the undying words;
The dawn, the garden, the enchanted fields,
Are gone, are vanished like a driven cloud,
And earth and all her fullness are forgotten. . . .[19]

QUESTIONS AND TOPICS FOR DISCUSSION

1. *In what connection have you come across Bialik's name before? Which of his songs do you know?*
2. *Describe what has happened to the "abandoned corners of our Exile."*
3. *Was the* Matmid's *life well spent?*
4. *Where may the* Matmid *be found now?*
5. *Why may study be considered a sacred calling?*
6. *Visit with a European trained Orthodox Rabbi and ask him to narrate his experiences at the* Yeshivah.

7. *Learn the singsong of the Talmudic chant which may be found in the music of* "Mai Ka Mashma Lan," (Yiddish Folk Songs, *Shack-Cohen, Bloch, N. Y. C.*).

THE IMMORTAL ORANGE
by Zalman Schneour

I

Two BOXES OF oranges are being shipped across the blue ocean. The oranges are Algerian, round, juicy, heavy, with a glowing red peel—the color of African dawns.

The oranges in the first box boast: "We are going to Warsaw, the ancient Polish capital. Oh, what white teeth will bite into us, what fine aristocratic tongues will relish us!"

The oranges in the second box keep silent; snuggle one against the other, and blush for shame. They know that their destination is a little village somewhere in Lithuania, and God knows into what beggarly hands they will fall. No, it was not worth drinking in so thirstily the warmth of the African sun, the cool dews of the Algerian nights, the perfumes of the blossoming French orange groves. Nimble brown hands of young Mulatto girls cut them off the trees, and flung them into bamboo baskets. Was it worth while? But we shall see who came off best: the oranges that went to Warsaw, or those that arrived later at Shklov[20]—a remote village in Lithuania. And we shall draw the moral.

So the first lot of oranges arrived at Warsaw and the fruit merchant set them out in pyramids. They glowed like balls of fire out of the window. But that did not last long. They were sold the same day. The tumultuous, thirsty street soon swallowed them up. Tired folks thrust them into their pockets, pulled off their juicy, golden peel with dirty fingers, and flung it on the slush-covered pavements. They swallowed the oranges as they walked along, like animals, without saying grace. The refreshing juice bespattered dusty beards, greasy coats. Their place in the shop is already taken by other fruits and even vegetables. No feeling for birth and breeding! Only bits of their beautiful peel still lay about in the streets, like the cold rays of a far-off, glowing sun. No one understood that these were greetings from distant sunny lands, from eternally-blue skies. They were trampled underfoot, horses stamped on them, and the street sweeper came with his broom, and swept them, ruthlessly, into the rubbish box. That was the end of the oranges! The end of something that had flourished somewhere, and drawn sustenance between perfumed leaves, and fell into bamboo baskets under a hot, luxuriant sky.

The second box of oranges arrived a few days later at Shklov. They were dragged along in little peasant wagons, and jolted in Jewish carts, until they had the honor of being shown into their new surroundings.

The wife of the spice-merchant of Shklov called over her husband: "Come on, my smart fellow. Open the oranges for the *Purim* presents."

Eli, the spice-merchant, despite his wife's sarcasm, was an expert at unpacking. He worked at the box of oranges for a couple of hours. Patiently, carefully he worked around the lid with his chisel, like a goldsmith at a precious case of jewels. His wife stood beside him, giving advice. At last the box was opened, and out of the bits of blue tissue paper gleamed the little cheeks of the oranges, and there was a burst of heavy, festive fragrance.

In a little while, the oranges lay set out in the little shop window, peeping out on the muddy market-place, the grey, lowering sky, the little heaps of snow in the gutters, the fur-clad, White Russian peasants in their yellow-patched, sheepskin jerkins. . . .

Aunt Feiga arrives with her woolen shawl about her head, and a basket in her hand. She sees the freshly unpacked fruit, and goes in to buy *Purim* gifts. And here begins the *immortality* of the orange!

Poor and grey is Lithuanian life. And the little natural wealth that sometimes falls into this place is used up a little at a time, reasonably, and with all the five senses. Not a drop of the beautiful fruit that has strayed in here goes to waste. No, if the orange had been no more than the wandering spirit of a sinful soul it would have found salvation at the home of Aunt Feiga.

II

"Then you won't take eight *kopeks*[21] either? Good day!"

The spice-merchant's wife knows full well that Aunt Feiga has no other place where she can buy; yet she pulls her back by the shawl:

"May all Jews have a pleasant *Purim* as surely as I am selling you golden fruit. I only want to make a start."

"We only want to make a start!" repeats Eli, the spice-merchant, the experienced opener of orange boxes.

"A *rouble* more or a *rouble* less." Aunt Feiga selects the best, the heaviest orange, wraps it up, and drops it carefully into the basket, between eggs, onions, and goodies for *Purim*. Aunt Feiga comes home, and the little ones clamor round her, from the eleven-year-old *Gemara*[22] student to the littlest one who is just learning the alphabet. They immediately start turning out their mother's basket.

"Mother, what have you brought? What have you brought?"

The mother silences them. One gets a smack in the face, because of the holiday; another a thump; and a third a tweak of the ear.

"What has happened here! Look at the locusts swarming around me!"

Yet, she shows them what she has brought.

"There! Look, you devils, scamps!"

Among the small town Lithuanian goodies, the orange glows like a harbinger of wealth and happiness. The children are taken aback. They still remember last *Purim,* and the fragrance of such a fruit. Now it has come back to life with the same fragrance and roundness. Here it is! They will not see the like of it again till next year.

They snatch at it with thin little hands; they smell it; they marvel at it.

"Oh, how delicious!" cries the youngest child. "Oh, how it smells!"

"It grows in Eretz Yisrael," puts in the *Gemara* student, and somehow feels proud and grave.

Aunt Feiga locks it into the drawer. But the round, fragrant, flaming fruit lives in the imagination of the children, like a sweet dream. It shines rich and new among the hard green apples and pickled cucumbers that the children have been seeing all winter.

When the *Purim* feast begins, the orange sits at the head of the table, among a host of little tarts, jellies, figs and sweets, and shines like a huge coral bead in a multi-colored mosaic.

Aunt Feiga covers it with a cloth, and gives it to the *Purim* gift-bearer to take away. The orange sticks the top of its head out of the cloth, as one might say: "Here I am. I am whole. A pleasant festival, children!" The children follow him on his travels with longing eyes. They know that it will have to pass through many exchanges, poor thing, until it is brought back to them by the beadle.

And so it was. One aunt exchanges the orange for a lemon, and sends it to another relative. And Aunt Feiga has the lemon. So she sends the lemon to another relative, and there it again meets the orange, and they exchange places. And Aunt Feiga gets her precious orange back again.

The cloth is removed. The orange, the cunning devil, sits in his former place, like the King of Bagdad, and rules over little cakes and sweets and raisins. The cold of the *Purim* night lies on him like a dew. He seems to be smiling a little wearily, a little chilled after his long journeying in so strange, snow-covered and unfamiliar a night:

"You see, children, I've come back! You needn't have been afraid."

III

When Purim is over, the orange lies in the drawer, still whole and feels happy. If relatives call, and Sabbath dainties are served up, the orange has first place on the table, like a prince among plebeian apples and walnuts. People turn him over, ask how much he cost, and give their opinion about him, like wealthy folks who are used to such fruits, and he is put back on his plate. The apples and the nuts disappear one by one, and the orange always escapes from the hands of the relatives, and remains whole. Relatives in Shklov are no gluttons—God forbid! They know what must be left for good manners.

About ten days after *Purim* there is a betrothal contract drawn up in Aunt Feiga's home. Aunt Feiga has betrothed her eldest daughter to a respectable young man. And again the orange lies on top, right under the hanging lamp, just as if he were the object of the whole party. True, one cheek is a bit withered by now, like that of an old general, but for all that, he still looks majestic. He lights up the table with his luxuriant, exotic strangeness. The youngsters, from the ABC boy to the eleven-year-old *Gemara* student, have already hinted repeatedly to their father and their mother that it is high time they had a taste of the orange. To say the blessing for a new fruit, that was all they wanted—only to say a blessing for a new fruit. But Aunt Feiga gave them a good scolding: "Idlers, gluttons! When the time comes to say the blessing over new fruit, we shall send a special messenger to notify you. Your father and mother won't eat it up themselves. You needn't be afraid of that."

The youngsters were all atremble at the betrothal party lest the bridegroom should want to say the blessing for the new fruit. Who can say what a bridegroom might want at his betrothal party? Mother always gives him the best portions.

But the bridegroom belongs to Shklov. He knows that an orange has not been made for a bridegroom to eat at his betrothal party, but only to decorate the table. So he holds it in his hand just for a minute, and his Adam's apple runs into his chin and runs out again. And the orange again is left intact.

But at last the longed-for Friday evening arrives. The orange is no longer so globular as it had been, nor so fragrant. His youth has gone. But it does not matter. It is still an orange. After the Sabbath meal the mood is exalted. No notification has been sent by special messenger; but the youngsters know instinctively that this time *the blessing over the new fruit will be said.* But they pretend to know nothing. One might think there was no such thing as an orange in this world.

Said Aunt Feiga to Uncle Uri:

"Uri, share out the orange among the children. How long is it to lie here?"

Uncle Uri, a bearded Jew with crooked eyes, an experienced orange-eater who has probably eaten half a dozen oranges, or more, in the course of his life, sat down at the head of the table, opened up the big blade of his pocket-knife and started the operation. The children stand round the table watching their father with reverent awe, as one watches a magician, though they would love to see the inside of the orange and taste it as well. They are only human beings, after all, with desires. But Uncle Uri has lots of time. Carefully and calmly he cuts straight lines across the fruit, from "pole" to "pole." First he cuts four such lines, then eight, one exactly like the other. (You must admit that he is a master at that sort of thing!) And then he begins to peel the orange.

Everybody listens to the crackling of the fleshy, elastic peel. Slowly the geometric pieces of red peel come off. But, here and there, the orange has become slightly wilted, and little bits of the juicy "flesh" come away with the peel. Uncle Uri says "Phut!" just as if it hurt him, thrusts the blade of his knife into the orange, and operates on the danger spot. The orange rolls out of its yellowish-white, fragrant swaddling-clothes, and is artistically divided up by the uncle piece by piece.

"Children," cries the newly-engaged girl, placing a big glass on the table, "don't forget the pips. Throw them in here. They will be soaked and planted."

She addresses her little brothers, but she means her father as well.

The youngsters undertake to assist their sister in her housekeeping enthusiasm, which seems to hold out a promising prospect. And they turn their eyes on the tender, rosy orange slices on the plate.

The first blessing is the prerogative of Uncle Uri himself. He chews one bite, and swallows it with enthusiasm, closing one crooked eye, and lifting the other to the ceiling, and shaking his head:

"A *tasty* orange! Children, come over here."

The youngest-born goes first. This is his privilege. Whenever there is anything nice, he is always first after his father. He says the blessing at the top of his voice, with a little squeak, flings the orange slice into his mouth, and gulps it down.

"Don't gulp!" says Uncle Uri very patiently. "No one is going to take it away from you."

"And where is the pip?" asks his betrothed sister, pushing forward the glass.

"Yes, that's right. Where is the pip?" Uncle Uri backs her up.

"Swallowed it," says the youngster, frightened, and flushes to his ears.

"Swallowed it?"

"Ye-e-s."

And the tears come into the little one's eyes. He looks round at his older brothers. They keep quiet.

But it is too late. He knows. No father can help him now. They will tease the life out of him. From this day on he has a new nickname: "Little pip."

Then the remaining portions of the orange are shared out in order, from the bottom upwards, till it comes the turn of the *Gemara* student. He takes his portion, toys with it a while, and bites into it, feeling that it tastes good and also that it is a sweet greeting from Eretz Yisrael, of which he has dreamed often at *heder*. Oranges surely grow only in Eretz Yisrael.

"And a blessing?" says Uncle Uri, catching him unawares, and fixing him with his crooked eyes.

"Blessed art Thou . . ." the *Gemara* student murmurs, abashed; and the bit of orange sticks in his throat. His greeting from Eretz Yisrael has had all the joy taken out of it.

But Uncle Uri was not yet satisfied. No. He lectured the *Gemara* student to the effect that he might go and learn from his youngest brother how to say a blessing. Yes, he might take a lesson from him. He could assure him that he would one day light the stove for his youngest brother. Yes, that he would, light his stove for him. And—

But he suddenly remembered:

"Feiga, why don't you taste a bit of orange?"

It was a good thing that he remembered; otherwise, who knows when he would have finished his lecture.

"It doesn't matter," Aunt Feiga replied. Nevertheless, she came up, said the blessing, and enjoyed it. "Oh, oh, what lovely things there are in the world!" And they started a discussion about oranges.

Aunt Feiga said that if she were rich, she would eat every day half an orange. A whole orange was beyond her imagination. How could anyone go and eat up a whole orange costing eight and a half *kopeks?* But Uncle Uri did things on a bigger scale. He had after all been once to the Fair at Nijni-Novgorod. So he smiled out of his slanting eyes: No, if he were rich, he would have the juice squeezed out of three oranges at once, and drink it out of a glass. There!

His wife and children were astounded at the richness of his imagination, and pictured to themselves a full glass of rosy, thick orange juice, with a white froth on top, and a pip floating about in the froth.

They all sat round the table in silence for a while, gazing with dreamy eyes at the yellow moist pips which the betrothed girl had collected from all those who had a share of the orange. She poured water over them, and counted them through the glass, one, two, three, four. She had nine in all. Next week she would plant them in the flower-pots; and after her wedding, she would take them with her to her own home. She would place them in her windows, and would let them grow under inverted glasses. . . .

You no doubt think that this is the end. Well, you have forgotten that an orange also has a peel.[23]

Questions and Topics for Discussion

1. Find the "image words" which show Schneour's rich imaginative descriptive talents. Show illustrations of his humor.
2. What picture of the Jews of Shklov does the author paint?
3. The home background painted above is not of a poor family. It was the average Jewish home in Europe. Compare it with the average American homes you know.
4. Compare the family life and the relationship between parents and children in the Lithuanian village with those of the modern Jewish family.
5. Which other fruits were immortalized in the Jewish home during certain holidays?
6. Why do we celebrate Hamishah Asar Be-Shevat?
7. How is it celebrated in your class? Your home?
8. What is the Hebrew blessing for an orange?

GREENS FOR *SHAVUOT*
by Shalom Aleikhem

ON THE EVE of *Shavuot* I induced my mother—peace be unto her!—
to let me go off outside the town, by myself, to gather greens for the
festival.

And my mother let me go off alone to gather the greens for the festival. May she have a bright Paradise for that! . . .

The day was so warm, the sun so beautiful, the sky so clear, the fields
so green, the grass so fresh, my heart so gay, and my soul so joyful that
I forgot completely I was a stranger in the field and had merely come to
cut green boughs for *Shavuot*. I imagined I was a prince, and the whole
field that my eyes rested on, and everything in the field, and even the
blue sky above it—all were mine. I owned everything, and could do what
I liked with it—I, and no one else. And like an overlord who had complete control of everything, I longed to show my power, my strength, my
authority—all that I could and would do.

*   *   *

First of all I was displeased with the tall giants with the yellow hats—
the sunflowers. Suddenly they appeared to me as my enemies. And all
the other plants with and without stalks, the beans and beanstalks, were
enemies too. They were the Philistines that had settled on my ground.
Who had sent for them? And those thick green plants lying on the
ground, with huge green heads—the cabbages, what are they doing here?
They will only get drunk and bring a misfortune upon me. Let them
sink into the earth! I do not want them. Angry thoughts and fierce
instincts awoke within me. A curious feeling of vengefulness took possession of me. I began to avenge myself of my enemies. And what a
vengeance it was!

I had with me all the tools I would need for cutting the green boughs
for the Festival—pocket-knife with two blades, and a sword—a wooden
sword, but a sharp one.

This sword had remained with me after *Lag Be-Omer*. And although
I had tarried it with me when I had gone with my comrades to do battle
outside the town, yet I could swear to you, though you may believe me
without an oath, that the sword had not spilled one drop of blood. It was

one of those weapons that are carried about in times of peace. There was not a sign of war. It was quiet and peaceful all around. I carried the sword because I wanted to. For the sake of peace, one must have in readiness swords and guns and rifles and cannon, horses and soldiers. May they never be needed for ill, as my mother used to say when she was making preserves.

*　　*　　*

It is the same the world over. In a war, one aims first at the leaders, the officers. It is better still if one can hit the general. After that the soldiers fall like chaff, in any event. Therefore you will not be surprised to hear that, first of all, I fell upon "Goliath, the Philistine." I gave him a good blow on the head with my sword, and a few good blows from the back. And the wicked one was stretched at my feet, full length. After that I knocked over a good many more wicked ones. I pulled the stalks from the ground, and threw them to the devil. The short, fat green enemies I attacked in a different manner. Wherever I could, I took the green heads off. The others I trampled down with my feet. I made a heap of ashes of them.

During a battle, when the blood is hot, and one is carried away by excitement, one cuts down everything that is at hand, right and left. When one is spilling blood, one loses one's self, one does not know where one is in the world. At such a time, one does not honor old age. One does not care about weak women. One has no pity for little children. Blood is simply poured out like water. When I was cutting down the enemy, I felt a hatred and a malice I had never experienced before. The more I killed the more excited I became. I urged myself to go on. I was so beside myself, so enflamed, so ecstatic that I smashed up, and destroyed everything before me. I cut about me on all sides. Most of all the "little ones" suffered at my hands—the young peas in the fat little pods, the tiny cucumbers that were just showing above ground. These excited me by their silence and their coldness. And I gave them such blows that they would never forget me. I knocked off heads, tore open bellies, beat, murdered, killed. May I know of evil as little as I know how I came to be so wicked. Innocent potatoes, poor things, that lay deep in the earth, I dug out, just to show them that there was no hiding from me. Little onions and green garlic I tore up by the roots. Radishes flew about me like hail. And may the Lord punish me if I even tasted a single bite of anything. I remembered the law in the Bible forbidding it. And Jews do not plunder. Every minute, when an evil spirit came and tempted me to taste a little onion or a young garlic, the words of the Bible came into my mind. But I did not cease from beating, breaking, wounding, and killing and cutting to pieces, old and young, rich and poor, big and little, without mercy. . . . I imagined I heard wails and groans and cries for mercy, and I was not moved. It was remarkable that I who could not bear to see a fowl slaughtered, or a cat beaten, or a dog insulted, or a horse whipped—I should be such a tyrant, such a murderer.

"Vengeance," I shouted without ceasing, "vengeance. I will have revenge of you for all the Jewish blood that was spilled. I will repay you for Jerusalem, for the Jews of Spain and Portugal, and for the Jews of Morocco.[24] Also for the Jews who fell in the past, and those who are falling today. And for the scrolls of the Torah that were torn, and for the. . . . Oh! oh! oh! Help! Help! Who has me by the ear?"

Two good thumps and two good smacks in the face at the same time sobered me on the instant. I saw before me a man who, I could have sworn, was Okhrim, the gardener.

*   *   *

Okhrim the gardener had for years cultivated fields outside the town. He rented a piece of ground, made a garden of it, and planted in it melons and pumpkins, onions and radishes and other vegetables. He made a good living in this way. How did I know Okhrim? He used to deal with us. That is to say, he used to borrow money from my mother every Passover eve, and about *Sukkot* time, he used to begin to pay it back by degrees. These payments used to be entered on a loose leaf inside the cover of my mother's prayer-book. There was a separate page for Okhrim, and a separate account. It was headed in big writing, "Okhrim's account." Under these words came the entries: *"rouble* from Okhrim. Another *rouble* from Okhrim. Half a *rouble* from Okhrim. A sack of potatoes from *Okhrim,"* and so on. And though my mother was not rich —a widow with children, who lived by money-lending—she took no interest from Okhrim. He used to repay us in garden-produce, sometimes more, sometimes less. We never quarrelled with him.

If the harvest was good, he filled our cellar with potatoes and cucumbers to last us all the winter. And if the harvest was bad, he used to come and plead with my mother:

"Do not be offended, Mrs. Abraham, the harvest is bad."

My mother forgave him, and told him not to worry. . . .

I used to rejoice when I saw Okhrim from the distance, in his high boots and his thick, white, warm woolen coat which he wore winter and summer. When I saw him, I knew he was bringing us a sackful of garden produce. And I flew into the kitchen to tell my mother the news that Okhrim was coming.

I must confess that there was a sort of secret love between Okhrim and myself—a sort of sympathy that could not be expressed in words. We rarely spoke to one another. Firstly, because I did not understand his language, that is to say, I understood his but he did not understand mine. Secondly, I was shy. How could I talk to such a big Okhrim? I had to ask my mother to be our interpreter.

"Mother, ask him why he does not bring me some grapes."

"Where is he going to get them? There are no grapes growing in a vegetable garden."

"Why are there no grapes in a vegetable garden?"

"Because vine trees do not grow with vegetables."

"Why do not vine trees grow with vegetables?"

"Why—why—why? You are a fool," cried my mother, and gave me a smack in the face.

"Mrs. Abraham, do not beat the child," said Okhrim, defending me.

That is the sort of Gentile Okhrim was. And it was in his hands I found myself that day when I waged war against the vegetables.

This is what I believe took place: When Okhrim came up and saw his garden in ruins, he could not at once understand what had happened. When he saw me swinging my sword about me on all sides, he ought to have realized I was a terrible being, an evil spirit, a demon, and crossed himself several times. But when he saw that it was a Jewish boy who was fighting so vigorously, and with a wooden sword, he took hold of me by the ear with so much force that I collapsed, fell to the ground, and screamed in a voice unlike my own.

"Oh! Oh! Oh! Who is pulling my ear?"

It was only after Okhrim had given me a few good thumps and several resounding smacks that we encountered each other's eyes and recognized one another. We were both so astonished that we were speechless.

"Mrs. Abraham's boy!" cried Okhrim, and he crossed himself. He began to realize the ruin I had brought on his garden. He scrutinized each bed and examined each little stick. He was so overcome that tears filled his eyes. He stood facing me, his hands folded, and he asked me only one solitary question:

"Why have you done this to me?"

It was only then that I realized the mischief I had done, and whom I had done it to. I was so amazed at myself that I could only repeat:

"Why? Why?"

"Come," said Okhrim, and took me by the hand. I was bowed to the earth with fear. I imagined he was going to make an end of me. But Okhrim did not touch me. He only held me so tightly by the hand that my eyes began to bulge from my head. He brought me home to my mother, told her everything, and left me entirely in her hands.

*　　*　　*

Need I tell you what I got from my mother? Need I describe for you her anger, and her fright, and how she wrung her hands when Okhrim told her in detail all that had taken place in his garden, and of all the damage I had done to his vegetables? Okhrim took his stick and showed my mother how I had smashed and broken, and trampled down everything with my feet, pulled the little potatoes out of the ground, and torn the tops off the little onions and the garlic that were just showing above the earth.

"And why? And wherefore? Why, Mrs. Abraham—why?"

Okhrim could say no more. The sobs stuck in his throat and choked him.

I must tell you the real truth, children. I would rather Okhrim with the strong arms had beaten me, than have got what I did from my mother before *Shavuot* and what the teacher gave me after *Shavuot*. And the shame of it all. I was reminded of it all year round by the boys at *Heder*. They gave me a nickname—"The Gardener." I was Yossel "the gardener."

This nickname stuck to me almost until the day I was married.

That is how I went to gather greens for *Shavuot*.[25]

QUESTIONS AND TOPICS FOR DISCUSSION

1. *Why is the child in this story so overwhelmed by the outdoors?*
2. *How does the story illustrate the rich inner life experienced by the Jewish child in the old country?*
3. *What does this story disclose about the relations between the average Jew and Gentile in the old country?*
4. *How was* Shavuot *observed in the synagogue and home then and now?*
5. *What new form of observance on* Shavuot *has been introduced in the synagogue?*

A STRIKE MEETING IN THE SYNAGOGUE
by I. J. Singer

[TIME: *The latter part of the Nineteenth Century.*
PLACE: *Lodz, a teeming metropolis populated by Jews engaged in the weaving industry. (Until destroyed by the Nazis, Lodz was the greatest textile center of Poland.)*

In the early days, the Lodz textile factories presented a very interesting scene—bearded Jews, wearing skull caps and Tzitzit, stood at their looms from early morning until night, weaving cloth and accompanying their work with the singing of synagogue hymns and Yiddish folk songs. Services were held at the factory three times daily.

One of the largest shops was run by Reb Abraham Hirsch Ashkenazi. His workers organized to improve their labor conditions, and to get an increase in wages. Their demands were not met, and they struck. The synagogue became a "union hall.". . .]

THEY ALL CAME. There was no danger in coming to the synagogue; that might be merely for the services. But they knew that after the services there would be something else, and whether or not they were ready for action, they wanted to be in on the excitement. And now the synagogue was jammed to the point of asphyxiation, and on the pulpit stood Tevyeh, not to read the week's portion from the Pentateuch, which he always did with great skill, but to initiate the great rebellion.

When he had at last obtained order, Tevyeh called up Nissan to read forth the manifesto. Nissan stepped up to the pulpit and unrolled a long document covered with fine script. The language was a highly Hebraized Yiddish, with a strong biblical background.

"Improvements demanded by the brotherhood of weavers, in the city called Balut.[26]

"(a) The weavers who pray in the synagogue *Ahavat Re'im,* as well as all the other weavers of Balut will not permit any reduction in their miserable wages. . . .

"(b) It is the will of the weavers of Balut that there shall not be any more work beyond midnight on Thursdays and Saturdays. . . .

"(c) On weekdays a weaver shall not work more than fourteen

hours a day. . . . The time taken out for afternoon and evening prayers shall be counted in the hours of work; and in winter, when it is too dark in the morning, the morning prayer shall be said in the factory, and that too shall be counted with the hours of work.

"(d) On Fridays and on the days preceding festivals the work shall st)p two hours before the lighting of the candles. . . .

"(e) Henceforth the pay for the week shall be given out regularly on Thursdays, so that on Friday the weaver's wife may make preparations for the Sabbath. . . .

"(f) Candles for work shall be bought by the employer, not by the worker.

"(g) It is forbidden for employers to call their workers by abusive names, for it is written that no man shall shame his brother. . . .

"(h) On feast-days the weaver shall work only till midday.

"(i) In the middle days of the Passover and the Feast of Tabernacles, the weaver shall work only till the time of the later afternoon prayers. . . .

"(j) The workers, apprentices, and seasonal workers who are lodged by their employers must be given food that is properly fried; likewise the coffee shall have milk and sugar in it. For if the workers are ill fed, and yet work is demanded of them, they are like the slaves in Egypt, who were bidden make bricks but were not given clay or straw. . . ."

When Nissan had done reading, a great tumult arose in the synagogue.

"Simple justice," shouted many. "Holy words those are."

"We'll never get it!" one despairing voice was heard.

"We will if we stand together!" came the cry from others.

Tevyeh banged on the pulpit till order had been restored again, and launched into a long harangue in which, taking his text from the manifesto, he compared the workers to the Jews in Egypt, and the employers to their taskmasters. He spoke passionately and at length, using words and figures with which they were all familiar, homely quotations and parables from the Bible. He spoke of the foremen and subcontractors as the overseers in Egypt, Jews themselves, but sworn to do the bidding of the tyrants. As the ancient Egyptians had forced the Jews to build their children as living sacrifices into the walls of Pithom and Ramses, so did the employers of Lodz force the weavers to build their children, too, into the system of slavery. For either the fathers, slaving day and night, were not able to feed their own children or else the young ones were handed over at a tender age to the taskmasters.

"It's true! It's true!" they cried. "As true as it is the Sabbath today in God's world!" . . .

Tevyeh glared triumphantly at the assembly and lifted his hand. "I will go to our Pharaohs and speak in the name of all. But let no man go with cunning, behind my back, to the bosses. Let no man go to work until our demands are granted."

"No one will sell you out, Tevyeh," someone screamed.

"I want an oath," shouted Tevyeh. "From all of you. Here, in this sacred place, before the Ark of the Torah, I want each one of you to swear that he will not take his brother's place at work."

An old weaver, with a tangled grey beard which looked like a mass of uncombed cottonwool, with eyes reddened by many years of work by smoky candles, struggled through to the pulpit and, with trembling hand uplifted, cried to the weavers, "Jews, hear me! It is forbidden to take an oath on the Sabbath, even for a true thing! It is a sin against heaven!"

But Nissan thrust him aside, shrilling: "That is a lie! When there is danger to life it is specifically permitted even to break the laws of the Sabbath. And the lives of your wives and children are in danger. Therefore you may take the oath, even though it were on the very Day of Atonement."

Without waiting another moment Tevyeh flung toward the Ark, took out the scroll in its shabby velvet mantle, and laid it before him on the pulpit.

"By the Law of God, and in this holy place, we swear that we will not return to work except by the consent of all. I swear it for all who are here!" He turned to the assembly. "Answer me!"

"We swear it!" came back a roar of voices.[27]

QUESTIONS AND TOPICS FOR DISCUSSION

1. *Look up any encyclopedia and report on the role played by Lodz as a textile manufacturing center in Europe.*
2. *From the strike demands indicated above reconstruct the life of the Jewish working class. Compare with present day working conditions.*
3. *Show how the textile workers were rooted in Jewish traditions. Compare with the Jewish labor class of today.*
4. *What happened to Lodz during World War II?*
5. *What role have the Jews played in the development of labor unions in America?*

I GO TO *HEDER*
by Shmarya Levin

IT WAS A HAPPY Sunday morning in the early spring, soon after the Passover. My body still had on it the taste of the new suit, with the real pockets. That morning my mother woke me early, gave me a bite to eat —I was still considered young enough to eat before prayers—and sent me off with father to the *shul* (synagogue). There I sat down right next to him—a privilege which I seldom enjoyed—and he bade me follow the *Hazan* with the closest attention. Some of the responses I already knew by heart. When prayers were over my father led me to Mottye the *melamed,* and there the formal introduction took place: "Mottye, this is your youngest pupil. Schmerel, this is your *melamed.* . . ."

Immediately after *melamed* and pupil had been officially introduced, the entire company, relatives and friends, with Grandfather Solomon at the head, repaired to our house. There a fine table had been prepared, with sweetmeats and drinks. I was seated in the place of honor, and a toast was drunk. My mother herself served the guests. To me was handed a prayer-book. Two of the pages had been smeared with honey, and I was told to lick the honey off. And when I bent my head to obey, a rain of copper and silver coins descended about me. They had been thrown down, so my grandfather told me, by the angels. For the angels, he said, already believed in me, knew that I would be a diligent pupil, and were therefore prepared to pay me something in advance. I was immensely pleased to hear that my credit with the angels was good, and I stole a look at my mother. A sweet, tender smile played on her lips, and I could not make out whether it was my credit with the angels which pleased her so, or whether she was keeping back some happy secret of her own.

When the ceremony was over, my father lifted me up, wrapped me from head to foot in a silken *Talit,* or praying-shawl, and carried me in his arms all the way to the *heder.* My mother could not come along— this was man's business. Such was the custom among us. The child was carried in the arms of the father all the way to the *heder.* It was as if some dark idea stirred in their minds that this child was a sacrifice, delivered over to the *heder*—and a sacrifice must be carried all the way.

Mottye the Melamed had his own house, standing on a little hill.

The house seems to have been patterned after Mottye, and not after his wife: it was small, dilapidated and overgrown with moss: the moss was the counterpart of his sparse goat-beard. The door was small, but Mottye went through without bending. My father had to stoop. Inside, he sat me down without further ceremony, gathered up the prayer-shawl, and left the *heder*. There I was, on a small, hard wooden bench, with nine other children, two of them my first cousins—Gershon, the son of Uncle Meyer, and Areh, the son of Uncle Schmerel—both of them a year older, but also beginners, like myself. There and then, without preliminaries, I was plunged into the work.

The table in front of the bench consisted of rough, unplaned planks, and the heads of the big nails which fastened them together stuck out, so that it was easy to get caught on them. The children sat on two benches, five on each side of the table, and Mottye the Melamed sat at one end. He had taken off his topcoat, and had replaced his hat with a pointed skull-cap: thus his face lay between two points, the upper point of the skullcap and the lower point of his goat-beard. In one hand he held a wooden pointer. He did not sit still, but swayed back and forth as he taught. He bade us keep our hands above the table, look out for the nails, and sit respectfully.

In the same room stood the large oven for baking, and above the oven was the usual alcove where one might sleep on frosty winter nights. An odor of fresh-baked bread filled the room. On one wall hung the leathern thongs, and toward one side was a small bench, just large enough for the boy whom evil fortune should befall. Then the *rebbi* made the round of the table, administered a friendly pinch to the cheek of every boy, seated himself in his place, and began the singsong lesson. And this was our induction into the immortal temple of the Jewish Torah, which is wider than all the earth and deeper than the sea. . . .

The children had to be broken in, for it was impossible to drag them away abruptly from their play. So during the beginning we were in *heder* for only half days; that is to say, from nine in the morning until four in the afternoon. But later, when the class was divided into groups, we would get only brief intervals of liberty during the day, taking turns at study and play.

But I remember that in spite of that love of study which my mother, by the songs she sang and the stories she told, had instilled in me, I was happy when Mottye dismissed the class, and I could get away from the "bean," from the face with its pointed skull-cap above and its pointed beard below. On that first day the ten of us burst out of *heder* in the afternoon, filled with joy, singing the crooning melodies which enfolded our first lessons.

Ten young "mighty men of Israel" ran out into the street, and ten powerful young throats filled the air of Swislowitz with music:
"*Kametz Aleph A-a, Kametz Bet Ba-a, Kametz Gimel Ga-a, A-a, Ba-a, Ga-a,* here we all are."[28]

QUESTIONS AND TOPICS FOR DISCUSSION

1. *Ask your father, grandfather or some one else who went to* heder *in the old country to describe it and tell you some of his experiences.*
2. *Describe the ceremony of beginning* heder *in the old country. Would you urge that a celebration be arranged nowadays at home and in school when a child begins* heder? *Why?*
3. *Describe your feelings on your first day at Hebrew school. Was there any ceremony at home or at school when you began to study Hebrew?*
4. *Why does the author consider the child beginning* heder *as a "sacrifice"?*
5. *Compare the* heder *and* melamed *of old with the modern Hebrew school and Hebrew teacher.*

SIMON, THE SHOEMAKER, FIRST CITIZEN
by A. S. Sachs

[*Simon the Shoemaker was a very poor, ordinary Jew, limited in learning and ability. He was the kind of person who would pass unnoticed and would be lost in a crowd. Yet he was a "pillar of the community" without whom the town "would have borne an entirely different appearance." It would have been "so to speak, minus its heart." Simon constantly sought the friendship of the town policeman, who was in charge of the local prison. He had a good reason for doing it . . .*]

THE *etape*[29] usually arrived in town either in the late night hours or early in the morning. But Simon the shoemaker would always be found at his post, never missing the golden opportunity of meeting it. No matter what the weather—rain, frost, thunder, lightning or wind—Simon was always there. He performed his self-imposed task faithfully and joyfully, and with inward happiness. It was at this time that he at once became thoroughly aware of his own worth; of the true cause of his being here upon God's earth.

When people saw Simon dressed in his Sabbath clothes, running through the market place in the direction of the police station, they knew at once that a new *etape* had arrived in town, and that Simon was bent on an errand of succor to these unfortunates. At that moment Simon the shoemaker became the most important personage of the town. He would become transformed into a veritable giant; a giant towering above everyone, even above the rabbi and Reb Nottel, who regularly bemoaned the destruction of the Temple in the midnight watches and, wearing his *tefilin* and his *talit,* studied the Torah all through the long day. Everyone now instinctively felt that Simon the shoemaker stood head and shoulders above him and was of far greater service to the community than all the rest of them. Every one envied him his extraordinary good fortune. On Fridays and Saturdays even more than on any other day of the week, Simon would be busy with the *etape.* On Fridays, Simon's home was like a busy market place. Yahe, his wife, cooked fish for the prisoners, and was as busy as if she were making ready for a wedding feast. Some of the housewives would come in to assist her, so that the work would be done more expeditiously, though with no less care. Simon himself, in the meanwhile, would be scurrying about the town, collecting white bread for the prisoners. With a generous sized pillow-case thrown over his shoulder, Simon would tramp from door to door collecting rolls and loaves for the unfortunates. Every one would contribute willingly, no one refusing his mite. People would leave the half baked or burned loaves for themselves, and give only of their choicest to Simon. Besides the pillow-case, Simon carried a large bottle for the *kiddush* wine. This privilege of supplying the *kiddush* wine was, by the way, duly claimed by Mottele the wine dealer, who refused to part with it for all the wealth in the universe.

But smooth sailing did not always attend this venture. Now and again it would indeed happen that the police captain would insist on sending the *etape* forward on the very eve of the Sabbath. The townlet would be thrown into a turmoil. Every one would become excited and deeply indignant with this evil doer. The communal conscience of the townlet would become awakened, urged on to greater activity, while Simon the shoemaker would go about as if in a daze and keep mumbling to himself and sighing continually: "On the road on the Sabbath, and among Gentiles! Without *kiddush,* without wine, without *halah* and fish, and to subsist on mouldy bread and water! How can one allow this to happen?"

He would run to the rabbi, to the householders and to the communal leader. He would implore, beg, cajole and threaten to cause a stoppage in the reading of the Torah on the Sabbath. "You will see!" he would threaten and plead at one and the same time, "you will yet see what I will do. I will not let you 'read' tomorrow. I won't let you take the Scroll out of the Ark. What do you expect, indeed?"

Simon's warnings usually had the desired effect. The leader would be obliged to leave his business and run to the police captain, in order to prevail upon him to rescind his evil decision; not, however, without the outlay of some bribe money to the official. But who cared for money when the observance of the Sabbath was at stake?

On the Sabbath, Simon the shoemaker would rise early, attend the early morning service, and, together with a few other artisans who desired to participate in this *mitzvah,* would proceed to carry the bags of *halah* and the platters of fish to the prison. If the guard did not permit them to enter the prison proper, they would pass the individual portions through the grating of each cell. A considerable crowd would then collect about the prison building; a crowd that would look pityingly at the unknown but unfortunate persons who had been thus forcibly separated from their fellow men and put behind the cruel bars of this dingy and clammy prison.

At three o'clock in the afternoon, the hour when everybody else had already had his afternoon siesta and was ready to go to the synagogue for the *Minhah* service, Simon still hadn't had his breakfast. His *halah* had not yet been broken and the sealed-up dishes were still in the oven.[30] For Simon the shoemaker had been busily preoccupied with the *Mitzvah* of the Redemption of Captives and was utterly unaware of gnawing hunger.[31]

QUESTIONS AND TOPICS FOR DISCUSSION

1. *Describe some one you know who may be likened to Simon the Shoemaker.*

2. *What was the importance of the* mitzvah *of redeeming captives during the Middle Ages?*

3. *Relate Simon's work to that of Henrietta Szold of Youth Aliyah fame during World War II.*

4. *What institutions have we in the modern American Jewish community which are supposed to do work similar to that of Simon?*

5. *Were Simon's townspeople justified in regarding him as superior to the Rabbi and Reb Nottel?*

IN THE RUSSIAN ARMY BARRACKS
by Irving Fineman

[At 68, Joseph, a very successful lawyer and father of a family of 7 children, each of whom is outstanding in the artistic, professional or business world, decides to write the life story of his first 25 years in the old country. His aim in writing it is to record, for the sake of his children, the origins and traditions that have made them what they are. His story depicts the beauty and the terror of Jewish life in Russia in the 19th Century. At the age of 25, he had been compelled to flee from the servitude of the Russian army because . . .]

MY THIRD CALL to appear for military service came in the autumn of 1887. It was the time when the revolutionary spirit was spreading in the Russian universities. Student nihilists went about throwing bombs; and suspect revolutionaries were drafted into the army to serve as common soldiers. There by contrast they would learn how truly free was the life of a citizen of the great Russian empire. The tales one heard of the inhuman treatment meted out to soldiers threw an unholy terror of the army into every young man.

But I set out for Prashnitz without anxiety, certain of release, for I was still under the required chest measure. It may be imagined that for some months I had not been gorging. I had been living mainly on thin gruel; and on the advice of Uncle Avrom had smoked incessantly. He brought me my first cigar but when this made me violently ill, I took to smoking the long, stiff-collared Russian cigarettes. . . .

But in Prashnitz I found my father anxious. Something unlooked for had happened. A calamity.

On a Monday morning, just before the hour of opening the offices, the clerks in the Town Hall were talking together as they prepared to begin the day's work. And among them was the Jew, Goldwasser, whose rich father the Poles had shot in the revolution; a keen young man, educated in Russian, ambitious to make his way in Russian circles, upstanding and of good physique. He was telling some tale, and the others were smoking a last cigarette before turning to their duties, when suddenly and quite unexpected at that hour the Russian *natchalnik*, the military governor, appeared, shining and bristling in his uniform. Never before had this arrogant autocrat come less than two hours late.

"What's this, you worthless creatures!" he barked.

They scrambled to their feet and stood at attention. But, his eye falling upon the Jew among them, he continued with the standard Russian greeting to the Jew—of which Gorky has somewhere said that a tax of a quarter of a cent exacted for each use of it would have covered all the expenses of the Russian government. . . .

Young Goldwasser, in the act of raising his hand in military salute when addressed by the officer, suddenly lost his head and launched his clenched fist at the mouth spewing corruption upon him. He landed just two blows; and the officer carried a bruised lip and a blackened eye. The young man had been seized and taken away to prison.

What his end was I never knew, any more than he knew of the turn his blows had given my fortunes. Another military officer had been sent down to investigate the incident, and stayed to take charge of the conscription examinations. This one saw fit, "in view of the mutinous act of the young Jew," to avenge the Russian government by the strictest dealing with all Jews who appeared this time. Regardless of regulations he took every one of us for service; even Yankel, the blacksmith's son, who though a ruddy youth was known to be subject to epileptic fits. As for me, when the doctor said I lacked an inch of the required chest measure, the officer looked up and said, "That doesn't matter; they know how to deal out good blows, these little Jews. I'll accept him on my own responsibility." I was declared a soldier of the Czar.

Contrary to custom we Jews—for fear of desertion—were not permitted to return home before induction into the army. I was turned over forthwith in charge of a guard, an ignorant Russian peasant who, gun in hand, led me like a prisoner to the nearest barracks. What I felt then is not to be described. Dazed by this blow, I could not gather my wits to think clearly, to consider what was happening to me. I remember as I was led out of the building how, hearing a cry, I turned and saw a soldier push my mother aside as she tried to come to me. I pictured the downfall of Zion, the destruction of the holy Temple, when the Romans seized the Jews and carried them off as slaves. My world was falling in ruins about me. It came to my mind, as I went beside that clod of a soldier, that the *Gemara* says that just as one offers a prayer of thankfulness, a blessing for whatever good comes, so should one also say a prayer of acceptance for evil. And how Rashi further explains this to mean that one should accept both with equal joy, since a man can never know what is truly good and what is evil. Numbly I told myself: God's judgments are ever right; and walked with a sinking heart beside the guard who stood in my mind, in his brutish ignorance, in his inescapable strength, for Russia—the power that held me in its toils.

In the barracks the stink of the unclean men and the evil smelling grease with which they smeared their boots almost stopped your breath. The long dormitory was full of the stifling smoke of soldiers who lay sprawling or sat on their disordered cots. Several Jewish recruits stood huddled in one corner staring timidly at the new world they had fallen into. Since recruits were ordinarily required to report for service only six weeks after acceptance, we Jews who were being illegally held, were not yet entitled to receive the clothing or provisions of a soldier. We got, of course, the usual blows and curses during that period. But we had to go to the corporals and ask to be provided with food. We were entirely at their mercy.

In the morning an officer came to take the soldiers out for exercise. I went up to him and begged for his consideration. I declared, respectfully, that I had left behind me a business; that I needed an opportunity to make arrangements to liquidate it, to pay outstanding debts, receive moneys and so on. Could I not be permitted a few days' leave? He listened with such interest that I was encouraged. When I stopped he smiled and said softly, "And that you have left a little black-eyed Jewess behind . . . you do not say"; and finished with the Russian greeting to the Jew. . . .

I took myself away, the blood boiling in my veins. Is this, I thought, the sort of government to which the Tana[32] in Avot[33] referred when he said: "You shall pray for the well-being of your government; for she guards the lives of her citizens."

When the officer had gone, one of the guards came to me. He had overheard us. "Foolish Jew," he said, "you should know that a soldier can get from an officer that sympathy which a pig gets from a dog. You better talk to us. Will there be in it a nip of vodka, a good supper, and a few coppers for tobacco? Then we'll help you to where you want to go." I promised what was necessary, and a soldier was provided to take me to my father's house. . . .

In several days all of us Jewish recruits were sent to a central garrison. There we were separated, and distributed among distant garrisons. I was assigned to Yamburg in Russia, up near the Gulf of Finland, about seven hundred miles from home. We travelled by a long circuitous route with the distributing party, which went from one barracks to another, leaving some recruits at each. At the first stopping place, Praga, a suburb of Warsaw, we were led into an immense armory. Clouds of dust, raised by the crowd of shuffling feet, and the smell of horses settled like a suffocating fog on my spirit. The tumult in that great vaulted place was deafening. All sorts of soldiers were gathered there. I saw all manner of faces such as I had never seen before. Terrible, wild faces, brutish faces and indescribably unhappy faces, wan, weary, sad. . . . In the middle of the huge floor many·sacks of straw were laid out in a square, one right beside the other. These were our beds for the night. The filth was unbearable; insects swarmed in untold numbers as in the third of Egypt's plagues. When I sat down to rest, in a minute my fine broadcloth coat was covered with them. I felt the last of my powers ebbing from my over-burdened heart. I was trapped, bereft of wife and children, cut off from the decent life of men.

We stood in line and to each three men was given a black bread weighing eight or nine pounds. Then they set us to work. A thin little Jew was called out and put to the task of carrying water to the kitchen. For a partner he was given a tall powerful soldier; so that each time they raised the large wooden pail, slung on a frame of poles, the big fellow hoisted his end up on to his shoulder with one swing which sent the cold water cascading on to the little fellow and bowled him over. The soldiers stood round to watch the fun with hand-clapping and shouts of laughter. "Pick it up, little Jew," they cried, and as he strained at the burden they encouraged him with their vile greeting. . . . My heart bled for my helpless people. And who knew when my own turn would come?

The soldiers began to bargain with the Jewish recruits. What would we pay to be free of their persecutions? We gathered together and made a wholesale rate of twenty coppers for each unmolested Jew.[34]

QUESTIONS AND TOPICS FOR DISCUSSION

1. *Why was there a spirit of rebellion in Russia in the latter part of the nineteenth and early part of the twentieth century?*

2. *How is the atmosphere in which Russian Jewry lived reflected in this selection?*

3. *Tell the agony of service in the Russian army and the measures taken to avoid it. Contrast with conditions in the American army.*

4. *Find someone who served in the Russian army and ask him to tell you of his experiences. Report on your interview to class.*

SUGGESTED BIBLIOGRAPHY FOR ADDITIONAL READING

Abramovitch, Raphael, *The Vanished World (Picture Album)*,
    Forward Association, 1947
Asch, Sholom, *Children of Abraham*, Putnam, N. Y., 1934
Asch, Sholom, *Salvation*, Putnam, N. Y., 1934
Berman, Hannah, *Ant Hills*, Payson & Clarke, N. Y., 1927
Bialik, Hayim, N., *Aftergrowth and Other Stories*,
    Jewish Publication Society, 1939
Cohen, Hyman, *Tents of Jacob*, McBride, N. Y., 1926
Gaer, Joseph, *The Legend Called Meryom*, Morrow, N. Y., 1928
Ginzberg, Louis, *Students, Scholars and Saints*,
    Jewish Publication Society, 1928
Iliowizi, Henry, *In the Pale*, Jewish Publication Society, 1897
Levin, Shmarya, *Youth in Revolt*, 1930; *The Arena*, 1932
Minkin, Jacob S., *Romance of Hassidism*, Macmillan, 1935
Millgram, Abraham E. (ed.), *Sabbath, the Day of Delight*,
    Jewish Publication Society, 1944
Morgenstern, Soma, *Son of the Lost Son*, Jewish Publication Society, 1946
Morgenstern, Soma, *In My Father's Pastures*,
    Jewish Publication Society, 1947
Opatoshu, Joseph, *In Polish Woods*, Jewish Publication Society, 1938
Peretz, I. L., *Bontshe the Silent*, McKay, London, 1928
Peretz, I. L., *Stories and Pictures*, Jewish Publication Society, 1906
Roback, A. A., *Story of Yiddish Literature*,
    Yiddish Scientific Institute, 1940
Roth, Joseph, *Job, the Story of a Simple Man*, Viking, 1931
Samuel, Maurice, *The World of Sholom Aleichem*, Alfred A. Knopf, 1943
Schneour, Zalman, *Song of the Dneiper*, Roy Publishers, N. Y., 1945
Schneour, Zalman, *Noah Pandre*, Furman, 1936
*Schwarz, Leo (ed.), *The Jewish Caravan*, Farrar and Rinehart, 1935
*Schwarz, Leo (ed.), *A Golden Treasury of Jewish Literature*,
    Jewish Publication Society, 1937

*Schwarz, Leo (ed.), *Memoirs of My People,*
    Jewish Publication Society, 1943
Sholom Aleichem, *The Old Country,* Crown, 1946
Singer, I. J., *The Sinner,* Liveright, 1933
Spiegel, Shalom, *Hebrew Reborn,* Macmillan, 1930
Steinberg, J. L., *In Those Days,* Jewish Publication Society, 1915
Vishniac, Roman, *Polish Jews* (Picture Album), Schocken Books, 1947
Wolfenstein, Martha, *Idylls of the Gass,* Jewish Publication Society, 1901
Wolfenstein, Martha, *A Renegade and Other Stories,*
    Jewish Publication Society, 1905
Zunzer, Miriam S., *Yesterday,* Stackpole, 1939

*Books suggested also for Parts II and IV.

PART TWO

The New World

God built Him a continent of glory and filled it with treasures untold;
He carpeted it with soft-rolling prairies and columned it with thundering
    mountains;
He studded it with sweet-flowing fountains and traced it with long-
    winding streams;
He planted it with deep-shadowed forests, and filled them with song.
Then He called unto a thousand peoples and summoned the bravest
    among them.
They came from the ends of the earth, each bearing a gift and a hope.
The glow of adventure was in their eyes, and in their hearts the glory
    of hope.
And out of the bounty of earth and the labor of men,
Out of the longing of hearts and the prayer of souls,
Out of the memory of ages and the hopes of the world,
God fashioned a nation in love, blessed it with a purpose sublime—
And called it America!

ABBA HILLEL SILVER

Introduction: NEW WORLD

FIRST TO GREET the eager, wide-eyed, weary immigrant at the threshold of America was the huge welcoming torch of the Goddess of Liberty. To the tired and the hounded its beckoning light meant welcome and freedom, freedom from the "stale and musty traditions" of the old country, freedom from the petrified class system of Europe. Years later they or their children may have learned about the promising message attached to the statue of the Goddess, entitled "The New Colossus," which had been written by one of our own, the poetess, Emma Lazarus.

America was indeed a rich land endowed with numberless opportunities by a kind Providence. America took the newcomer to its bosom. It accepted him in its teeming cities. It welcomed him to its broad fruitful plains where some of the immigrants pioneered in the newly opened frontier cities beyond the wide prairies. The magic of America also evoked the loftiest sentiments and aspirations among the young generation. The exciting stories of Washington and Lincoln were compelling and thrilling. The stories of the builders of America were sources of inspiration and stimulation to the sensitive and the gifted. To them the longed for freedom and the equality of opportunity offered by the public schools led to greater and wider fields of endeavor.

For most of the immigrants America meant the famed East Side, across the ferry from the gateway once called Castle Garden or Ellis Island. Indeed every large city had its East Side in which the "greenhorns" held together and lived their old life until they were gradually adjusted to the ways of the new land. In these self-imposed "ghettos" the immigrants learned the language, ways and customs of America. To their dismay they found that life in America was different from the old country. It conflicted with the simple life of the Russian Pale. In America things were practically topsy-turvy. Here the aggressive and big-fisted rose to the top of the heap while the shy student and self-effacing scholar were at the bottom. The struggle for a livelihood was intense and all-absorbing. The materialistic side of life was primary, while piety, study, and prayer were relegated to unimportant roles. On the East Sides of New York, Chicago, Philadelphia, and other large centers, the immigrant passed through the crucible of the sweat shop and the acid test of grinding poverty. Driven by the elemental need of earning bread for their families they sweated and toiled in shops the livelong day without even seeing their children. Many who could not stand up to the physical demands of the shop broke down and became a burden to their families and to society. Periodically they were scourged with that recurring great fear, "the plague of slack." Slack meant the scarcity of bread and the danger of eviction from home to sidewalk.

The teeming slums of the metropolitan centers were breeding places for gangs and gangsterism. The Jewish religious education of the children was casual and haphazard. It was left, in many cases, in the hands of ill-equipped and inept part time Hebrew teachers. No wonder that in many families there developed a wide rift between the immigrant generation and their children. There were also other negative aspects in this new America. For example, it was inevitable that America, which absorbed a medley of nationality groups, should have admitted among its immigrant groups some that brought over the poison of European anti-Semitism. Jew-baiters were therefore to be found in the large centers as well as in the small hamlets of America.

It did not take long, however, for the Jews to find themselves in this country and to learn its language, its culture, in short, to become Americanized. Viewing the adjustment period in retrospect, American Jewry may well be proud of its early Americanization period. For in their industry and their desire for learning and advancement, they overcame the handicaps of the ghetto and after a while were graduated into the larger American scene.

But unfortunately, to many immigrants, Americanization meant assimilation. They sought to lose themselves in the fascinating American environment, but they could not achieve complete identification with the people about them. Their lives were therefore made unhappy. While they tore themselves away from their own people and the satisfactions that come from active participation in its group life, they were not really accepted in the larger society about them. This usually led to loss of self-respect and to self-abasement, and created personality problems in their own lives and in the lives of their children. Frequently this condition also led to the disintegration of family life. The victims of this tragic process became creatures of two worlds—their own which they rejected and the non-Jewish world which spurned and did not want them. On the other hand, there were some who clung to their Jewish heritage during the process of Americanization. These were the most fortunate of the immigrants, since they remained rooted in their own culture while they were being enriched by the American civilization in which they soon felt at home.

THE JEWS AND AMERICA
by Solomon Schechter

ON THE DAY on which King Solomon married the daughter of Pharaoh, the Rabbis narrate, there came down the angel Gabriel. He put a reed in the sea, which, by means of the slime that adhered to it, formed itself, in the course of time, into a large island, on which the City of Rome was built—an event with which the troubles of Israel began. If our poets would have some of the imaginative powers of the Rabbis, they would have perceived in Columbus another Angel Gabriel, and in the discovery of America, not the triumph of Spain, but the punishment of Spain. For it was America which was destined not only to destroy the last political influence, but to give the death blow to all the principles for which Spain stood, and spared neither treasure nor lead to enforce them upon the world. Persecution and fanaticism were the things which Spain wished to enforce upon us. Liberty of conscience and tolerance were the doctrines which America gave to the world. These two contrasts could not exist on the side of one another. As the Rabbis say of Jacob and Esau, God's world, large as it is, is too small to keep both. When the one rises, the other falls.[1]

QUESTIONS AND TOPICS FOR DISCUSSION
1. *What is the underlying significance of the legend connecting the marriage of Solomon to Pharaoh's daughter and the beginnings of Rome? (For further reading about this legend see Louis Ginzberg's* Legends of the Jews, *J.P.S., 1936, Vol. IV, p. 136 f.)*
2. *What connection is there between the expulsion of the Jews from Spain and the discovery of America?*
3. *Was Christopher Columbus a Jew? Read Salvador de Madariaga's* Christopher Columbus: Being the Life of the Very Magnificent Lord, Don Christobal Colon, *The Macmillan Co., New York, 1940.*
4. *Read about the roles of such Spanish Jews as Abraham Zacuto, Luis de Santangel, Don Isaac Abravanel, etc., in the discovery of America. Refer to any Jewish history, encyclopedia, or to Cecil Roth's* The Jewish Contributions to Civilization, *U.A.H.C., 1940, Ch. IV.*
5. *Find out about the role of the Inquisition in the early days of Brazil, Mexico, and the other Spanish American dominions.*

A LETTER FROM AMERICA
by Leon Kobrin

[Somewhere in Lithuania nestled the village of B—, boasting a popula-
tion of several hundred Jews and a few gentiles. Thus begins Kobrin's
tale which depicts the idyllic story of a deeply rooted Lithuanian Jewish
community. Its death knell is sounded, however, when Orre, the black-
smith, and his young wife, Leah, accept the invitation of a rich brother to
come to America. Their parents move heaven and earth to stop them
from going, but to no avail. Some time later comes the first letter from
far away America. The letter leads to a flow of emigrants from B—.]

MOTTEL IS STANDING before his store, reading the letter in a loud voice,
with Mirke beside him, surrounded by all the storekeepers and the women
who own the market stands; all listen to the letter with mouths agape and
eyes distended in wonder. Mirke drinks in every word, smiles with enthusiasm, wipes her eyes, and every other moment interrupts Mottel's
reading. "Oh, thanks be to God! Do you hear? Well, what do you say
to that, ha? . . ."

And the rest shake their heads, smack their lips and murmur their
wonderment.

"My, my! Ay! Ay! . . ."

"Why not confess it?" reads Mottel. "Never in my life have I seen
what I saw at the home of my brothers-in-law in New York. On the
very sidewalk lay precious things such as I only wish you could have on
your table for the holidays. It's only too bad that people step all over
them with their feet. And there are golden mirrors here that reach to the
ceiling. And there isn't a trace of a lamp in all New York. And at night
you press the wall, and a lot of moons in glass cases light up, just like on
the ship on which we came across. . . ."

"Well!" interrupts Mottel. "What do you think of that? Ha? . . ."

"Do you hear?" adds Mirke, and her whole countenance is one smile
of exaltation.

"My! My! Ay, ay!" chorus the listeners.

Mottel resumes his reading: . . .

"And as for eating," the letter went on, "they eat of the very best here. They don't lack even bird's milk! Roast hens in the middle of the week and so many other dainty dishes that I don't know how to name them. . . ."

"There's a Rothschild existence for you!" interjects Mottel once more, continuing to read:

"And the buildings in New York are so high that even when you turn back your neck you can barely see the roof. And overhead run trains filled with people, and the people aren't afraid, and my brothers-in-law tell me that none of these trains has ever fallen down. . . ."

"My, my! Heavens! Ay, ay!"

"—And they rented a home for us in which even a count might live. Six rooms in a fine building. And in three of the rooms, on the floor they've laid down a kind of oil-cloth with such nice squares, and in the hall on the floor they put a big piece of velvet with flowers painted on it. I don't let anybody into the house, because I don't want them to step on it. Then I've got chairs, a bureau and what not else, which they sent in. It simply dazzles your eyes to look at them. And mother-in-law is living with us. And there's water in our house. All you have to do is turn a faucet and water comes from the wall. And you don't need any lamps either. When you want light, you simply turn a sort of screw and you bring a match to it and it gets light. And there's no oven here, either. When you wish to cook you turn another screw, and pretty soon the stove is hot and you put your pots on top of it and you make the finest dishes. And my brothers-in-law have taken Oree into their factory, where they make iron ceilings and stairs for the buildings, and they pay him, thank God, twenty dollars a week. In our money that's every bit of forty rubles."

"Listen, folks! Just listen to that!" cries one of the women. "I could pinch my cheeks. . . ."

"Read on, Reb Mottel!" urges Mirke with ardor, drying her eyes.

Mottel continues:

"Yes, where was I? 'In our money that's every bit of forty rubles. And later, say my brothers-in-law, he'll get even more'."

Mirke can no longer restrain her sobs.

"Well? Ha? Well?"

"—I hope to God that I'll be able to send for all of you, and bring you across. And my brothers-in-law tell me that in New York there are a good many Jewish policemen, too. . . ."

"That's so," cries Mottel. "I heard that a long time ago,—that Jews over there have equal rights!"

"Really?" asks one. "And they have Jewish policemen there, too?"

"What do you think?" shouts Mottel in reply, his voice ringing with confidence. "Even Jewish intelligence-officers. . . ."

"You don't say!"

"It would pay to pawn our wives and children and take a trip over there!" jests one of the men.

"And the men, too!" retorts one of the women. "But I'm afraid Berel Itsye the money-lender wouldn't advance a penny on them."

The rest of the women burst into laughter. . . .

Mirke now stands with the letter in her hand, taking no part in the general merriment. She feels provoked that they should not now be talking of her daughter's good fortune. For a moment she remains thus, then she remarks:

"And I, fool that I was, tried to keep her from going! . . ."

"Hush! Here comes the lord with the brass buttons!" . . .

The sergeant issues forth from the apothecary's, stops and eyes the crowd around the shops.

And when the sergeant disappears, Mottel cries to one of his neighbors, in a voice breathless with wonder:

"And in America there are even Jewish policemen. There's no grief of Exile over there. Full rights. . . ."

For the next few weeks there was talk of this letter all over the town, and of the "full rights," and on a certain Saturday morning, when Mottel caught hold of little Shlayme in the synagogue and asked him: "Well, youngster, are you going to sail to America, too?" Shlayme replied, "You bet! I'll be a policeman there!"[2]

QUESTIONS AND TOPICS FOR DISCUSSION

1. *How does the "letter" reflect conditions of Jewish life in the Lithuanian town?*

2. *Ask your parents, grandparents or someone who immigrated to this country what their reactions were to such American everyday conveniences as "water faucets," "gaslight," "electric bulbs," "furniture," "elevated trains," etc.*

3. *Letters like these arrived in thousands. What would be the effect of such letters on the towns in the "pale"? How would they lead to emigration?*

THE GREENHORN'S FIRST DAY
IN AMERICA
by Abraham Cahan

[*At the age of 19, Abraham Levinsky, born and reared in abject poverty, leaves the* Yeshivah *and the study of the Talmud for America. He travels steerage and arrives in New York with four pennies in his pocket. The year is 1885.*]

TEN MINUTES' WALK brought me to the heart of the Jewish East Side. The streets swarmed with Yiddish-speaking immigrants. The signboards were in English and Yiddish, some of them in Russian. The scurry and hustle of the people were not merely overwhelmingly greater, both in volume and intensity, than in my native town. It was of another sort. The swing and step of the pedestrians, the voices and manner of the street peddlers, and a hundred and one other things seemed to testify to far more self-confidence and energy, to larger ambitions and wider scopes, than did the appearance of the crowds in my birthplace.

The great thing was that these people were better dressed than the inhabitants of my town. The poorest looking man wore a hat (instead of a cap), a stiff collar and a necktie, and the poorest woman wore a hat or a bonnet.

The appearance of a newly arrived immigrant was still a novel spectacle on the East Side. Many of the passers-by paused to look at me with wistful smiles of curiosity.

"There goes a green one!" some of them exclaimed. . . .

I understood the phrase at once. And as a contemptuous quizzical appellation for a newly arrived, inexperienced immigrant, it stung me cruelly. As I went along I heard it again and again. Some of the passers-by would call me "greenhorn" in a tone of blighting gaiety. But these were an exception. For the most part it was "green one," and in a spirit of sympathetic interest. It hurt me, all the same. Even those glances that offered me a cordial welcome and good wishes had something self-complacent and condescending in them. "Poor fellow! He is a green one," these people seemed to say. "We are not, of course. We are Americanized."

For my first meal in the New World I bought a three-cent wedge of coarse rye bread, off a huge round loaf, on a stand on Essex Street. I was too strict in my religious observance to eat it without first washing the hands and offering a brief prayer. So I approached a bewigged old woman who stood in the doorway of a small grocery store to let me wash my hands and eat my meal in her house. She looked old-fashioned enough, yet when she heard my request she said with a laugh:

"You're a green one, I see."

"Suppose I am," I resented. "Do the yellow ones or black ones all eat without washing? Can't a fellow be a good Jew in America?"

"Yes, of course he can, but—well, wait till you see for yourself."

However, she asked me to come in, gave me some water and an old apron to serve me as a towel, and when I was ready to eat my bread she placed a glass of milk before me, explaining that she was not going to charge me for it.

"In America people are not foolish enough to be content with dry bread," she said.

While I ate she questioned me about my antecedents. I remember how she impressed me as a strong, clever woman of few words as long as she catechised me, and how disappointed I was when she began to talk of herself. The astute, knowing mien gradually faded out of her face and I had before me a gushing, boastful old bore.

My intention was to take a long stroll, as much in the hope of coming upon some windfall as for the purpose of taking a look at the great American city. Many of the letters that came from the United States to my birthplace before I sailed had contained a warning not to imagine that America was a "land of gold" and that treasure might be had in the streets of New York for the picking. But these warnings only had the effect of lending vividness to my image of an American street as a thoroughfare strewn with nuggets of the precious metal. Symbolically speaking, this was the idea one had of the "land of Columbus." It was a continuation of Cortez and Pizarro in the sixteenth century, confirmed by the successes of some Russian emigrants of my time.

I asked the grocery woman to let me leave my bundle with her, and, after considerable hesitation, she allowed me to put it among some empty barrels in her cellar.

I went wandering over the Ghetto. Instead of stumbling upon nuggets of gold, I found signs of poverty. In one place I came across a poor family who—as I learned upon inquiry—had been dispossessed for non-payment of rent. A mother and her two little boys were watching their pile of furniture and other household goods on the sidewalk, while the passers-by were dropping coins into a saucer placed on one of the chairs to enable the family to move into new quarters.

What puzzled me most was the nature of the furniture. For in my birthplace chairs and a couch like those I now saw on the sidewalk would be a sign of prosperity. But then anything was to be expected of a country where the poorest devil wore a hat and a starched collar.

I walked on.

The exclamation "A green one" or "A greenhorn" continued. If I did not hear it, I saw it in the eyes of the people who passed me.

When it grew dark and I was much in need of rest I had a street peddler direct me to a synagogue. I expected to spend the night there. What could have been more natural?

At the house of God I found a handful of men in prayer. It was a large, spacious room and the smallness of their number gave it an air of desolation. I joined in the devotions with great fervor. My soul was sobbing to Heaven to take care of me in the strange country.

The service over several of the worshippers took up some Talmud folio or other holy book and proceeded to read them aloud in the familiar singsong. The strange surroundings suddenly began to look like home to me.

One of the readers, an elderly man with a pinched face and forked little beard, paused to look me over.

"A green one?" he asked genially.

He told me that the synagogue was crowded on Saturdays, while on week-days people in America had no time to say their prayers at home, much less to visit a house of worship.

"It isn't Russia," he said, with a sigh. "Judaism has not much of a chance here."

When he heard that I intended to stay at the synagogue overnight he smiled ruefully.

"One does not sleep in an American synagogue," he said. "It is not Russia." Then, scanning me with an air of compassionate perplexity: "Where will you sleep, poor child? I wish I could take you to my home, but—well, America is not Russia. There is no pity here, no hospitality. My wife would raise a rumpus if I brought you along. I should never hear the last of it."

With a deep sigh and nodding his head plaintively he returned to his book, swaying back and forth. But he was apparently more interested in the subject he had broached. "When we were at home," he resumed, "she, too, was a different woman. She did not make life a burden to me as she does here. Have you no money at all?"

I showed him the quarter I had received from the cloak contractor.

"Poor fellow! Is that all you have? There are places where you can get a night's lodging for fifteen cents, but what are you going to do afterward? I am simply ashamed of myself."

"Hospitality," he quoted from the Talmud, " 'is one of the things which the giver enjoys in this world and the fruit of which he relishes in the world to come'. To think that I cannot offer a Talmudic scholar a night's rest! Alas! America has turned me into a mound of ashes."

"You were well off in Russia, weren't you?" I inquired, in astonishment. For indeed, I had never heard of any but poor people emigrating to America.

"I used to spend my time reading Talmud at the synagogue," was his reply.

Many of his answers seemed to fit, not the question asked, but one which was expected to follow it. You might have thought him anxious to forestall your next query in order to save time and words, had it not been so difficult for him to keep his mouth shut.

"She," he said, referring to his wife, "had a nice little business. She sold feed for horses and she rejoiced in the thought that she was married to a man of learning. True, she has a tongue. That she always had, but over there it was not so bad. She has become a different woman here. Alas! America is a topsy-turvy country."

He went on to show how the New World turned things upside down, transforming an immigrant shoemaker into a man of substance, while a former man of leisure was forced to work in a factory here. In like manner, his wife had changed for the worse, for, lo and behold! instead of supporting him while he read the Talmud, as she used to do at home, she persisted in sending him out to peddle. "America is not Russia," he said. "A man must make a living here." But, alas, it was too late to begin now! He had spent the better part of his life at his holy books and was fit for nothing else now. His wife, however, would take no excuse. He must peddle or be nagged to death. And if he ventured to slip into some synagogue of an afternoon and read a page or two he would be in danger of being caught red-handed, so to say, for indeed she often shadowed him to make sure that he did not play truant. Alas! America was not Russia.[3]

QUESTIONS AND TOPICS FOR DISCUSSION

1. *Describe the feelings of the "green one" during his first day in America.*

2. *Find a newcomer to America and ask him to tell you about his "first day" in America.*

3. *Contrast the differences between the way of life on the East Side of New York and in the Old World ghetto, as seen through the eyes of the "green one."*

4. *Many a prosperous businessman today has had similar experiences to those described above. Arrange for an interview with such a person and report on it in class.*
5. *In recent years a number of immigrants from Germany and Western Europe have arrived in this country. In their case the contrast between the new country and the old is not so great. Find one who can tell you his tale and report it to class.*
6. *When were the doors of America closed to immigration and why? Are you in favor or against free immigration into this country? State your reasons.*

MY SON
by Morris Rosenfeld

I have a little son,
The lad is good and fine.
And when I look at him I think
The whole world is mine.

But only rarely, waking,
I see him, my delight.
I always find him sleeping.
When I see him it is night.

My work brings me out early.
It is late when I come back.
And my own flesh is strange to me,
My own child, alack!

I come home tired and weary,
With darkness round my head,
My pale wife tells me how the boy
Was playing, what he said.

And all the questions he has asked:
"Tell me, dear mother, when
Will daddy come and will he bring
A penny for me again?"

I jump up from my chair and cry,
It is a crime such things should be!
It is a sin that any child
His father cannot see.

I stand beside his cot and watch.
And suddenly I hear
The lad is speaking in his sleep:
"Where is my daddy dear?"

I kiss his blue eyes, and he wakes:
"Look, child, your daddy!" And
He sees me, he has seen me! Then
Is back in slumberland.

"Look, child, here is your daddy! Look!
Here is a penny, here!"
The child sleeps, and in his sleep he speaks:
"Where is my daddy dear!"

I feel my heart is breaking—and
"My child!" I cry, "my dear!
One day you will awake, and I
Will be no longer here!"[4]

Questions and Topics for Discussion

1. *What was the "sweat shop"? What were the conditions of work in it?*
2. *Compare Rosenfeld to the English poet, Thomas Hood, in his poem, "The Song of the Shirt."*
3. *Contrast the sweatshop to the modern shop. In the light of your findings evaluate the role of the Jewish labor leaders and especially the work of the Amalgamated Clothing Workers Union, the International Ladies Garment Workers Union, etc., in the improvement of labor conditions. Name several outstanding Jewish labor leaders in America.*
4. *How did Rosenfeld's work help in furthering the movement to improve the lot of labor in general and the Jewish labor class in particular?*

A M O N G   K E N T U C K Y   N E I G H B O R S
by I. J. Schwartz

[*Joshua, a newly arrived immigrant, leaves the crowded city and sweat-shop and, pack on back, becomes an itinerant peddler in the Midwest. Although handicapped by his ignorance of the language and his strict observance of Jewish tradition and ritual, he is nevertheless welcomed by the simple folk in the far-flung farms and hamlets of Kentucky and elsewhere. One night he is given board and lodging by a Gentile farmer who is very much impressed with Joshua's story and his piety. Late that day. . . .*]

When daylight faded by degrees
And sunset tinged the mottled sky,
The neighbors, country folk, met;
They were the owners of the land.
Men corpulent, with clumsy hands,
With necks and faces florid-red,
All wore white trousers loosely cut
And shirts wide open at the throat.
Enormous straw hats decked their heads
But one, the pastor, tall and frail,
Remained aloof. His raiment, black
And buttoned to the neck, revealed
The qualities of rank and birth. . . .
All took their seats upon a porch,
The men and women grouped apart. . . .

The Jew, the lonely stranger, sat
Embarrassed, shy; his eyes observed
The stalwart, virile, rustic-men
Like oaks deep-rooted in the ground.
He felt forlorn. An aching sense
Of keen regret weighed on his mind.

He sat distressed, engrossed in thought.
Just then the host began to speak,
"Good neighbors," trilled his friendly voice,
"I've told you all about the Jew.
He's here alone within our midst,
What can we do to help him?" Then
The pastor, kind and gentle, spoke,
"Let's listen to the Jew, and then
We'll see." The listeners agreed
And all exclaimed, "He's right, indeed."
The Jew retold his narrative.
The tone and tremble of his voice
Impressed the audience—but more
The sadness welling in his eyes.
The frequent speechless sigh, a word
A phrase commingled with the sound
Of foreign accent—and the grief,
The sorrow of the homeless, reigned
In tone, in each misspoken word.

And when his tale came to an end,
The audience, heads bowed, sat still
In twilight's changing, fading glow.
Though hardened by their daily chores
They felt a fellow's checkered life.
From early days of youth they, too,
Had known the lot of wretchedness
Heard from their fathers and their kin,
The early pioneers who fought
The redman—tales of horror, tales
Of violence, of lurking foes,
Of burning homes and tomahawk.
The sorrow of the homeless Jew
Had stirred their brave responsive hearts.
Again the kindly pastor rose.
He touched his forehead, paused and spoke,
Each word intoned and eloquent.
He spoke of Jews—the Patriarchs,
The Prophets, Levites and the Priests;

Of Joseph exiled from his home;
Of David—psalmist, lyrist, king;
Of Moses and the Ten Commandments.
His theme concluded, "Render help
And homage to your fellow-man."

One of the neighbors, Tompkins, old
And grizzled, heavy browed, his face
The picture of a lion, spoke,
"My house and silo by the lake
Are vacant. Let our friend, the Jew,
Move in and carry on his trade.
No recompense, no rent required.
Should he desire to buy the place,
I'll sell the structure very cheap."
"Good, very good."
The host sincerely thanked the man.
"Your place is old and broken down.
It is in danger of collapse.
Let's not incur the loss of life,"
The latter said half-jokingly.
"I shall supply the lumber," spoke
The village lumberman—"enough
To keep the house in perfect shape."
"We will repair the house and barn,"
Consenting voices filled the air.
The host kept on, "But funds, my friends,
Are as important as the house."
"I'll sell some goods," replied the Jew,
"And that will be sufficient."
"Well spoken, stranger, excellent!
Ay, mother, get the vendor's pack."

The Jew's possessions, sundry goods,
Were spread before the rural folk.
Wool jackets for the women folk
In splendid colors, rose and green;
Apparel of the finest silk;
Fine table-cloths, striped red and blue

And fringed with twisted golden threads;
Striped shirts for men; tobacco pipes
Of amber—yellow, ecru, buff—
And watches of a by-gone day.
Long strings of beads that fell in lines
Of rainbow colors; pocket knives
With blades of stainless steel and toys
For children, trinkets and the like.
The sunset's splendor cast its glow
Upon this colorful display.
The people stood with half-closed eyes,
Amazed and blinded by the glare.
Some smacked their lips and others smiled.
The women, still and reticent,
Turned their heads from side to side.
"Here, women, now you have your chance.
Come over, choose the things you like."
All rose, came nearer to the show.
At first, they were complacent, calm,
But soon enough revealed their zeal,
The mood of barter and exchange.
Their treble voices rose in force.
Their eyes were sparkling and alive.
Quick moving fingers spoke of skill.
Each wrapped a package for herself.
The hostess, flushed and busy, moved
Among the buyers. Now and then
Addressed her questions to the Jew.
"Just tell me what the garment cost,
And I shall set the retail price."
The Jew sat bashful, among
The sturdy tillers of the soil.

When dusk enveloped home and grove
The buyers' ardor slowly sank.
The women folk assumed their role.
Sedate, they sat upon the porch.
Again their faces grew demure.
They slowly rose, sat down again,

> And silently began to leave.
> The men in front with lighted pipes;
> The women lingering behind.
> One gently touched the stranger's back:
> "Your name, good friend?"
>   "Joshua"
> "Fine name, indeed,
> From now on let us call you 'Josh'."
> The night engulfed the parting friends.[5]

QUESTIONS AND TOPICS FOR DISCUSSION

1. *Show the influence of the Bible on the lives of the farm folk described above.*
2. *How does the plight of the Jew remind them of their early pioneering days?*
3. *Find instances of similar friendly treatment of Jewish immigrant peddlers by native Americans and report your findings to class.*
4. *Where do you think are Jews welcomed more, in the city or in rural areas?*
5. *Give instances of good will between Christians and Jews that have come to your attention.*

FIRST STEPS IN THE NEW LANGUAGE
by Hyman and Lester Cohen

[*Aaron Traum is the story of a twelve-year-old immigrant boy who comes to this country in the 80's and settles with his family on the East Side of New York. Although a talented student and artist, he is compelled to go to work on the second day of his arrival.*

He undergoes a series of heartbreaking experiences as worker in sweat shops and as peddler and newsboy. Even though he works 12-14 hours a day, he nevertheless finds time to teach himself English with the aid of a German-English dictionary and by the reading of cheap dime novels. His struggles and suffering until he finally finds himself is the story of many an immigrant. The following two excerpts depict two incidents in his endeavors to learn English and to become Americanized.]

THAT NIGHT he (Aaron) took the German-English dictionary out of its drawer.

And now he began crawling on all fours before a language. . . .

He cleared a corner of the kitchen table, spread out the front page of *The World,* put the German-English dictionary at his elbow—and began to materialize the laborious dream of mastering two strange tongues. First he copied the German alphabet. Within a week he was feeling over guttural syllables that had a familiar ring, guessing at German meanings, dimly apprehending a few English words and saying them to himself dozens of times, scribbling over endless sheets of foolscap, often realizing, in a bewildered way, that he had guessed wrong and dismissing half the definitions into which he had been betrayed by Yiddish-sounding words that held strange meanings under their familiar, blasé faces.

Soon he had picked up the courage to make another attempt at the library. . . .

Like the others, he walked along the walls, looking at book after book. After a while he became nervous about it. He didn't know what to do next.

The white-cuffed young woman came up to him. "Is there any particular book you want?" she inquired.

He was flustered. He felt himself sinking into a deep excited shame.

Out of his little store of English he could only conjure up one word.

"This," he said, pointing to a thick volume in front of him.

He took the book, stood off in a corner, and excitedly opened it. Its pages might as well have been blank. As it was, they were given over to diagrams, here and there an *x* marked a dotted line. . . .

So, he reflected, he had run up against another problem! How was he to get at the books he wanted? Ah—he had it! He would come here, night after night, notebook and pencil in hand. And beginning with the section nearest the door—he would list every book, put down the name of its author, make a note of where it was to be found.

It was weeks before he stumbled onto the printed catalogues. By that time he had catalogued a wing of the library.

*   *   *

The next evening, after coming home from the stand, he washed up, and went down for his lesson. He was somewhat shamefaced about it, feeling that his attitude was not quite sterling. In his heart of hearts he knew that it wasn't only teaching he wanted. He hoped, somehow, to be taken into the charmed circle of the Bobrikoffs.

"In what branch do you wish instruction?" Sonya inquired.

Branch? Wasn't a branch a tree? "I don't know."

"Oh . . . well." And she walked across the room and got a book. "You can read?"

He nodded.

Sonya didn't seem to know what to do next. "Well," she decided, "we shall see how you read." She opened her little volume, and handed it to him. "There," she said, "read that."

Aaron found himself staring down at *Kubla Khan*.

"Aloud," she said.

He began:

> "In Xanadu did Kubla Khan
> A stately pleasure-dome decree:
> Where Alph, the sacred river, ran
> Through caverns measureless to man
> Down to a sunless sea."

He stuttered and stammered, and shifted from foot to foot. Then he looked at her.

"But you don't read with feeling," she said. "You know—a little feeling!"

He nodded.

"You know what feeling is?"

He nodded again. Yes, he knew—feeling.

She sat in her chair by the window, looking up at him. "Now stand straight. And try it again."

He perked up, fished around for feeling, and got as far as:

"In Xanadu . . ."

"Oh, no!" she exclaimed. "That X in Xanadu is not an X. It's a Z."

Aaron glared down at the X. "It's an X," he said.

"Z, please. We pronounce it as Z. Z-z-z-Zanadu!"

"Z-z-z," he went, "Zanadu!"

"That's right!" And she smiled a thin little smile. "Go on."

He got as far as Alph, the sacred river.

"Please," she said, "the river is sacred. Do you know what that means? Sacred means holy. Now, please make the sacred holy!"

Aaron made the sacred holy.

She let him struggle through the rest of the piece, now and again suggesting some elocutionist's gesture. On the whole she seemed unhappy about the lesson. "It'll be better next time," she said.

Aaron went out, feeling ragged and flustered. "Coleridge," he thought, "certainly must be a great man, but . . ."

The next evening he went to the Grace Aguilar Library and hunted through the atlas and numerous books on geography. He was looking for Xanadu. He wanted to trace the course of that sacred river, the Alph.

No Xanadu.

No Alph.

It being that Aaron Traum had to discover most things for himself, he didn't stumble upon poetic license until he tried to write verse. But that took several years.[6]

QUESTIONS AND TOPICS FOR DISCUSSION

1. *How do these selections illustrate the thirst and zeal of the immigrant child for learning?*
2. *Have you had, or heard of, similar experiences?*
3. *From your observations, is the second generation of American Jews as zealous and as eager for success as the first? Wherein are they superior? Inferior?*

AN EAST SIDE *HEDER*
by Henry Roth

"Odds!" said Izzy.

"Evens!" said Solly.

"Skinner!" said Izzy. "Don' hold back yuh fingers till yuh see wad I'm puttin' oud."

They were gambling for pointers as usual, and David stood by watching the turns of fortune. In other corners of the yard were others engrossed in the same game. There were a great many pointers in circulation today—someone had rifled the rabbi's drawer. Nothing else had been taken, neither his *Tefilin,* nor his clock, nor his stationery, nothing except his pointers. He had been furious, but since everyone else had looked blank, he hadn't been able to convict anyone. Yet here they were, all gambling for them. David was amused. In fact, everything that had to do with pointers amused him. They were one of the few things that relieved the dullness of the *Heder.* He had thought when he first saw them that the rabbi whittled them out himself, but he soon found out he was wrong. The rabbi broke so many that that would have taken all day. No, the pointers were just ordinary lollipop sticks, and even that had been amusing. An incongruous picture had risen in his mind: He saw his severe, black-beared rabbi wearing away an all-day sucker. But his fellow pupils soon enlightened him. It was they who brought the rabbi the lollipop sticks. A gift of pointers meant a certain amount of leniency on the rabbi's part, a certain amount of preference. But the gift had to be substantial, else the rabbi forgot about it, and since few of his pupils could afford more than one lollipop a day, they gambled for them. Izzy's luck today was running high.

"Naa. Dey's two goils in my class, an' anudder kid—a *Goy.* So dey all bought lollipops, and de *Goy* too. So I follered dem aroun' an' aroun' an' den we'en dey finished, dey trowed away de sticks. So I picked 'em up."

"Lucky guy," they said enviously.

It took more than luck though, as David very well knew. It took a great deal of patience. He had tried that method of collecting lollipop sticks himself, but it had proved too tedious. Anyway he didn't really have to do it. He happened to be bright enough to avoid punishment, and could read Hebrew as fast as anyone, although he still didn't know what he read. Translation, which was called *Humash*, would come later.

"Yowooee!" The cry came from overhead this time. They looked up. Shaih and Toik, the two brothers who lived on the third floor back had climbed out on their fire-escapes. They were the only ones in the *heder* privileged to enter the yard via the fire-escape ladders—and they made the most of it. The rest watched enviously. But they had climbed down only a few steps, when again the cry, and now from a great height —

"Yowooee!"

Everyone gasped. It was Wildy and he was on the roof!

"I tol' yuh I wuz gonna comm down higher den dem!" With a triumphant shout he mounted the ladder and with many a flourish climbed down.

"Gee, Wildy!" they breathed reverently—all except the two brothers and they eyed him sullenly.

"We'll tell de janitor on you."

"I'll smack yuh one," he answered easily, and turning to the rest. "Yuh know wad I c'n do if one o' youz is game, I betcha I c'n go up on de fawt' flaw an' I betcha I c'n grab hol' from dat wash-line an' I betcha I c'n hol' id till somebody pulls me across t' de wash-pole an' I betcha I c'n come down!"

"Gee, Wildy!"

"An' somm day I'm gonna stott way over on Avenyuh C an' jump all de fences in de whole two blocks!"

"Gee!"

"Hey, guys, I'm goin' in." Izzy had won the last of the pointers. "C'mon, I'm gonna give 'im."

"How many yuh god?" They trooped after him.

"Look!" There was a fat sheaf of them in his hand. They approached the reading table. The rabbi looked up.

"I've got pointers for you, rabbi," said Izzy in Yiddish.

"Let me see them," was the suspicious answer.

"Quite a contribution you're making."

Izzy was silent.

"Do you know my pointers were stolen yesterday?"

"Yes, I know."

"Well, where did you get these?"

"I won them."

"From whom?"

"From everybody."

"Thieves!" he shook his hand at them ominously. "Fortunately for you I don't recognize any of them."[7]

QUESTIONS AND TOPICS FOR DISCUSSION

1. *Compare the modern Hebrew School with the* heder, *the modern Hebrew teacher with the* melamed *described above.*
2. *Do Jews still live in the type of tenements depicted above? Contrast the Jewish community of today with the one described above.*
3. *In depicting present-day Jewish children would the author be justified in using the above dialect? If not, why not?*

SEDER NIGHT IN LONDON
by Israel Zangwill

Prosaic miles of streets stretch all around
Astir with restless, hurried life, and spanned
By arches that with thund'rous trains resound,
And throbbing wires that galvanize the land;
Gin-palaces in tawdry splendour stand;
The newsboys shriek of mangled bodies found;
The last burlesque is playing in the Strand—
In modern prose all poetry seems drowned.

Yet in ten thousand homes this April night
An ancient people celebrates its birth
To Freedom, with a reverential mirth,
With customs quaint and many a hoary rite,
Waiting until its tarnished glories bright,
Its God shall be the God of all the earth.[8]

QUESTIONS AND TOPICS FOR DISCUSSION

1. *Paraphrase the above poem in a few paragraphs.*
2. *How does the poet contrast the Seder ceremony in the Jewish home with the general Gentile environment?*
3. *Show other examples where Jewish life resembles an island in the midst of a Gentile sea.*

SHENANDOAH
by Delmore Schwartz

[*The Fish family is preparing for the* Brit Milah *(circumcision) of their new-born son, and the mother, Elsie, is looking about for a name. The play is cast in the Greek tradition. Shenandoah, philosopher-poet, is the narrator, or Greek messenger, whose role it is to relate the incidents in the play to the past, to the world about, and to foreshadow the future.*

Originally, Mrs. Fish planned to give her son the name of her father-in-law. She is finally dissuaded from doing so because her father-in-law insists that if his grandson is named Jacob, it would be his "death warrant." The following dialogue takes place between her and Mrs. Gold-mark, a neighbor.]

MRS. G.: That's the way it is, that's old age for you.

ELSIE: But now I must find a new name for my boy before the guests come. My husband's relatives are coming and some of the men who work for my husband, with their wives. Mrs. Goldmark, you gave your children such fine names, maybe you can think of a name for me.

MRS. G.: Thank you for the compliment. I like the names of Herbert and Mortimer more all the time. They are so distinguished and new and American. Do you know how I came to think of them? I was reading the newspaper in bed after my first boy was born. I was reading the society page, which is always so interesting.

ELSIE: Let's get the morning paper and we will see what luck I have. I wish my husband were here, I must have his approval. He gets angry so quickly. (*Mrs. Goldmark goes into the living room at the right and returns with the newspaper.*)

ELSIE: (*To herself.*) I wonder where Walter is.

MRS. G.: Now let us see what names are mentioned today.

SHEN.: *While they gaze at their glamorous ruling class,*
I must stand here, regardant at an angle,
I must lie there, quite helpless in my cradle,
As passive as a man who takes a haircut—
And yet how many minds believe a man
Creates his life ex nihilo, *and laugh*
At the far influence of deities, and stars—

MRS. G.: "Mr. and Mrs. Frederick Somerville sailed yesterday for Havana—" What a life! to be able to enjoy sunshine and warmth in the middle of winter: one would never have colds—

ELSIE: Maybe some day you too will be able to go south in the winter. Who would have believed we would all be as well as we are, ten years ago? Read some of the first names, one after the other.

MRS. G.: Russell, Julian, Christopher, Nicholas, Glenn, Llewellyn, Murray, Franklin, Alexander: do you like any of those?

ELSIE: I like some of them, Mrs. Goldmark, but I might as well pick one from a whole many. Read some more.

MRS. G.: Lincoln, Bertram, Francis, Willis, Kenneth—

ELSIE: Kenneth: that's a fine name—

MRS. G.: I don't like it: it sounds Scandinavian—

ELSIE: What's wrong with that?

MRS. G.: You should hear some of the things my husband tells me about the Scandinavians! Marvin, Irving, Martin, James, Elmer, Oswald, Rupert, Delmore—

ELSIE: Delmore! What a pretty name, Mrs. Goldmark—

MRS. G.: Vernon, Allen, Lawrence, Archibald, Arthur, Clarence, Edgar, Randolph— . . .

MRS. G.: . . . Elliott, Thomas, Maxwell, Harold, Melvin, Mitchell, Tracy, Norman, Ralph, Washington, Christopher—

ELSIE: I like those names, but none of them really stands out. How do you think they would sound with Fish? Washington Fish? Christopher Fish? I would like an unusual sound. . . .

MRS. G.: . . . Do you know, I could read the society page for weeks at a time? If I am ever sick, I will. I feel as if I had known some of the members of the Four Hundred, the Vanderbilts and the Astors, for years. And I know about the less important families also. I know their friends and where they go in winter and summer. For instance, the Talbot Brewsters, who are mentioned today: every year they go to Florida in January. Mr. Brewster has an estate in the Shenandoah Valley . . .

ELSIE: Shenandoah! What a wonderful name: Shenandoah Fish!

(The baby begins to howl.)

MRS. G.: It is not really the name of a person, but the name of a place. Yet I admit it is an interesting name.

ELSIE: He will be the first one ever to be called Shenandoah! Shhhh, baby, shhhh: you have a beautiful name.

SHEN.: *Now it is done! quickly! I am undone:*
This is the crucial crime, the accident
Which is more than an accident because

It happens only to certain characters,
As only Isaac Newton underwent
The accidental apple's happy fall—

[As before, the spotlight shines on Shenandoah, the scene itself is left in a half-light, Elsie Fish gives Shenandoah the crying child and leaves the dining room with her neighbor. Shenandoah steps to the footlights, goes through motions intended to soothe the crying child, and speaks as if to the infant.]

Cry, cry, poor psyche, eight days old:
Primitive peoples, sparkling with intuition,
Often refuse to give the child a name,
Or call him "Filth," "Worthless," "Nothingness,"
In order to outwit the evil powers.
Sometimes a child is named by the event
Which happened near his birth: how wise that is—
This poor child by that rule would thus be named
"The First World War"—Among the civilized,
A child is often named his father's son,
Second and fresh identity: the wish is clear,
All men would live forever—Some are named
After the places where they live, tacit
Admission of the part the milieu plays
And how it penetrates each living soul—
Some are called the professions, some after saints
As if t'express a hope of lives to come:
But everywhere, on all sides, everyone
Feels with intensity how many needs
Names manifest, resound, and satisfy—
The Jews are wise, when they called God "The Nameless"
(He is th'anonymous Father of all hearts,
At least in my opinion). Legal codes
Are right too when they make most difficult
The change of names, flight from identity—
But let me now propose another use,
Custom, and rule: let each child choose his name
When he is old enough? Is this too great
An emphasis upon the private will?
Is not the problem very serious?[9]

QUESTIONS AND TOPICS FOR DISCUSSION

1. *What is the Jewish tradition of naming a child? What customs are followed in choosing a name?*
2. *What is your Hebrew name? Your name in English? After whom were you named?*
3. *Are you in favor of giving children Biblical names? Explain.*
4. *What is your opinion about Jews changing their names so that they sound non-Jewish?*
5. *Contrast the spirit and mood in the naming of the boy as described in the above selection with the naming of Ud and Niemand in the first selection of Part III. Explain the difference.*

ARTHUR REALIZES HIS MISTAKE
by Ludwig Lewisohn

[*Arthur Levy, M.D., a son of Americanized Jewish parents, marries Elizabeth Knight, daughter of a devout Christian clergyman. Two years later, their son, John, is born. After his birth, Elizabeth resumes her literary work and becomes a very popular magazine writer. She is accepted in the so-called "genteel" literary circles of New York. Gradually, Arthur and Elizabeth become estranged from each other.*]

ELIZABETH WAS ALREADY at home when he returned. She seemed rested and softened. She clung to him for a moment when they met and he blamed himself for feeling even in that clinging the presage of farewell. The child was still in Far Rockaway and so Arthur and Elizabeth were alone together as they had been during the early days of their union. . . .

They were silent for a while. He put his hand over hers.

"What are we going to do, Elizabeth?"

"Don't know yet, darling. Do you mind this uncertainty terribly? Of course, it depends a little, or rather more than a little on you."

He withdrew his hand. "It's not for me to be impatient or intolerant, Elizabeth. I only know that I seem to be living in a void. And it seems to me more and more as though many Jews are living in a void. Now what they do is to settle down and establish a real home in the quite old-fashioned sense and cling to that and so shut out the sense of emptiness and of not belonging anywhere. I have the same impulse, but it seems that this complete settling down is repugnant to your instincts. You don't need it. You're not living in a void. You belong somewhere and in fact everywhere. Even if you forced yourself to do outwardly as I wish, I doubt whether that would solve the problem. I'm on the edge of perceptions that I dare not admit even to myself. They are so extreme that you would laugh at them. They are so extreme that my father and mother would think that I'd lost my mind; my Jewish colleagues would be quite sure of it. So, you see, I have no more certitude than you have. I have less, in fact, far less. Who am I to be impatient?"

She looked at him earnestly. "I'm a fairly intelligent human being, Arthur. Why don't you tell me what's really in your mind?"

"I will as soon as it is clear and so articulate. Today it isn't. I don't know enough. I'd like to spend a quiet winter, too, and take up some studies that have nothing to do with either medicine or psychiatry. But I want to raise a practical problem that cuts into the root of the matter: How are we going to bring up John?"

She nodded. "Dad raised the same question. But I put him off. He is afraid of course, that John's soul won't be saved. Well, we're not."

"I am." He saw her utterly astonished look. "You're saved, Elizabeth, because you live in a stream of tradition that is native to you. The stream changes. You don't believe what your father believes. The intellectual processes and accents are different. But the stream is the same. You are an American Protestant. Your divergence from your ancestors are normal divergences within the native tradition of your race and blood and historic experience. But I and many like me have tried to live as though we were American Protestants or, at least, the next best thing to that. And we're not. And the real American Protestants know we're not. And so we live in a void, in a spiritual vacuum. The devil of it is we don't know exactly what we are. Now, to come back to John. I'd be perfectly willing to have him brought up as a partaker in your tradition and have him feel at home in his country and its life as a Protestant American. But I can't help to bring him up that way. And what's worse, his name *is* Levy and the more of a Protestant American he were in his heart and soul the more disastrous to him would be the things which in a Protestant American civilization are bound to happen to some one named Levy. I don't see all that clearly enough yet. But I see it."

Her eyes were wide. "I think I see what you mean, Arthur. But don't you think you overestimate the prejudice?"

"No, I'm afraid not. Your international literary crowd in New York is no criterion."

A look of fear, instinctive and unavertable, came into Elizabeth's eyes. "You don't mean to say, Arthur, that you would think of having John brought up as a religious Jew?"

He did not answer at once.

"Tell me, Arthur," she repeated. "Is that what you mean?"

"I'm not prepared to go as far as that. I told you that I was only on the edge of perceptions. But your instinctive terror at the very thought is enormously instructive."

She drew herself up. "It's all a nightmare. Can't we all just be human?"

Arthur smiled. "What is it to be human? Nothing abstract. Show me a human being who isn't outwardly and inwardly some *kind* of a human being, dependent, though he were the most austere philosopher, in his human life on others of more or less the same *kind*. There is no place of *kindless* people in the world. And if you established a colony of extra-religious and supra-national philosophers and sages, male and female, their extra-religiousness and supra-nationalism would establish their kind and their inner kinship, and, far from having broken up the families of mankind, we would have added but another family—a magnificent one, I grant you—to those that already exist. In a word, this vague cry, let us be human—it's a favorite cry among Jews—means nothing and gets you nowhere."

Elizabeth smiled. "How brilliant you are, Arthur. You ought to write something about that. It would make a gorgeous article."

They laughed together.

"You know I don't write. And, anyhow, what good would that do John?"

"Poor little John," she teased. "Don't let's be so solemn and intellectual about it all. I have a notion that it will all take care of itself in some natural way. As Dad always says, God is good."

A few days later the elder Levys returned to the city and the child with its nurse came home. The summer had done the little fellow good. He was sturdier and more vivid. He looked more and more like Hazel. His nose was almost as straight as Elizabeth's. But he was, in coloring and expression, a Jewish child. . . .

Arthur sat beside the child's crib until late that night. He sent the nurse to bed and watched the sleeping child hour after hour.

He did not think; he did not reason. Neither can it be said that he indulged in vivid emotion. He brooded over the child, over himself. He recalled his own childhood and boyhood and its difficulties and he wondered how this boy of his would adjust himself, by what inner means of adaptation or resistance he would adjust himself to a hostile and complicated world. . . He remembered his own clinging to his father's house, later to streets and squares. John did not even have a house to cling to, only an apartment, an office, a passageway. . . But perhaps he would not need that sense of protection and refuge; perhaps, like his mother, he would be at home in the world. . . At home in the world . . . at home in the world. . . How did one achieve that? His father and mother had it upon some terms that Arthur could not quite make clear to himself. His generation had lost it. . . Where would be the spiritual dwelling-place of his boy? . . .[10]

QUESTIONS AND TOPICS FOR DISCUSSION

1. *Wherein is Arthur different from Elizabeth?*
2. *From your observations and acquaintances can you generalize as to the distinctions between Jews and Gentiles?*
3. *How does Arthur describe the atmosphere of the set in which he moves?*
4. *Is Elizabeth right in stating that Arthur overestimates the prejudice he fears?*
5. *Do you agree with Arthur's statement, "Let us be human . . . means nothing and gets you nowhere"?*
6. *Judging from this selection and perhaps from your own knowledge, what problems are caused by intermarriage? What problems and difficulties are met by the children who are born in such families?*

ANTI-SEMITISM IN OTTUMWA
by Edna Ferber

[*As a child, Edna Ferber lived in Ottumwa, Iowa, not far from Des Moines. In her auto-biography,* A Peculiar Treasure, *from which the following selection is taken, Miss Ferber writes that the seven years between 1890-97 "must be held accountable for anything in me that is hostile toward the world in which I live." They were years of adversity created by brutal and ignorant neighbors.*]

ON SATURDAYS, and on unusually busy days when my father could not take the time to come home to the noon dinner, it became my duty to take his midday meal down to him, very carefully packed in a large basket; soup, meat, vegetables, dessert. This must be carried with the utmost care so as not to spill or slop. No one thought of having a sandwich and a cup of coffee in the middle of the day, with a hot dinner to be eaten at leisure in the peace of the evening.

This little trip from the house on Wapello Street to the store on Main Street amounted to running the gantlet. I didn't so much mind the Morey girl. She sat in front of her house perched on the white gatepost, waiting, a child about my age, with long red curls, a freckled face, very light green eyes. She swung her long legs, idly. At sight of me her listlessness fled.

"Hello, Sheeny!" Then variations on this. This, one learned to receive equably. Besides, the natural retort to her baiting was to shout, airily, "Red Head! Wets the bed!"

But as I approached the Main Street corner there sat a row of vultures perched on the iron railing at the side of Sargent's drugstore. These were not children, they were men. Perhaps to me, a small child, they seemed older than they were, but their ages must have ranged from eighteen to thirty. There they sat, perched on the black iron rail, their heels hooked behind the lower rung. They talked almost not at all. The semicircle of spit rings grew richer and richer on the sidewalk in front of them. Vacant-eyed they stared and spat and sat humped and round-shouldered, doing nothing, thinking nothing, being nothing. Suddenly their lackluster eyes brightened, they shifted, they licked their lips a little and spat with more relish. From afar they had glimpsed their victim, a plump little girl in a clean starched gingham frock, her black curls confined by a ribbon bow.

Every fiber of me shrieked to run the other way. My eyes felt hot and wide. My face became scarlet. I must walk carefully so as not to spill the good hot dinner. Now then. Now.

"Sheeny! Has du gesek de Isaac! De Moses! De Levi! Heh, Sheeny, what you got!" Good Old Testament names. They doubtless heard them in their Sunday worship, but did not make the connection, quite. They then brought their hands, palms up, above the level of their shoulders and wagged them back and forth, "Oy-yoy, Sheeny! Run! Go on, run!"

I didn't run. I glared. I walked by with as much elegance and aloofness as was compatible with a necessity to balance a basket of noodle soup, pot roasts, potatoes, vegetable, and pudding.

Of course it was nothing more than a couple of thousand years of bigotry raising its hideous head again to spit on a defenseless and shrinking morsel of humanity. Yet it all must have left a deep scar on a sensitive child. It was unreasoning and widespread in the town. My parents were subject to it. The four or five respectable Jewish families of the town knew it well. They were intelligent men and women, American born and bred, for the most part. It probably gave me a ghastly inferiority, and out of that inferiority doubtless was born inside me a fierce resolution, absurd and childish, such as, "You wait! I'll show you! I'll be rich and famous and you'll wish you could speak to me."

Well, I did become rich and famous, and have lived to see entire nations behaving precisely like the idle frustrated bums perched on the drugstore railing. Of course Ottumwa wasn't a benighted town because it was cruel to its Jewish citizens. It was cruel to its Jewish citizens because it was a benighted town. Business was bad, the town was poor, its people were frightened, resentful and stupid. There was, for a place of its size and locality, an unusually large rough element. As naturally as could be these searched for a minority on whom to vent their dissatisfaction with the world. And there they were, and there I was, the scapegoat of the ages. Yet, though I had a tough time of it in Ottumwa and a fine time of it in New York, I am certain that these Ottumwa years were more enriching, more valuable than all the fun and luxury of the New York years.

New England awoke, horrified and ashamed, after its orgy, of witch-burning. Ottumwa must feel some embarrassment at the recollection of its earlier ignorance and brutality. A nazi-infested world may one day hide its face at the sight of what it has wrought in its inhuman frenzy.[11]

QUESTIONS AND TOPICS FOR DISCUSSION

1. *What experiences have you had of the kind presented above?*
2. *How did you meet them?*
3. *What should you have done now as you look back at them?*
4. *How does anti-Semitism tend to give the Jew a sense of inferiority?*
5. *Why is the Jew "the scapegoat of the ages"?*

SONG TO BE SUNG AT DAWN
by Abraham M. Klein

Heigh Ho! the rooster crows!
The rooster crows upon the thatch;
A dog leaps up to pull at a latch;
The dew is on the rose.
The daisies open: they shine like money;
The bees are busy gathering honey;
The pigeons hop on their toes.
The birds chirp underneath the eaves;
They sing from their nests among the leaves;
The sun is in the skies!
The barn is bright; the meadow sunny;
The sun smiles into every cranny.
A little boy rubs his eyes,—
A little boy rubs his eyes and nose,
And says his *Modeh Ani*.[12]

GIFT
by Abraham M. Klein

I will make him a little red sack
    For treasure untold,
With a velvet front and a satin back,
    And braided with gold,
    His *Tefilin* to hold.

I will stitch it with letters of flame,
With square characters:
His name, and his father's name;
And beneath it some terse
Scriptural verse.

Yes, singing the sweet liturgy,
He'll snare its gold cord,
Remembering me, even me,
In the breath of his word,
In the sight of the Lord.[13]

QUESTIONS AND TOPICS FOR DISCUSSION

1. *How does the last line in "Song to Be Sung at Dawn" strike you? How does it illustrate Klein's "at homeness" both in English literature and in Jewish life?*
2. *Compare this poem to Longfellow's "Daybreak" and other similar verse.*
3. *Which lines of the above poems do you like best?*
4. *How does Klein illustrate the best synthesis of Judaism and the new world?*

SHABBAT
by E. Grindell

This is it
To come from the blazing sunlight
Into the dim quiet of the synagogue.
To sit with my grandfather, his thin shoulders
Sharp against his white silk Talit.
To hear the murmur of old
And the rising melancholy song of the cantor;
The crying song of God and of prayer.
This is the great warmth the great at-homeness;
This is the knowledge of belonging;

The loneness merging into a strong oneness.
One lost drop of water finding its way into the sea.
The Torah gleams white and silver, and we stand
Singing and praying,
Our hearts warm with peace,
Our spirits quiet in the quietness of *Shabbat*.
This is the end of the week and its beginning.
This is the moment of pause,
The refilling of the empty vessel,
The renewing of the empty spirit
This is the remembering:
The shared memory of two thousand years
And the shared embarking upon two thousand more.
This is the hearth, the gathering together;
The pain and the joy,
The tears and the gentle laughter.
This is the benign wisdom in an old man's eyes
And the hope in a boy's fresh voice,
The roots into the past
And the arms stretched forward into the future.
We shall live forever and ever.
We shall wander from land to land,
From nation to nation,
Sometimes driven, sometimes tormented;
We shall suffer sharp blows and many deep-hurting wounds.
But this place will be with us
And this warmth
And this rejoicing. . . .
For this is the great, the many-faceted, the bottomless *Shalom*.[14]

QUESTIONS AND TOPICS FOR DISCUSSION

1. *Have you ever had a similar emotional experience when you entered a synagogue? Describe when and how it happened.*
2. *Have you ever felt a "great at-homeness" in a synagogue? If so, describe it.*
3. *Which word-pictures and lines do you like best in the above selection?*
4. *Paraphrase this poem in your own words.*
5. *Contrast the spirit of the Sabbath, described above, with that of "Sabbath at Merhaviah" in Part IV.*

SUGGESTED BIBLIOGRAPHY FOR
ADDITIONAL READING

Antin, Mary, *The Promised Land*, Houghton Mifflin, 1912
Asch, Shalom, *The Mother*, Putnam, 1937
Bisno, Beatrice, *Tomorrow's Bread*, Jewish Publication Society, 1938
Bogen, Boris D., *Born a Jew*, Macmillan, 1930
Ferber, Edna, *Fanny Herself*, Stokes, 1917
Golding, Louis, *Day of Atonement*, Alfred Knopf, 1925
Golding, Louis, *Magnolia Street*, Farrar and Rinehart, 1932
Harrison, Samuel B., *Yonder Lies Jericho*, Appleton-Century, 1933
Hobson, Laura Z., *Gentleman's Agreement*,
      Simon and Schuster, 1947
Janowsky, Oscar I., *The American Jew*, Harper, 1942
Kohut, Rebekah, *My Portion*, Albert & Charles Boni, 1925
Leonard, Oscar, *Americans All*, Behrman, 1944
Levinger, Elma E., *Grapes of Canaan*, Stratford, 1931
Levy, Harriet Lane, *920 O'Farrell Street*, Doubleday and Co., Inc., 1947
Lewisohn, Ludwig, *Upstream*, Boni and Liveright, 1923
Lewisohn, Ludwig, *This People*, Harper, 1933
Lewisohn, Ludwig, *Trumpet of Jubilee,* Harper, 1937
Lewisohn, Ludwig, *Among the Nations*, Jewish Publication Society, 1948
Manners, William, *Father and the Angels*, E. P. Dutton and Co., 1947
Meller, Sidney, *Roots in the Sky*, Macmillan, 1938
Miller, Arthur, *Focus*, Reynal, 1945
Pinsky, David, *Generations of Noah Edon*, Macauley, 1931
Reznikoff, C., *By the Waters of Manhattan*, Boni, 1930
Rosten, Leo C., *Education of Hyman Kaplan*, Harcourt Brace, 1937
Schneider, Isidore, *From the Kingdom of Necessity*, Putnam, 1935
Seid, Ruth, *Wasteland*, Harper, 1946
Singer, Jeanne, *This Festive Season*, Harcourt, 1943
Tobenkin, Elias, *God of Might*, Balch, 1925
Zangwill, Israel, *Selected Works (Children of the Ghetto; Ghetto
      Comedies; Ghetto Tragedies)*, Jewish Publication Society, 1938

PART THREE

Tragic Years

Introduction: TRAGIC YEARS

WHILE THE PAST century was swept by fresh gusts of liberalism, our century has been battered by waves of anti-Semitism and hatred. Europe and Western civilization as a whole began to fester early at the turn of the century. This festering was ushered in with the Dreyfus case[2] and the Russian pogroms. A mean egoism and a sordid envy were growing in the hearts of the peoples of Europe. The Old World became increasingly intolerant, and reverted more and more to the dark days of medievalism. A narrow, bitter nationalism was enthroned in almost every land. Small nations and minority groups were pushed around and trampled on by unfeeling, greedy neighbors. European Jews found their living space becoming smaller and smaller. As the century progressed, disaster followed disaster. Radar-like, the Jews were the first to feel these oncoming catastrophies. First came World War I which drowned humanity in a sea of blood, and sowed the seed of an even greater and costlier war. In the Twenties and the Thirties came the great world depression which gave birth to fascism, nazism, and finally World War II, from which it will take decades to recover.

The World War of 1914, which ironically was fought to make the world "safe for democracy," is to all intents and purposes still going on for our people. The aftermath of the war led to pogroms in the Ukraine and Poland, pogroms which decimated hundreds of thousands of the Jewish people. Poland, for whose birth and freedom thousands of Jews shed their blood, has from its infancy been intolerant and indecent. There were bloody, monotonous repetitions of pogroms and riots and persecutions. In Communist Russia, the Jews, who were largely a middle class group, were dispossessed of their property and business and made into outcasts. Hebraists, Zionists and religious Jews were sent into exile to isolated outposts in Siberia. But it was left to Hitler and to cold-blooded, efficient Germany to sanction anti-Semitism as an accepted, legalized, and regulated system. Anti-Semitism became a pseudo-science. It soon infected the whole body of Germany and, in fact, almost the entire world. It ended, as is well known, in the most horrible tragedy of Jewish history. The gruesome story is too fresh in our minds to need repetition. A full forty percent of our people were exterminated in the most tragic years in our history, 1939-1945.

Words cannot describe the depths to which Nazi bestiality sank. But the years of the Nazi terror also witnessed acts of heroism and self-sacrifice which stand high in the epic story of our people. Sealed off from the world in ghettos surrounded by high, thick, stone walls topped with broken glass, they were subjected to hunger, fear, disease and wanton killing. As the war progressed, they were deported in hundreds of thousands to the extermination camps of Treblinka, Auschwitz, Lublin and other places, the names of which make one shudder. When the tortured Jews of Warsaw were reduced from 500,000 to less than 40,000, they rose like one man in rebellion. The Revolt of the Warsaw Ghetto has already become a shining episode in Jewish history. The rebellion was hopeless and doomed from the beginning. But it lighted a flame in the hearts of world Jewry and will remain an everlasting light in the years to come. The stories of brave Tzivia Lubetkin, Haya Grossman, Mordecai Anielewicz of the Warsaw Ghetto,[3] Hanna Senesch[4] and Enzo Sereni[5] of the underground, and countless other nameless fighters and partisans are living testimony to the heroism and faith of those who fought the battle against the Nazis to redeem the world.

And now, two years after the war, heroic battles are still being fought, in the D.P. camps of Europe, in the refugee camps of Shanghai and the Far East, in the Mediterranean against the British blockade of the so-called "illegal" immigration, in Cyprus, in Eretz Yisrael and in America where we are mobilizing the wherewithal for our far-flung battlefronts.

Withal, the spirit of the Jew is still unbroken. The Jew still sings of man. He still believes in man. Like the prophets of old, he believes that some day mankind will arise from its ruins and "peace, girdered with justice, shall come back to earth."

UD
by Marie Syrkin

IN DAPHNE I met Ud. Daphne is a Jewish agricultural settlement in Upper Galilee; Ud is a baby. The queer monosyllable by which he is known was not bestowed capriciously; nor is it a pet-name. *Ud* is a Hebrew word which means "the last brand," the ember plucked from the burning.

The boy and girl who were the parents of Ud had escaped from the Warsaw ghetto, after taking part in its last stand. Together they reached Palestine and in that land their son was born. They named him Ud. When I saw him he was a jolly, chubby baby of ten months, and he gurgled as happily as any baby with a less tragic and significant name. But the sign was upon him. Perhaps as he grew older he would resent his parents' dramatic choice, as children always resent the peculiar or the passionate in regard to themselves. No doubt child psychologists would seriously question the wisdom of involving a young life from the outset in the catastrophe from which his parents had miraculously escaped. However that might be, there he was, and I wondered if his mother, as she caressingly called his name—"Ud, Ud"—was aware each time of its terrible meaning and history.

I thought of still another child, born seven years earlier, in the fall of 1938. His mother had been one of a group of Jews driven out of the Sudeten area in one of the first of such expulsions. Because the family had been unable to get admission into any border town, the child's birth-place was a ditch. His mother named him Niemand, the German for "nobody."

The incident made something of an impression at the time. This was before the Nazi slaughterhouses had, among their other victims, destroyed the capacity for fellow feeling. We could still sense the anguish of this nativity, the terror of this Jewish mother's annunciation that the man-child she had borne was No One. In the years that have passed, I have often wondered about the fate of Niemand. Did he live? Did he escape the gas chambers? It is unlikely. There were so many ways for him to die; at any rate, I have not read his name among the few rescued. But he is unforgettable, as Ud is unforgettable.

From the German *Niemand* to the Hebrew *Ud*—there is the core of the calamity that befell my people. The symbolically named babies stand at either end of the great carnage, framing it with an artistic completeness which suggests a considered plan rather than the accident of a mother's despair or hope: Niemand, the prophetic name presaging the immense annihilation, and Ud, the small remnant![5]

QUESTIONS AND TOPICS FOR DISCUSSION

1. *Why is this excerpt appropriate as the opening selection for this section of the book, even as it served as the opening chapter of* Blessed Is the Match?

2. *What procedures do Jewish parents follow in naming their children?*

3. *Are you as impressed as the author with the significance of the names Ud and Niemand?*

4. *The closing chapter of* Blessed Is the Match *is entitled "The Seventh City." Read it for a note of hope and encouragement. Present a digest of its contents to class.*

THE RETURN HOME
by I. J. Singer

[*World War I caught Max (the former Simhah Meyer) Ashkenazi in Russia. By dint of superhuman effort and extraordinary ability, he succeeds in transporting the machinery of his factories in Lodz to Petrograd (now Leningrad), the Russian capital, where he erects a new textile empire. During the Bolshevik revolution, however, he is thrown out penniless and is later imprisoned. Saved from death by a lifelong rival and enemy, his twin brother, Jacob Bunim, he is "smuggled" out of Russia into Poland and is about to return to Lodz.*]

"EVERYBODY OUT!" the German conductor shouted. "We're a couple of kilometres from Lapy. This train doesn't go any farther."

The passengers climbed out. Close to the railroad track was a wooden hut, and outside the door a soldier, with the Polish eagle fastened to his cap, stood guard. Between two trees was stretched a linen streamer, with a welcome to the returning Poles. The crowds of Poles burst into the national anthem. . . .

"Well, we're 'at home,' " muttered Yakob.

The crowd straggled along the sandy road parallel with the railroad for several kilometres. In front of the station of Lapy, over which fluttered a white and red flag, stood a squad of gendarmes, with long swords dangling at their sides.

"Jews and Bolsheviks to one side!" the corporal shouted. . . .

The gendarme looked up at the two Jews, and an expectant leer distorted his face.

"Well, where do you two Sheenies come from?" he asked.

Yakob took out his papers and laid them on the table. The gendarme didn't even look at them.

"Get undressed!" he ordered, curtly.

The two brothers looked at each other in stony silence. The waiting room was jammed. At the wooden table, next to the gendarme, sat a girl in uniform. The gendarme banged on the table and yelled to his men: "Strip them naked."

Amid the laughter of the crowd the soldiers threw themselves on

Max and Yakob and began to tear the clothes from them. The gendarme at the table was suddenly replaced by an officer, a young, thin-faced Pole, with a sharp nose and little mustache. He wore, slung across one shoulder, the coat of a Hungarian hussar. Yakob broke free from the soldiers who were tearing off his clothes and flung himself toward the officer.

"Lieutenant!" he cried. "My brother and I are manufacturers of Lodz. We own houses there. We place ourselves under your protection."

The officer threw off his hussar's coat, and removed his cap, revealing a mop of blond, stiff hair which stood out like pig's bristles. He looked out of his narrow grey eyes at the big, dignified figure of Yakob.

"So, manufacturers of Lodz, and owners of your own houses," he repeated. "Not Bolsheviks at all, then."

"God forbid, lieutenant," said Max, thrusting eagerly forward. His coat and vest had been ripped from him. "I've just come from Russia, where I was imprisoned by the *Cheka*. Here are my papers to prove it."

"Very well, we'll see," said the thin officer. "Shout at the top of your voice: 'To hell with Leon Trotsky!'"

"To hell with him by all means!" said Max Ashkenazi, fervently.

"I told you to shout it!" said the officer, angrily. "At the top of your voice."

"To hell with Leon Trotsky!" repeated Max Ashkenazi, more loudly.

"Louder!" yelled the officer.

Max Ashkenazi repeated the words again, but the officer was still not satisfied.

"Louder, you filthy Jew! Louder! Till your teeth rattle!"

Max Ashkenazi shouted with all his remaining strength, amid the laughter of the soldiers and of the girl in uniform.

"Now shout: 'To Hell with all the *Yids!*'" the officer commanded. "At the top of your voice!"

The sweat was streaming down Max's face. He could not open his lips. His breath came in spasms. The officer smacked him across the face with his hat.

"Shout! Or I'll tear the guts out of you!"

Yakob tried to twist himself free from the soldiers who held him. They tightened their grasp on him.

"Shout!" yelled the officer again.

Max Ashkenazi looked around at the excited mob of peasants and soldiers. He saw the delight on their faces, the frenzied desire to crush and humiliate him. He gave way.

"To hell with all the *Yids!*" he whispered. Then louder, and louder again, he repeated the words.

The mob neighed with happiness.

"That's fine!" said the little officer. "Now you can give us a little dance, Mr. Manufacturer and house-owner of Lodz. A little dance and song, to entertain our soldier boys here. Come on, now, lively!"

Again Yakob tried to tear himself free from the men who held him, and again they tightened their grasp, driving their fists into his ribs.

"Don't, Max. Don't do it!" he shouted.

Max did not hear him. He cast round him, at the mob of tormentors, a look in which all the poisonous contempt in his soul found expression; and he did as he was told. He turned and twisted before all the soldiers.

"Faster, livelier!" they shouted, clapping their hands.

Max went on twisting and turning until he collapsed and lay on the floor covered with perspiration and panting brokenly.

"Let him lie there!" the officer commanded. "Now for the other Jew."

The gendarmes brought Yakob forward and released him. He stood deathly white, but erect and dignified.

"Go on with the dance," the officer commanded.

Yakob did not budge.

"Dance, you dirty Jew!" the officer shouted, and brought his fist down on the table. "Dance or it will be worse for you."

Still Yakob did not budge.

The blood rushed into the little officer's face. The soldiers were all looking now, from him to the big, silent, dignified man and back again, waiting to see what would be the upshot of the struggle between these opposed wills. The officer rushed round the table and grabbed Yakob by the beard.

"Dance!" he shouted, and tried to pull Yakob down.

At that instant Yakob tore himself free, stepped back, lifted his arm, and slapped the officer with such force that the latter staggered back until he was brought up against the wall.

The audience was paralyzed, and a mortal silence filled the room. Only the girl in uniform rose and ran over to the officer. Then Max Ashkenazi, on the floor, crawled toward his brother. "Yakob! Yakob!" he whispered, his voice filled with fright.

The officer straightened up, his face contorted. With a trembling hand he fumbled at his holster and drew out his pistol. It took him a long time to get his pistol free. Then he lifted it and screamed: "Stand back!"

The gendarmes made a rush away from Yakob Ashkenazi. Several times the officer shot point-blank at the big, white silent figure. Then he turned. "My hat and coat!" he gasped. They were handed to him. Without donning them he rushed from the room.

Max Ashkenazi had crawled over to the bloody figure of his brother and was holding him in his arms.

"Why did you do it, Jacob Bunim?" he wailed. "Why?" And he tried to lift the body. But there was no response. A thin trickle of blood ran out from his forehead over the beard. Yakob was dead. . . .

Max Ashkenazi lay wailing on his brother's body, oblivious of his surroundings. The crowd stood silent, wretched little creatures suddenly aware of their meanness and smallness. Smallest of all felt Max Ashkenazi, as he lay on the corpse of his twin brother, who had triumphed over him again, but now for the last time.[6]

Questions and Topics for Discussion

1. *Describe the characters of Max and Yakob as depicted in this selection.*
2. *In your modern Jewish history book find out the facts about the attitude of Poland to its Jews between the First and Second World Wars. Report on your findings.*
3. *What is meant by the term a "Mah Yafit Jew?"*
4. *What is the condition of Jewish life in Poland now?*

GERMAN PUBLIC SCHOOL, 1920
by H. W. Katz

[*The Fishmans, who emigrated from Galicia, lived in a little town in central Germany. The time is the period following World War I. Germany is in the throes of unrest. Jacob, in his desire to become identified with the rising German nationalism, endeavors to join the Jungsturm, which is the National Socialist Youth Movement. However, he and two other Jewish pupils of the class are rejected and ostracized; they are regarded as non-existent. It must be remembered that this occurs in 1920, before the rise of Hitler.*]

NEW RECORDS were being compiled in our school, and everyone had to give his name, his father's name, his birthplace and birthdate. First the Protestants of the class were called on to give the necessary information, then the two Catholics, finally the three Jews.

"What is your name?"

"Benno Nadel."

"What is your father's name?"

"M. Nadel."

"So it's Moses Nadel," Professor Opel sneered. He stuck his thumbs into his vest and spoke through his nose. "The son's name is Benno, and the father's name is Moses."

The class laughed, roared, applauded. Only the three Jews were still.

"No," said the hunchback, biting his protruding lower lip. "His name is M. Nadel."

"Maybe M. stands for Isidor in your language, my Benno *leben?*"

The class was almost hysterical. Some literally moaned with laughter.

"Quiet!" ordered Professor Opel. "What is there to laugh about? I am not being funny, am I?" Complacently he looked over toward his particular favourites.

Benno was sobbing.

"What a sissy you are, my Benno *leben!*" said Professor Opel with assumed tenderness, and went down the aisle. "What pretty black curls!" he said, stroking Benno's hair with an air of extreme caution. "Stop your crying!"

He removed his hand from Benno's head, held it out carefully before him as though it were a soiled towel, and washed it carefully at the basin, letting the water flow over it a long time. Benno's tears, too, kept flowing. Professor Opel seemed to soap his hands for an eternity, all the while winking and grimacing at the guffawing class.

"Now, now, sit down, little Benno, darling. Are there any more Jews in the class?"

"Two!" everybody shouted, pointing to Heinz Levy and myself.

"What's your name?" Professor Opel asked me.

"Jacob Fishman."

"Is your father's name Moses, too?"

No one was laughing yet. Everybody awaited my answer with intense expectation. I pondered it carefully. I was in no hurry. Finally I said: "No. Joseph."

"Are you sure?"

"Yes, sir."

"Where were you born?"

"In Strody."

"Where is that?"

"In Galicia."

Professor Opel, with a look of distaste, put down the class register and his pen, and came toward me.

"So you are an Eastern Jew?"

I could hear the vileness in his voice. I could feel the curiosity of the pupils around me. I was silent.

"What does your father do?"

"He is a merchant."

"Naturally! And what does he sell, your father *leben?*"

My ears began to hum as if bees were buzzing in them. I thought: I mustn't sob like Benno. Opel would be only too pleased if I did. From now on I won't answer. What can he do about it? Nothing. . . .

"Did you hear me? What is your father's business, what does Herr Moses Fishman from Galicia do?"

I looked into his fat face. I read in it the self-satisfied smugness of a man who fancies he is God-knows-what just because he was not born a Jew, just because he belongs to the non-Jewish majority. His satisfaction, his joy at my helplessness were clearly visible. The beast, I thought, is nearly fifty years old, and I am almost thirteen, but at thirteen a Jew is a man, I thought. . . . He may be as funny as he likes, but I'd rather be beaten dead than say a word, than answer him. Besides, he won't kill me, this cowardly pig, I thought. . . . I mustn't be scared by his shouting! The more excited he gets, the calmer I will be! He can't control himself, but I can! He won't draw a word out of me today!

"Did you hear me? I asked you a question!"

I looked straight into his eyes as he stood there in front of me, not much bigger than I was. When we played Indians nobody was allowed to blink his eyes, not even when tied to the post, and that was not so easy; the others would fire an air pistol at a target placed a few inches above the head of the "pale-faced prisoner." . . . I thought: You are a mangy Sioux, you're in conspiracy with criminals who bought you for a barrel of firewater, but now you're going to tremble at the sight of my eagle eye. . . . And so it turned out! Opel's eyes began to blink!

"Sit down!" he hissed, and turned away from me. Slowly he walked back to his desk. "I'll talk to you again, you good-for-nothing!" he threatened, staring at me as if only he and I were in the classroom. Then he yelled:

"Next Jew!"

"Heinz Levy," murmered Heinz Levy, standing up slowly.

"Repeat it! Louder!" shouted Opel.

"Heinz Levy."

"And what is your father's business?" The question was pronounced in a casual tone; this time Opel's voice had nothing sharp in it, it was a sly, calculating voice.

"I don't quite understand you," said Heinz Levy.

"Are you hard of hearing, Levy?"

"No, sir."

"So what is Herr Levy Senior's business?"

"He was killed at the front in 1916."

Professor Opel turned pale.

Nervously he rustled the pages of the old register.

"Sit down," he said hoarsely. "Sit down. Right. It's noted here."

But Heinz Levy did not sit down.

"I only wanted to give you my dead father's name. It was neither Moses nor Joseph. And it wasn't Abraham, either. His name was Ernst Levy, he was called Ernst—just as you are, sir. But he died for the Fatherland."

Only then did he sit down, Heinz Levy, the third Jew of the class.[7]

QUESTIONS AND TOPICS FOR DISCUSSION

1. *Analyze the personalities of the three Jewish boys from their reactions to the anti-Semitic teacher.*

2. *How would you have behaved under similar circumstances?*

3. *Have you observed unfair treatment and unreasonable humiliation of pupils in public school? Give details. What were your personal reactions and the reaction of the class?*

BOYCOTT DAY IN NAZI GERMANY, APRIL 1, 1933[8]
by Lion Feuchtwanger

[*Professor Edgar Opperman, world renowned throat specialist and member of an aristocratic German Jewish family, is the chief of the throat department of a leading Berlin hospital and clinic. Like other members of his family and his set, he is not frightened by "the old wives' tales" of the "popular blockhead" and his "few thousand young ruffians who roam about the streets." He is convinced that a whole nation of 65 million people will not be influenced by the "tomfoolery" of a few fools and scoundrels. The tragedy of the Oppermans, like the tragedy of German Jewry, strikes suddenly. One fine sunny day . . .*]

THE CITY LOOKED as though it were a public holiday. People were jostling one another in the streets in order to watch the boycott in operation. He (Prof. Edgar Opperman) passed innumerable placards: "Jew." "Don't buy from Jews." "Death to Judah." The Nationalist mercenaries stood about overbearingly, their legs encased in high boots, and bawled in unison, their silly young mouths wide open:
"Until the last of the Jews is dead
There'll be no work and there'll be no bread." . . .
There were twenty-four Jewish doctors attached to the clinic. They were all there, even little Jacoby. Everyone was in a hurry, as usual. No one mentioned the boycott. But Edgar could see the suppressed excitement on the apparently indifferent faces. Little Jacoby was pale. In spite of all the measures he had taken to prevent it, his hands that day were perspiring slightly.
"Get Case 978 ready," Edgar instructed Nurse Helene. Dr. Reimers suddenly put in an appearance. In a low voice, in his good-natured, rather blunt way, he made his request to Edgar. "Better pack up and go, Professor. There's absolutely no sense in your staying here. No one knows what the mob may do if they get out of hand. If you go, perhaps

I shall be able to get little Jacoby away too. It's simply suicidal of that fellow to have shown up here."

"All right, my dear Reimers," replied Edgar. "Now you have spoken your piece, we can get on with Case 978."

He began the operation.

Scarcely had the patient been wheeled back into his ward when they arrived. They had a list of the twenty-four physicians who officiated at the municipal clinic. They asked for them. But the staff resorted to passive resistance and refused to disclose their identity. A search was conducted under the guidance of a few Nationalist students. Whenever they found one of the Jewish doctors, they seized him and took him outside of the building. They did not allow the doctors to take off their white smocks. In fact, if they caught one without his smock, they forced him to put it on. Outside, before the main entrance, an enormous crowd was gathered. Whenever another white-smocked figure appeared, it was greeted with catcalls, whistling, and lewd insults.

Presently they found Edgar. "Are you Professor Opperman?" he was asked by one who had two stars on his collar.

"Yes," said Opperman.

"He's number fourteen," said another, with satisfaction, striking the name off his list.

"You are to leave this hospital at once," said he of the two stars. "Come along."

"Professor Opperman has just finished an operation," interrupted Nurse Helene. Her voice was not as low as usual, her brown eyes were wide with anger. "It is important," she added quietly, "that the patient remain under his observation for some time yet."

"We have orders to drive the man into the street," said the two-starred man. "Our business is to evict these twenty-four Jewish doctors and thus help purify Germany," he went on solemnly, as though reading from a document and avoiding the use of dialect as well as he could. "That is final," he said.

Meanwhile one of the nurses had informed Privy Councillor Lorenz of what was happening. He loomed large before the intruders, his white coat billowing about him, his red face thrust forward. He looked like a moving mountain. "What's the matter here?" burst from his gold-filled mouth, the words sounding like a small avalanche. "How dare you take such liberties? I am the master here, remember that." Privy Councillor Lorenz was one of the most popular doctors of the country, perhaps the most popular. Even some of the Nationalists recognized him from his pictures in the illustrated papers. The two-starred man had greeted him with the ancient Roman salute.

"There is a national revolution, Herr Professor," he explained. "The Jews are to be kicked out. We have orders to clear twenty-four Jews out of here."

"Then you'll have to clear out twenty-five men, gentlemen, for old Lorenz will go with 'em, see?"

"You can do as you like about that, Herr Professor," said the two-starred man. "We have our orders."

Old Lorenz was helpless; for the first time in his life he was completely helpless. He realized that Professor Opperman had been right: it was not an acute disease the nation was suffering from, it was a chronic one. He tried to compromise. "At least let the Professor here go free," he said. "I'll guarantee that he will leave the building." The two-starred man was undecided for a moment.

"Very well, then," he said at last. "I'll take the responsibility. You guarantee, Herr Professor, that the man will not touch another Aryan and that he will be out of the building in twenty minutes. We'll wait until he is." His followers released Edgar and went off.

But twenty minutes later they were back again. "Who," they wanted to know, "who was shameless enough to allow himself to be operated on by a Jew today?" Old Lorenz had gone.

"Now listen to me, please, gentlemen," Dr. Reimers demanded in his place; he was not quite able to control his voice; there was a snarl in it.

"Hold your tongue until you are spoken to," the two-starred man warned him. One of the students led them to the man who had been operated on. They entered the ward. Reimers followed. Edgar, a bit dazed, brought up the rear with heavy, mechanical step.

The administration of an anaesthetic for an operation on the air passages is difficult. Opperman had developed his own method for such cases. The patient, Peter Deicke, was conscious but he was full of morphia. His head looked like one huge white bandage, and from this his glazed, dull eyes peered forth at the intruders. Terrified, her arms spread out protectingly, the attendant nurse stood before the bed. The mercenaries marched up to her with a firm tread and thrust the trembling, speechless woman to one side. The Nationalists are people who know how to organize to the smallest detail; they had prepared everything; they even had their rubber stamps with them. "You swine!" they said to Peter Deicke, and on his bandage stamped the words: "I have been shameless to allow myself to be treated by a Jew." Then they shouted: "Heil Hitler!" and tramped down the stairs.

Edgar, as though hypnotized, as though he were being manipulated by wires, continued to follow them mechanically, his gaze vacant, confused. Nurse Helene caught him by the arm and drew him into the directors' room. She fetched old Lorenz. The two men stood opposite each other. They were both very pale.

"Forgive this, Opperman," said Lorenz.

"You are not to blame, colleague," replied Opperman, with an effort, in a dry hoarse voice and shrugging his shoulders several times, heavily, automatically. "Well, I suppose I'd better go now," he added.

"Won't you take off your smock?" Lorenz suggested.

"No," returned Edgar. "No, thank you, colleague, I'll take that with me, at any rate."[9]

QUESTIONS AND TOPICS FOR DISCUSSION

1. *When and what was Boycott Day in Germany?*
2. *From the events that happened during the Hitler Era, show how the poison of Nazism spread until it enveloped Europe and led to the extinction of 6,000,000 Jews and the destruction of European Jewry.*
3. *Read "Wear It With Pride," an editorial which appeared in the leading German-Jewish periodical three days after Boycott Day. You will find it in Ludwig Lewisohn's* Rebirth, *Harper, 1935. Report on its contents to class.*
4. *Do you agree with Prof. Opperman that "it was not an acute disease the (German) nation was suffering from, it was a chronic one"?*
5. *Find out how the world reacted to the Dreyfus Affair, to the Kishinef Pogrom, to the Nazi atrocities from 1933 to 1939. How can we explain the difference in reaction?*

THE LETTER OF
THE NINETY-THREE MAIDENS
by Hillel Bavli

[*Out of the Nazi ghettos, the concentration and extermination camps of Europe have come many stories of incredible heroism and self-sacrifice. But the sacrifice of the 93 maidens, students and teachers of the Beth Jacob Schools,[10] is the most dramatic of all. The story was told in a letter by Haya Feldman, one of the 93 who gave up her life for* Kiddush Ha-Shem. *The Germans saved these girls from extermination in order to keep them for a life of shame. When they learned the shameful future that awaited them, they recited the* Viduy *(prayer before death) and committed suicide, thus sanctifying God's name in death as they did in life.*

This translation is from the Hebrew poem by Hillel Bavli (b. Lithuania, 1893) which is based on The Letter. *Hillel Bavli is Professor of Hebrew Literature at the Teachers Institute of the Jewish Theological Seminary of America and is recognized as one of the leading Hebrew poets of this country.*]

We washed our bodies and we grew clean.
We purified our souls and we grew quiet.
Death does not terrify us; we go out to meet it.
We served our God while we were alive;
We shall know how to sanctify Him by our death.
We made a covenant in our hearts, all the Ninety-Three:
Together we learned the Torah, together we will meet our end.
We read the Psalms together, we read and we felt relieved.
We confessed our sins together, and steady grew our hearts.
Now we feel well prepared and ready to breathe our last.
Now may the unclean come to defile us; we are not afraid.
We will drink the cup of poison and perish in front of their eyes,
Pure and undefiled, as is the law with the daughters of Israel.
To Mother Sarah we will come and lovingly clasp her knees:

Here we are! We stood the test, the test of the binding of Isaac!
Arise and pray for our people with us, for the nation of Israel:
Pity oh merciful Father! Oh pity the people that knew Thee!
For there is no more pity in men.
Reveal Thy hidden kindness and save Thy downtrodden children:
Save and keep Thy world!
The hour of *Neilah*[11] is come, and quiet grow our souls.
One more prayer we utter: Brethren, wherever you are,
Say the *Kaddish* for us, for the Ninety-Three daughters of
Israel.[12]

QUESTIONS AND TOPICS FOR DISCUSSION

1. *Give other instances of* Kiddush Ha-Shem *in Jewish history.*
2. *Read about the Jewish community of Worms and its act of* Kiddush Ha-Shem *during the period of the Crusades.*
3. *Read the book* Kiddush Ha-Shem *by Sholom Asch and compare the sanctification of God's name as described in that book with that of the 93 Maidens.*
4. *What other instances do you know of Jewish heroism in World War II?*

POEMS BY CHILDREN IN THE WARSAW GHETTO

[*Although living under inhuman conditions the Jews in the Nazi ghettos conducted schools, organized theatrical groups and printed newspapers. One stands in awe and humility before the manifestations of their courage, heroism and nobility. Below are poems written in Yiddish by young children in the Warsaw ghetto. These poems touch the heart. They express poignantly the silent suffering, the dreams, the courage of little children. In the few years of the Nazi reign of terror, over 1,000,000 innocent children were exterminated.*

These poems were translated from the ghetto newspaper by Marie Syrkin and first published in English in the Jewish Frontier, *November, 1942.*]

MOTELE

From to-morrow on, I shall be sad
From to-morrow on!
To-day I shall be gay.
What is the use of sadness—tell me that?—
Because these evil winds begin to blow?

Why should I grieve for to-morrow—to-day?
To-morrow may be so good, so sunny,
To-morrow the sun may shine for us again,
We will no longer need to be sad.

From to-morrow on, I shall be sad
From to-morrow on!
Not to-day; no! to-day I will be glad.
And every day, no matter how bitter it be,
I shall say:
From to-morrow on, I shall be sad,
Not to-day!

NATASHA

It is twilight. I sit with my dolls by the stove and dream.
I dream that my father came back and will no longer go away.
I dream that my father lives with us now.
He comes home from work; he takes me on his knee.
He will tell me stories. He will play with me.

Mamma, mamma, how good it is to have a father.
I don't even know where my father is. Does he remember me?
If only a letter came from him.
Suddenly there is a knock at the door. . . .
I think—perhaps my father has come back.
I run to the door; I dance; I throw down my dolls!
My heart beats so—I think I hear my father. . . .
A beggar-man is standing at the door!

MARTHA

I must be saving these days,
(I have no money to save)
I must save health and strength,
Enough to last me for a long while.
I must save my nerves,
And my thoughts, and my mind
And the fire of my spirit;
I must be saving of tears that flow—
I shall need them for a long, long while.

I must save endurance these stormy days.
There is so much I need in my life:
Warmth of feeling and a kind heart—
These things I lack; of these I must be saving!
All these, the gifts of God,
I wish to keep.
How sad I should be,
If I lost them quickly.

QUESTIONS AND TOPICS OF DISCUSSION

1. *What happened to the Jewish children of Europe?*
2. *Which of these poems touches your emotions most?*
3. *Have your class write to the American Association for Jewish Education, 1776 Broadway, New York, N. Y., for information on how you can establish contacts with our child survivors.*
4. *Tell about the work of the Hadassah Youth Aliyah and how it helped save Jewish children.*
5. *For the background material to these poems read Marie Syrkin's* Blessed Is the Match, *Chap. IV, entitled, "The Ghetto Battle."*

CONFESSIONS OF A SURVIVOR
by Mark Dworzecki

IT IS NIGHT. My thoughts give me no rest. Images rise in my mind. Like my grandfathers before me, I rise at midnight to weep for the Destruction. It is the age-long ceremony of *Hatzot*[13] in a new form and with a new content. I recall verses from Jeremiah, who wandered over the graves of my forefathers, those verses which my fathers and my grandfathers used to recite, and my mind goes back to the graves of only yesterday. I hear voices from "over there," from those who have disappeared, asking me: "We are gone—why have you remained? How did you manage to survive?" . . .

"I don't know," is my reply. I myself cannot understand it. My thoughts drive me mad. I seem to feel everyone's eyes riveted on me with the question: "Why have you survived?" It seems to me they all must ask that question, they cannot help it! . . .

It was a combination of circumstances in which there was nothing striking or unusual. A mere succession of accidents. I always believed that I would live, that I would survive. But then all those who were led to the Fonar mountains refused to believe that this was their last trip. . . . And I saw death many times in the ghetto and in the concentration camps. Yet always the way out would come suddenly, as if by a miracle. Always a fellow-sufferer would appear to help out in a dangerous situation, by giving a hand, by offering advice, by saying a kind word; in days of hunger, by sharing a few potatoes and a spoonful of soup; in sickness, by bringing a piece of ice for my head; once—I shall never forget that—

a friend, risking his own life, brought me a dose of anti-tetanus serum.

I waited for death, many times, in the garrets and in the hiding places, during the early days of the Vilna Ghetto, in 1941, when the gunmen of the Gestapo were already knocking at our hideout. One more knock and we would have been discovered. But we were not discovered. . . .

I expected death as I burned in a fever from spotted typhus in the Kureme camp in Estonia, in December, 1943, when the most stalwart inmates of the camp, in the midst of their delirium, suddenly fell down like cut trees. Yet death did not come.

In March, 1944, I felt its wings come down upon me—during the long "march of evacuation" in the winter on the way to the Goldfilz camp in Estonia, when, thoroughly exhausted by typhus, frozen, with trembling knees and unsteady gait, as I walked, I saw the sky and the trees and the wind mingle in one mist—and I felt that I would be unable to continue this endless march, that I would not reach its destination, and that it did not matter, and that all I wanted was a minute's rest in the snow (and a bullet from the S.S. to put an end to me as it did to those who fell in the snow) when suddenly a comrade's hand caught me, dragged me for a few miles until we reached the enclosure of the camp. . . .

I saw it, in the summer of 1944, in the Goldfilz camp as we marched for "selection," and the chief physician of the camps, Dr. von Bottmann, looked deep into my eyes and declared: "You are too old," and pushed me towards the left side, for death—but the S.S. leader of the camp said: "He hasn't any gray hair yet," and pushed me back towards the right side for life. . . .

I awaited death in January 1945, in the sick division of the extermination camp of Dautmergen, in Southern Germany, where I lay suffering from general blood poisoning and a broken arm caused by the blows of a labor superintendent. Near me lay the intellectual leaders of Vilna Jewry, whose lives went out like candles one by one. Of the twenty Jewish physicians in Vilna, who were my schoolmates, only four remained in the camp, and each one wondered when his turn would come. . . . But my turn failed to come. . . .

I waited for it in April of 1945, during our camp uprising, on the road to Dachau, when the S.S. bullets pursued those who fled into the forests, and stricken comrades fell by the wayside, in the last hour before liberation—but the bullets did not strike everyone.

And that is how I have survived! Then how am I to blame?

And yet it seems to me that I carry an ineffaceable stain. It is the shame of my survival when the others are gone. . . .

* * *

Quoth my conscience:

"Is that how you survived? And how did you manage to receive your life-certificate?[14] Are you sure you haven't somewhere, somehow, betrayed me, your own conscience, on the road of sorrow, in hours of trial, in the ghetto or in the concentration camps? Did you perchance sell me at a price of survival—by serving the foe, by delivering your fellow-Jews?

"Were you perchance among those Jews, in the ghettos and concentration camps, who sold their own brothers to the *Molokh?*"

"I think I can look you straight in the eye, my conscience," I countered, "I am not guilty of selling you or betraying you."

Perhaps it was Fate which kept me from those inhuman trials which some people were unable to resist.

Now listen to me and give me your verdict.

The time came when only those could remain in the Vilna ghetto who were in possession of so-called "life certificates." There were very few certificates, far fewer than there were people who wanted to live— but I did not buy mine nor receive it as a gift—I won it in a lottery. The dice were thrown as between myself and my friend, Dr. Kolodner, and the two of us sat and waited for our verdict. Among others present there were Dr. Godburt from Vilna and Dr. Lazar Finkelstein from Kovno. My lot fell to be among the living, my friend's to die. . . .

For a long time I kept to Dr. Kolodner, in the ghetto and in the concentration camps in Estonia, where we slept on hard boards together, and on a Passover evening, by the small candle light in the Goldfilz camp, we chanted the verses of the *Song of Songs,* and on *Purim* we read together the *Book of Esther* and of Haman's downfall.

No, I did not seek any salvation for myself in the ghetto by joining the Jewish police. And when I was offered the position of chief of the Jewish ambulance service in the Vilna ghetto, I rejected it although it would have assured me of being among "the last survivors of the ghetto." . . .

And when I worked as a district physician in the Health Department of the Vilna Ghetto, and was ordered to compile a list of the old people in my district (I had a presentiment of the purpose of that list), I failed to find any old people in my district and resigned from my post. . . .

And in the Vaivara camp in Estonia, when the S.S. camp leader sought to appoint me as *Kapo* (Labor Superintendent), I informed him that very day that I was not capable of giving orders—and I remained at work as a latrine cleaner, while other Jews did find a way of ordering me how to do my work well and fast. . . .

*   *   *

Quoth my conscience:

"Thus you seek to exonerate yourself by proving that you haven't done any harm; but where were you when the Partisan Movement came into being, and how did you happen to get into a concentration camp, and where is your active resistance as befits a Jew?"

And I reply: "Your question has been harassing me for long. Now listen to me and tell me your verdict."

When they came, they were like the lava of a volcano that floods everything and swallows everything. We were trampled underfoot, humiliated and shamed, without honor, without weapons, not knowing what was going on in the world around us. And our neighbors, the Poles and the Lithuanians, with but few exceptions, showed fiendish joy at our misfortune, jeering and laughing as they saw us go into the ghettos, robbing our houses, and submissiveness reigned all around us.

On the third day of the Vilna Ghetto when we called a meeting of the comrades of our movement in the old *Hurva*, we thought that the mere secret nature of our activities made it a resistance movement.

And when we called memorial meetings in the ghettos for Herzl and Bialik and Trumpeldor, and told of their dreams and deeds—we thought it was a resistance movement.

And when during the days of sorrow in the ghetto we came to the despondent and discouraged Jews with a vision of a dignified Jewish existence, in a national home of freedom and labor, and with a vision of a free world, a world of justice and equality and human brotherhood— and when we appealed for courage and endurance and preached contempt for the enemy—we thought we were doing resistance work.

And when other groups arose in the Ghetto and when all of them together helped to build up a Jewish school system, a theater, a choir, an orchestra, and carried on cultural activity with lectures and literary symposia, at a time when every vestige of cultural activity among the non-Jews had died, we felt proud of it and we thought that that, too, was resistance.

At that time we also thought that every rescued Jew, every hiding place built up and every false passport made to deceive the enemy, was an act of resistance.

Only later we realized that all those things were merely aspects of the larger whole, and that the main part of resistance consisted in taking up arms even when there was no chance of victory.

And the Partisan Movement came into being.

I was a soldier among soldiers, a comrade in a cell and an instructor in a circle of partisan nurses. The leader of my group was Jehiel Scheinbaum. I used the ring I had bought as a wedding present for my wife to buy a gun. And life in the ghetto took on a new meaning, a new light, and it became as sacred as the closing hour of the service on the Day of Atonement.

But then came the day when the Jewish ghetto police came into the Jewish hospital, pretending to check up on the physicians. Then—with loaded revolvers—they led the physicians out in pairs to the hospital gates, to the gates of the ghetto and to the train. Among them, I, too, found myself in a transport going to a concentration camp in Estonia....

And I waited and waited for that day when I could exonerate myself, and those days did come.

When I was in the Kureme camp, in Estonia, where I had the "good fortune" to work as a physician, when the S.S. man Scharfetter came to me demanding a list of incurable people, he was told that there were no such people in the camp....

And when an epidemic of spotted typhus broke out in the same camp, then I (knowing the fate of those in Kovno who were ill with spotted typhus) concealed the facts from the authorities by making out false charts and by painting the typhus spots with iodine solutions and with solutions of Sefsa and Ichthiol. And when a Jewish camp superintendent warned me that after an S.S. inspection the responsibility would fall on my head (which meant a bullet) I answered him: "It has not been my privilege to take part in the ghetto uprising or to go to the partisans into the woods. Then let this be my medical work of resistance. I accept the responsibility and the penalty."

But now at night it occurs to me that I see them, the shades of Mordecai Tannenbaum from Warsaw and Jehiel Scheinbaum from Vilna and Fruma Plotnicka from Bendzin, and I hear them talk to me aloud: "We have perished—and you are here!"

"Tell me, my conscience, what can I answer to Mordecai and Jehiel and Frumka?"[15]

QUESTIONS AND TOPICS FOR DISCUSSION

1. *How many Jewish survivors were left in Europe after the defeat of the Nazis? Where were they found?*
2. *Describe, if only from this one selection, the inhuman tortures of the Jews under the Nazi occupations.*
3. *How did they organize to keep up their morale in the Nazi-made ghettos? Was that type of "resistance" heroic?*
4. *What was the role of the Jews in the "Partisan" war against the Nazis?*
5. *Read other stories or books written by survivors or interview one who has survived and report what you read or heard to class. An outstanding book of this type is* Blessed Is the Match *by Marie Syrkin.*

THE OLD PRAYER BOOK
by Jacob Kahan

The old tear-stained prayer book will I take in my hand
And call upon the God of my fathers
In my distress.
To the God of my fathers who was their Rock and Refuge
In ages past,
I will pour out my woe
In ancient words, seared with the pain
Of generations.
May these words that know the heavenly paths
Bring my plaint to the God above,
And tell Him that which is hidden in my heart —
What my tongue is incapable of expressing.
These words, faithful and true, will speak for me
Before God.
They will ask His pity.
And God in heaven who has heard the prayers
Of my fathers,
The God who gave them power and strength —
Perchance He will hear my prayer, too,
And my distress,
And will be a Shield unto me as He was unto them.
For, like them, I am left a spoil unto others,
Degraded and despised,
A wanderer over the face of the earth.
And there is none who can help and sustain me
Except God in heaven.[16]

QUESTIONS AND TOPICS FOR DISCUSSION
1. *Find in your prayer book "ancient words, seared with pain," and report on them to class.*

2. *Would you say that there has been a return to religion in recent years? If so, how do you acount for it?*

THE PARACHUTISTS FROM ERETZ YISRAEL
by Marie Syrkin

[*In* Blessed Is the Match, *from which the following excerpt is taken, Marie Syrkin writes that until August 1942, when the first horrible reports of the extermination of Jews in Nazi Europe reached Eretz, no one in the outside world knew what was happening to our people. These reports, brought by a group of Polish exchange prisoners, were so incredibly horrible that they were not believed by the non-Jewish press and radio. The Jewries of America, England and elsewhere, however, organized protest meetings, began actively to seek and publicize the facts, and to collect funds for relief. It was left to the* Yishuv, *however, to make direct contacts with our dying people behind the thick walls of the fortress of Europe. By dint of superhuman effort and self-sacrifice they succeeded finally in penetrating the sealed, weird ghettos with the help of the underground and the resistance forces. But it was not until 1943 that the Jews of Eretz Yisrael finally persuaded the British military authorities to drop Jewish parachutists into the Balkan countries in order to organize an underground army. The aim of those who volunteered was twofold: to help organize resistance and to rescue their brethren.*

The story of some of these parachutists is told vividly by Marie Syrkin in her book, and in Seven Who Fell *by Dorothy and Pesach Bar-Adon. The story of Avi, one whose life was saved, was selected for this collection as "a sample of the scope and magnificence of the attempt."*]

AVI STARTED training as a parachutist with considerable misgivings. He had been anything but a sportsman. The leisurely pace of tending sheep was hardly preparation for a life of strenuous physical activity. . . . His wife, his child, his sheep, had filled his life. But the cry of the Jews of Europe kept reaching him in the fields of the Emek. . . . Avi told me that he found strength in remembering the favorite characters of Jewish folk-lore — simple men who performed miracles for the nation, shoe-makers or tailors who became capable of fantastic acrobatic feats in a moment of exaltation! "You see," he said to me, "it is not the wonder-rabbis who became our saviors. In the legends, it is the plain, humble man, the shoemaker who is able to perform *kefitzat ha-derekh* (leap over the road, that is, annihilate distance); he is the original parachutist!"

In the fall of 1943, after a brief training period, Avi and Arye, another Palestinian, were dropped in Rumania. According to the original plan they were to jump in the vicinity of Timisoara, where members of the Jewish underground were supposed to receive them. Documents and facilities for the later transfer of the parachutists to Bucharest had been prepared. Owing to bad visibility, however, they were dropped not on the designated point but amidst anti-aircraft fire in a small Rumanian town. Arye fell in the courtyard of a police station where he was promptly seized. Avi landed on a rooftop, breaking his leg in the fall. In the morning, he too was arrested.

This seemed like a hopeless end to the mission. What could be accomplished by a prisoner of war lying with his leg in a cast in a Rumanian prison hospital? The first problem, naturally, was to prevent the Rumanians from discovering his identity or the nature of his mission. Since he was captured in uniform—that of a British lieutenant — Avi was in a position to insist on his rights as a prisoner of war. He claimed that he and his companion had been obliged to bail out because of engine trouble. As a Palestinian, he could be a British airman without knowing English. The Rumanians, however, were suspicious. They accused him at once of being a Rumanian native, who knew the language and who had been deliberately dropped for some Allied task. Avi's great concern was to keep them from discovering that he knew Rumanian. He spoke only German to his interrogators.

The Rumanians kept trying to trap him by wearing him down physically and nervously. His leg was in a bad state—infected and badly fractured—and he was in great pain. Nothing was done to alleviate his suffering, on the pretext that the Rumanian nurses did not understand what he wanted. He would not be given the flask for urine and other necessities when he made the request, on the theory that in a moment of distress and impatience he would betray his knowledge of Rumanian. When the cast on his leg bothered him, the nurse would manipulate the leg in some particularly painful manner and ask in Rumanian "Does this hurt?"

When these devices failed to elicit the desired response, the Rumanians decided on a more drastic course. He was told that his leg would be X-rayed. In the elevator the nurse said to the porter in Rumanian: "If I could throw this ugly Jew down the shaft, I would do so." Avi had to pretend not to understand.

In the X-ray room, while the apparatus was being made ready, the physicians began a discussion in Rumanian as to whether they should arrange the machine in such a fashion that there would be an explosion. Apparently they had read Jules Verne. Finally they announced that they would remove the usual safeguards. During this discussion, they kept watching Avi, and he, though uncertain whether this was a trick or whether the doctors were in earnest, had to look calm and uncomprehending.

After the photograph had been made, the physicians told Avi that his leg would have to be stretched, and that he would be given an opiate. This was a real danger. Avi knew that under the influence of an opiate, he might readily answer a question in Rumanian. Only an enormous effort of the will could save him. He determined that, if possible, he would repeat only one German phrase: *Was wollen Sie?* (What do you want?) When they began giving him ether the doctors started counting in German and then switched to Rumanian, requesting him to repeat the numbers. He forced himself to say nothing. Then as he began to lose consciousness, they squeezed his body painfully, while asking in Rumanian: "Shall I stop?"

Somehow, Avi managed to get through this trial without betraying himself. Even when he regained consciousness he heard himself repeating mechanically: *Was wollen Sie?*

The net result of this episode was that the Rumanians began to fear that he was a German, involved in some Nazi double-cross of the Rumanians. This suspicion made his stock rise, and his life became more endurable.

His fellow-prisoners, however, who were for the most part American and British aviators, also got wind of his conduct under ether and began to suspect that he was a German spy. Fortunately, he had means of persuading them of his true identity.

Though bed-ridden, Avi managed to establish contact with the Jewish underground in Bucharest, and by that means to fulfill some of the purposes of his flight. First of all he had to discover a friendly soul among the guards and attendants. After tactful probing, he established good relations with a soldier and a nurse, both of whom began to assist him. The initial step was to get messages out of the hospital. A regular correspondence developed between Avi and centers in Bucharest, Istanbul and Cairo by means of those go-betweens, whose cooperation was absolutely trustworthy and who were inspired by a genuine desire to help rather than by the usual motive of a fat bribe.

Once Avi knew that his contacts with the outside world had been established and could be brought into play, he began to carry out a principal point in his program: to help in the escape of American and British prisoners of war. He made his presence and purpose known to an American major in the prison and began to work out plans for escape. At that time the prison camp had in it one hundred and twenty American prisoners of war, all of them aviators who had been downed in the costly bombardments of the Ploesti oil fields.

Shortly after that, a directive in code was received from American headquarters indicating to the Americans that Avi (this was not the name by which he was known in the camp) was to be obeyed by all United Kingdom and United States prisoners in matters of escape. This settled the question of his authority.

* * *

. . . As far as the Jews of Europe were concerned, the parachutists' appearance was the sign that the tomb in which they were perishing was not sealed.

Word of the parachutists reached every Jewish community. . . . The story of Avi spread throughout Rumania. Of course, all kinds of legends sprang up around the parachutists. Their numbers grew in the popular mind; the nature of their deeds assumed a more spectacular character.... For the Jews of Europe, as every rational expectation of help proved illusory, as no great power intervened, no "conscience of mankind" revolted, hope began to center on the resurgent "homeland" — the only place which offered welcome, if it could be reached. When the miracle took place, and the homeland voluntarily sent its sons and daughters into the abyss, it is readily understandable what emotions were aroused.

One of the songs chanted in the ghettos of Poland and in the extermination camps consists of a single statement reiterated over and over: "I believe the Messiah will come. Though his coming be delayed, I believe that he will come." Even on the way to the slaughterhouse the need to believe could not be crushed. And for many the young parachutists from Palestine were an affirmation of their faith (as expressed in the immortal lines of Hannah Senesch):

Blessed is the match that is consumed in kindling flame.
Blessed is the flame that burns in the secret-fastness of the heart.
Blessed is the heart with strength to stop its beating for honor's sake.
Blessed is the match that is consumed in kindling flame.[17]

QUESTIONS AND TOPICS FOR DISCUSSION

1. *Read the excerpts from the following books and report on them to class.*

a. *Marie Syrkin's* Blessed Is the Match, *Chapters on "The Para-chutists from Palestine," "Jewish Partisans in Eastern Europe" and "Western Europe" and "Resistance in Palestine."*

b. *Pierre van Paassen's* Forgotten Ally *(Dial Press) Chapter on "The Best Kept Secret of the War" (The Jewish Brigade).*

c. *Dorothy and Pesach Bar-Adon's* Seven Who Fell, *Palestine Pioneer Library, 1947.*

d. *Moshe Mosenson's* Letters From the Desert *(Sharon Books) Chapters on "Desert Victory," "Brother Meets Brother," etc.*

e. *Major Lewis Rabinowitz's* Soldiers From Judea *(American Zionist Emergency Council).*

THERE ARE TIMES
by Zalman Schneour

There is a time for the silence of sorrow—
Not for loud weeping for a people who died—
Butchered like beasts, entrapped in their lair. . . .

Ascend unto the mountain
Made high by our dead.
Scorn and spurn
The promises of a brave new world
Which holds such wonder in it!
So lying tongues proclaim.
No brave new world
Without repentance from the old;
No wonders bloom
Where conscience is debased.
No scent of rose or myrtle
Can sweeten the foulness of the jackal's den
Or add a clean aroma to the stench
Of child-devouring haunts.

Ascend again
Upon the hill of death.

Spurn and scorn
The long peace-mongering procession
Of politicians, leaders, diplomats —
This long black-coated crew with white cravats;
And all the smart-attired generals
Bloated with honors like sated cannibals,
For whom the bones of our martyrs
Were a fortress of defense.

Sooner, later,
Will your scorn
And the groan of all our dead,
Like a cloud-burst fall upon them
With a rain of lead.
Brave new world of base deceivers
Lusting for the blood of men.

And you our saintly grandsires,
The *Book of Lamentations* close;
The *Yahrzeit* light extinguish.
Fall upon the ground —
The silent witness of our latest *Tishah Be-Av,*
When temples in their thousands fell in flames,
And Warsaw, Wilna, Cracow,
Lublin and Minsk and Kovno
Were devastated like Jerusalem.

Arise!
And blow upon the *Shofar*
The ban of excommunication
To the four corners of this earth,
Till the sound shall stab each Jewish ear
And reverberating mingle with timeless tomorrows.

The murderer's vintage, made rich upon our ashes,
No Jewish lips shall taste;
Not for us to share his golden corn
Springing from soil by Jewish blood enriched,
Not for us his luscious fruit

Made sweet by Jewish pain;
His tongue not of our speaking,
His songs not of our singing.
Not for us his fine fabrics
Interwoven with the hair of our daughters.
No smile of ours shall ever light upon his babes
Conceived in vilest evil;
The light within their eyes is but the sparkle
Of their fathers' murderous knives.

Unclean their violence and crime;
Unclean their degradation;
Unclean their humiliation and their doom;
Unclean to the end of time shall even their repentance be.

Tekiah, Teruah, Tekiah Gedolah
Blow the *Shofar* loud!
Proclaim the sole revenge of a living people —
Eternality!
A people pledged to life—
Pledged to the uprooting of the evil within life.[18]

Questions and Topics for Discussion

1. *Compare this poem to Bialik's "In the City of Slaughter" which was written after the Kishineff pogrom.*
2. *"No brave new world without repentance from the old." Do you agree? What repentance would you expect?*
3. *Is the poet justified in his pessimism?*
4. *What was the Jewish practice of excommunication in former years? Which country was excommunicated by the Jews? What has happened to that country?*
5. *Would you recommend excommunication of Germany by our people?*

AMOS ON TIMES SQUARE
by Jacob J. Weinstein

[This prophetic poem was written in the first year of America's entry into the war.]

(With apologies to Amos for slight liberties with his text, and gratitude for the perennial freshness of his ideas.)

THE WORDS OF Amos, a farmer from Pleasantville, which he saw concerning the nation, and which he spoke to the crowds on Times Square, two weeks after the bombing of Pearl Harbor, in the days of Franklin Roosevelt and Adolf Hitler:

AND HE SAID:
   "The Voice has again come from Jerusalem,
   And the warning, from the high places in Zion
   That blood and sweat and tears shall pour abundantly,
   And the green pastures shall be whitened with the bones of youth."

THUS SAITH THE LORD:
   "For three transgressions of Nippon,
   Yea, for four, I will not reverse the Judgment of Doom;
   Because they took Manchukuo with deceit
   And threshed the patient Chinese with sledges of steel;
   And ignited dynamite of air and sea with the pipe of peace;
   So will I send a fire into the house of the Sun-Emperor,
   And it shall devour the palaces of Hirohito
   And the mighty houses of the Samurai.
   And the people of Kobe, Tokyo, and Yokohama shall pay sevenfold,
   And the rising sun shall set in darkness of blood."

THUS SAITH THE LORD:
   "For three transgressions of Italia,
   Yea, for four, I will not reverse the judgment of Doom,

Because they rained death upon the inhabitants of Ethiopia
And called the shell-shattered bowels of the dusky people
'Beautiful as orchids flaming from the ground';[19]
Because they played the jackal to the raging beast from the North;
And betrayed the brotherly Covenant for gains of Empire,
I will send a fire against the walls of Rome:

And it shall devour the strutting Caesar from the high balcony
And strip the black shirts from an enslaved people,
And purge the slow seeping poisons of Fascism like oil of castor:

Thus shall liberty be restored to the sons of Mazzini,[20]
Laughter and song to the people whose speech is sparkling wine
And melts like music in the ear."

THUS SAITH THE LORD:
"For three, aye, for thirty transgressions of Germania
I will not reverse the Judgment of Doom;
For they loosed the dogs of war on all mankind,
And branded the flesh of myriad innocents with a double cross;
They devised devilish devices of destruction,
Turned vaulted chambers into arsenals of death,
Streaked the wide savannahs of the air with furious dragons of fire.
Yea, they harness the waves of the air to parachutes of lies,
And drop the subversive word into the wells of living waters
To breed suspicion and rancor in the councils of free nations,
To set white against black; rich against poor; Gentile against Jew
And make of no effect the will of the fair-minded.

Terrible and dreadful is this bitter and impetuous nation
That marches through the breadth of the earth
To possess dwelling-places that are not theirs;
Their law and their majesty proceed from themselves;
But, lo, I have raised the Stalin rod of my vengeance,
The resolute Bear of the East, whose paws are hammer and sickle,
To pursue him with the fury of an east wind,
And hold his panzers in an icy grip,

Until the Lion and the Eagle have recovered their strength,

And the Day of final Reckoning shall be at hand,
And the sons of violence shall be winnowed like chaff."

The Day of Judgment and of Reckoning; the Day of the Lord, indeed.

But think not, oh people of America, that this will be a day of light and rejoicing—a day of carousing and carnival. It will be a day of penitence and deep searching of soul—a day of confession and true atonement. Think not that ye are the chosen of the earth, inasmuch as I have cast your lives in pleasant places, and given you the kidney fat of wheat and the rich corn, that ye have become the millers and meat-packers for the world. Think not that ye are set above my other children. For your people are but branches of my planting in lands across the seas. Ye are a nation of nations—in you is all of Europe and Asia and Africa. Think not that the cushions of water about your lands are shields from the pestilence that walketh by day, or the arrow that flieth by night.

Egypt was mighty in its day, and Babylon no less. Assyria called itself "Invincible Eagle," and Rome anointed herself "Mistress of all Lands and all Seas." Yet, I destroyed these mighty Empires, their fruit from above, and their roots from beneath. Their names are but faded echoes in the ear of Time, and their vauntings, the babbling of children.

People of America, take this to heart and consider it well. Ye have I endowed more richly than all other nations. Ye have I given soil veined with silver beneath and crowned with fields of golden grain. Ye have I given forests of good wood, and lakes and rivers abounding in fish. And I have brought you tested men to match my mountains. Therefore, do I expect of you a double responsibility, and will visit upon you all your iniquities.

For, have ye not heard that the Earth is mine, and all that is therein? Hath it not been proclaimed aforetime that the Lord God is Father to all; that the children of Manchuria, Ethiopia and Andalusia are as dear unto me as the children of England and America: Wherefore, then, did ye smugly wrap thy oceans about thee and turn thy broad back on Europe's woes, that time my servant Woodrow Wilson pleaded that ye rise to your high-born part and create a *League of Nations,* in the image of the United States? Where was thy brotherly heart when the Chinese perished, and the Ethiopians were murdered and the Spanish massacred by the unrepentant sons of Edom, the stream-lined barbarians of earth? Did you not say, as Cain of old: "Am I my brother's keeper?" Two mighty oceans of water will not dilute the brother blood in the heart of my creatures. Therefore, the very ground cries out with the blood of the innocent, and will not open itself to thee until every drop of blood drawn from my abandoned children is recompensed by one drawn from those who were callous of heart. It will go ill with thee, but by Justice, and Justice alone, can the Earth endure.

> "The voice of sorrow will be heard in the land
> As the mourning for an only son.
> And the end thereof as a bitter day.
> Thus shall all the stored-up violence be expressed
> And the ancient wrongs be requited in blood.
>
> Then will the remnant of the people be sound,
> And get them a heart of wisdom at last,
> And raise up again the fallen tabernacle of David;
> A permanent Assembly for all nations;
> A Court of Justice for all peoples.
> And Peace, girdered by Justice, shall come back to earth,
> And men will turn their swords into plow-shares,
> And breathe freedom from the four winds,
> With none to make them afraid.
>
> Behold, the abundant days come,
> That the plowman shall overtake the reaper,
> And the treader of grapes, him that soweth seed;
> And I will restore the captive peoples to their lands,
> And Israel to his long-promised land.
> And men shall build the waste cities and inhabit them;
> They shall make gardens, and eat the fruit of them.
> And Man shall no more be plucked up out of the land which is
>   his home.
> On that day alone shall man inherit the earth,
> And be worthy of his God."[21]

QUESTIONS AND TOPICS FOR DISCUSSION

1. *Compare this selection to Amos, Chap. I and II.*
2. *This selection was written in the midst of the war. How does it illustrate the viewpoint that the words of our prophets are as fresh and timely now as they were when first uttered?*

3. *What message does this selection offer now?*
4. *What ideas would Amos stress were he to speak forth from Times Square now?*
5. *Explain the various allusions such as the* Sons of Mazzini, *the* Lion, *the* Eagle, *etc.*

UNIVERSAL DECLARATION OF HUMAN RIGHTS
United Nations General Assembly Second Session, December 6, 1948
(Doc. A/811)

[*Out of the agony and indescribable suffering of World War II came again the age-old dream of the prophets, the United Nations. The misery and horror of the war might be atoned for if Isaiah's vision of peace "when nation would not lift up sword against nation" were fulfilled, and the peoples of the earth could learn to live together in peace. With bated breath, mankind, praying for justice and peace, awaited the fateful deliberations of the United Nations.*

When the Universal Declaration of Human Rights, adopted by the General Assembly on December 10, 1948, was received, the world offered up a prayer of thanks. For the Declaration is an extension of the great teachings of the Bible that man is created in God's image and that we must respect the dignity, rights and freedom of our fellow men.

The following are some of the articles of this Declaration:]

THE GENERAL ASSEMBLY

Proclaims this Universal Declaration of Human Rights as a common standard of achievement for all peoples and all nations, to the end that every individual and every organ of society, keeping this declaration constantly in mind, shall strive by teaching and education to promote respect for these rights and freedoms and by progressive measures, national and international, to secure their universal and effective recognition and observance, both among the peoples of Member States themselves and among the peoples of territories under their jurisdiction.

ARTICLE 1.   All human beings are born free and equal in dignity and rights. They are endowed with reason and conscience and should act towards one another in a spirit of brotherhood.

ARTICLE 2.   Everyone is entitled to all the rights and freedoms set forth in this Declaration, without distinction of any kind, such as race, colour, sex, language, religion, political or other opinion, national or social origin, property, birth, or other status. . . .

ARTICLE 3.   Everyone has the right to life, liberty and security of person.

ARTICLE 4.   No one shall be held in slavery or servitude: slavery and the slave trade shall be prohibited in all their forms.

ARTICLE 5.   No one shall be subjected to torture or to cruel, inhuman, or degrading treatment or punishment.

ARTICLE 7.   All are equal before the law and are entitled without any discrimination to equal protection of the law. . . .

ARTICLE 9.   No one shall be subjected to arbitrary arrest, detention, or exile.

ARTICLE 11.   Everyone charged with a penal offence has the right to be presumed innocent until proved guilty according to law in a public trial at which he has had all the guarantees necessary for his defence. . . .

ARTICLE 17.   1) Everyone has the right to own property alone as well as in association with others. 2) No one shall be arbitrarily deprived of his property.

ARTICLE 18.   Everyone has the right to freedom of thought, conscience, and religion; this right includes freedom to change his religion or belief, and freedom either alone or in community with others and in public or private, to manifest his religion or belief in teaching, practice, worship, and observance.

ARTICLE 20.   1) Everyone has the right to freedom of peaceful assembly and association. 2) No one may be compelled to belong to an association.

ARTICLE 21.   1) Everyone has the right to take part in the government of his country, directly or through freely chosen representatives. 2) Everyone has the right of equal access to public service in his country. 3) The will of the people shall be the basis of the authority of Government; this will shall be expressed in periodic and genuine elections which shall be by universal and equal suffrage and shall be held by secret vote or by equivalent free voting procedures. . . .

ARTICLE 23.   Everyone has the right to work, to free choice of employment, to just and favorable conditions of work, and to protection against unemployment. . . . Everyone has the right to form and to join trade unions for the protection of his interests.

ARTICLE 24.   Everyone has the right to rest and leisure, including reasonable limitation of working hours and periodic holidays with pay.

ARTICLE 25.   Everyone has the right to a standard of living adequate for the health and well-being of himself and of his family, including food, clothing, housing, medical care and necessary social services, and the right to security in the event of unemployment, sickness, disability, widowhood, old age or other lack of livelihood in circumstances beyond his control. . . .

ARTICLE 26.   1) Everyone has the right to education. Education shall be free, at least in the elementary and fundamental stages. Elementary education shall be compulsory. Technical and professional education shall be made generally available, and higher education shall be equally accessible to all on the basis of merit. 2) Education shall be directed to the full development of the human personality and to the strengthening of respect for human rights and fundamental freedoms; it shall promote understanding, tolerance, and friendship among all nations, racial or religious groups, and shall further the activities of the United Nations for the maintenance of peace. 3) Parents have a prior right to choose the kind of education that shall be given to their children. . . .

ARTICLE 28.   Everyone is entitled to a social and international order in which the rights and freedoms set forth in this declaration can be fully realized.

QUESTIONS AND TOPICS FOR DISCUSSION

1. *Trace some of the above articles to their origins in the Bible. For example, compare articles 1 and 2 to Genesis 1:27; article 4 to Leviticus 25:10; article 7 to Exodus 22:20-23; articles 5-11 to Leviticus 19:11-18; article 24 to Exodus 20:8-11, etc.*

2. *Trace the basic ideas of this Declaration adopted in 1948 to the United States Constitution and Bill of Rights adopted in 1787 and 1791 respectively.*

3. *Write to the United Nations, New York City, and find out about its work and what role you can play to help realize its aims and aspirations.*

SUGGESTED BIBLIOGRAPHY FOR ADDITIONAL READING

Berg, Mary, *Warsaw Diary*, L. B. Fischer, 1945

Berges, Max L., *Cold Pogrom*, Jewish Publication Society, 1939

Bettauer, Hugo, *The City Without Jews*, Bloch, 1926

Davis, Mac, *Jews Fight Too!*, Doubleday, 1945

De Lacretelle, Jacques, *Silbermann*, Boni and Liveright, 1923

Golding, Louis, *Mr. Emmanuel*, Viking, 1939

Golding, Louis, *Elsie Silver*, Dial, 1945

Hashomer Hatzair, *Youth Amidst the Ruins*, Scopus, 1941

Hecht, Ben, *A Guide for the Bedevilled*, Scribner, 1944

Hirschmann, Ira, *Life Line to a Promised Land*,
        Jewish Book Guild of America, 1946

Jackson, Ada A., *Behold the Jew*, Macmillan, 1944

Katz, H. W., *The Fishmans*, Viking, 1938

Kertzer, Morris N., *With an H on My Dog Tag*, Behrman House, 1947

Kolitz, Zvi, *The Tiger Beneath the Skin*, Creative Age Press, 1947

Kulkielko, Renya, *Escape From the Pit*, Sharon, 1947

Lewisohn, Ludwig, *Breathe Upon These*, Bobbs-Merrill, 1944

Padover, Saul K., *Let the Day Perish*, J. Cape and R. Ballou, 1932

Pat, Jacob, *Ashes and Fire*, International Universities, 1948

Popkin, Zelda, *Small Victory*, Lippincott Co., 1947

Rontch, Isaac E. (ed.), *Jewish Youth at War*, Marstin, 1945

Schneour, Zalman, *Downfall*, Roy, 1944

Shoskes, Henry, *No Traveler Returns*, Doubleday, 1945

Singer, I. J., *East of Eden*, Knopf, 1938

Singer, I. J., *The River Breaks Up*, Knopf, 1938

Stone, I. F., *Underground to Palestine*, Boni and Gaer, Inc., 1946

Taylor, Kressman, *Address Unknown*, Schuster, 1939

Werfel, Franz, *Jacobowsky and the Colonel*, Viking, 1944

PART FOUR

The Promised Land

Refrain thy voice from weeping,
And thine eyes from tears,
For thy work shall be rewarded, saith the Lord;
And they shall come back from the land of the enemy.
And there is hope for thy future, saith the Lord;
And thy children shall return to their own border.

JEREMIAH 31: 17-18

Introduction: THE PROMISED LAND

EUROPE IN THE Nineteenth Century beckoned to the Jews with promises of liberty, equality and fraternity. But these promises proved will-o'-the-wisps that would not be caught. The nightmare of oppression and persecution continued in Russia, Roumania, Poland and later was to culminate in the bloody horror of Nazi Germany. And our people yearned, and prayed for a haven of refuge, for peace and rest. Already in the latter part of the Nineteenth Century Jews began to migrate in large masses. While the great majority took the westward route to America, a small group moved southward. Some 7000 Jews settled in Eretz Yisrael—the largest number on record to return since the fateful year of 70 C.E.

The miracle of present day Eretz Yisrael began haltingly in the last two decades of the preceding century. Long before Herzl, dreamers and idealists formed the vanguard of our seven hundred thousand builders of the present *Yishuv*. They were the *Biluim*.[1] They swore that they would work only on the land and only as members of a cooperative group. Overnight the *matmid*[2] became a watchman on horseback; the *Yeshivah* student a road-builder; the delicate, sheltered Jewish maiden a bricklayer and hod carrier. The flame kindled by Hess,[3] Smolenskin,[4] Pinsker and Herzl of a brave, free, reborn people on its old-new soil flared up in the hearts of the *Biluim* into an unshakable resolve to redeem that land. The wonder tales of those early years are indeed of epic proportions.

As persecution in Europe increased, wave upon wave of immigration beat upon the shores of Eretz. In 1881 it was the enactment of the Russian May Laws that marked the First *Aliyah*.[5] In 1903 it was the climactic Kishinef Pogrom[6] and the growing realization of the hopelessness of Jewish life in Russia that led to the idealistic Second *Aliyah*. The Second *Aliyah* emphasized the ideas of collective group living and the "conquest" and "religion" of labor; it stressed the primacy of the Hebrew language and the principle of self-reliance in every phase of life. By the time the first World War broke out the dream of Eretz was becoming a reality. To paraphrase the words of Weizmann, when the Jew finally became reunited with the soil of Eretz Yisrael energies were released within him "which had been stored up or suppressed for thousands of years." These energies are recreating a land and ideals that are inspiring not only our people but "may be of service even to rich and more fortunate countries."

It cannot be over emphasized that Eretz Yisrael did not represent to the *Biluim* and those who followed simply a haven, a homecoming in a physical sense. It was a spiritual experience. The return to Eretz Yisrael reached into the deepest emotion of the Jew. It meant rebirth, self-fulfillment, a release of the pent up dreams and energies of our people.

The miraculous achievements of our *halutzim* have been described elsewhere in word, picture, radio and cinema. Their feats have been acclaimed by Jew and non-Jew, by friend and foe alike. But even greater than the miraculous physical restoration of the land has been the miracle of the rebirth of our people in language, literature, art, music and dance. It is these values of Eretz which have made it a dynamic force whose life-giving rays have brought light and energy to the Jewish world.

Lurking in the background however (now very much in the fore-front!) was the problem of learning how to live with the Arabs. In the first groping years the Arabs were an enigma to the European Jew, as indeed the Jew was a source of wonder and fear to the Arabs. Gradually, after many bitter experiences, the need for a mutual understanding grew and became intensified. The problem is now agitating the Jewish world and the family of nations as never before.

In a short span of fifty years Eretz Yisrael has become a crucible where new forms of social and economic living are being created and where a new Jewish tradition is being developed. In the communal villages and cities, the Sabbath and Jewish holidays have taken on new forms of observance and new dynamic significance. Eretz Yisrael has fired the imagination of our young people to sacrifice themselves for the cause of Zion rebuilt. Because of Eretz, life for the Jew has assumed new meaning and new significance. Eretz Yisrael has become a fascinating mixture of dream and reality, of the ideal and the practical, of the humble and the exalted.

And all the achievements in Eretz have been made despite heart-breaking odds. Cities have been built on desert land, fields and vineyards planted on wasted soil, bare hills afforested, dry soil irrigated, and malaria-ridden marshes dried. The *Yishuv* has overcome the corrupt Turkish rule, the instigated Arab riots, the betrayal of the British, and the duplicity of anti-Jewish colonial officials. With the decline of world civilization in the thirties, Eretz Yisrael became a pawn in the deadly game of the Fascists. Then came the three terrible years (1936-1939) of murder, pillage and burning. The *Yishuv's* self-defense which gave rise to the magnificent new concept of *havlagah*[7] will be immortalized in our long history. That period of terror culminated in the cruel British White

Paper of 1939 restricting immigration and land purchase. Despite these heart-breaking obstacles, however, the record of Eretz as the Middle-East arsenal for the democratic countries during the war, and the heroic story of the Jewish Brigade will be our everlasting pride and glory.

The most recent phases of Jewish heroism are the *ha'apalah,*[8] so-called "illegal" immigration into Eretz, and the *Haganah,* the armed struggle carried on by the *Yishuv* against British duplicity and Arab terrorism. During the post-war years, the *Yishuv* struggled against almost insuperable forces in order to gain admittance for the helpless and despairing victims who had escaped from the flaming hell of Hitler Europe and who, but for Eretz, were without hope as without home. Once more our brothers rose to great heights. Then, in the midst of the pain and suffering, the strife and travail, came the fateful U.N. decision of Saturday, Kislev, 16, 5708 (November 29, 1947). The dream and the prayer of centuries was declared a reality by the nations of the world. To us has been given the privilege and the opportunity of sitting at the cradle of history. May we be worthy of the historic task, and may we be equal to the responsibility which Providence has placed on our shoulders to establish our ancient people on its ancestral soil in dignity, freedom, peace and security. As these lines are being written our people are drenching the soil of Eretz with their blood. Blood, sweat and tears are indeed still the lot of our people. For us the war still goes on. But ours is the right and the faith!

MOURN NOT!
by David Shimonowitz

Mourn not, weep not at a time like this,
Nor bow your head.
Work! Work! Plow, O Plowman!
Sower, sow your seed!
In time of stress, redouble your toil;
Dig, and then plant; clear and fence.
Level and cast up the highway of freedom
Toward a new day of light.
For on the path of pain, redemption comes,
And the blood drawn by the tyrant's lash
Cries out to the soul of the people:
"Bestir yourself and work!
Be redeemed! Set others free!"[9]

QUESTIONS AND TOPICS FOR DISCUSSION
1. *Compare this poem to the words of the prophet Jeremiah 32: 14-15.*
2. *Compare this poem with Einstein's address on p. 197.*
3. *How is this poem particularly appropriate to the period of the Arab atrocities in 1936-1939? To the Arab war against Israel following Nov. 29, 1947?*
4. *Compare the story of the upbuilding of the Second Commonwealth as told in Nehemiah, Chapter 4, with the experiences of the Yishuv in the upbuilding of the Third Jewish Commonwealth.*

AUTO-EMANCIPATION
by Leo Pinsker

OUR PLIGHT IN THE PAST AND PRESENT

THE NATIONS of the earth could not destroy us bodily, yet they were able to suppress in us every sense of national independence. So now we look on with fatalistic indifference when in many countries we are refused such recognition as would not lightly be denied to Zulus. . . . We were the shuttle-cock which the peoples tossed in turn to one another. The cruel game was equally amusing whether we were caught or thrown, and was enjoyed all the more as our national respect became more elastic and yielding in the hands of the peoples. . . .

When we are ill-used, robbed, plundered and dishonored, we dare not defend ourselves, and, worse still, we take it almost as a matter of course. When our face is slapped, we soothe our burning cheek with cold water; and when a bloody wound has been inflicted, we apply a bandage. When we are turned out of the house which we ourselves built, we beg humbly for mercy, and when we fail to reach the heart of our oppressor we move on in search of another exile.

When an idle spectator on the road calls out to us: "You poor Jewish devils are certainly to be pitied," we are most deeply touched; and when a Jew is said to be an honor to his people, we are foolish enough to be proud of it. . . . If no notice is taken of our descent and we are treated like others born in the country, we express our gratitude by actually turning renegades. For the sake of the comfortable position we are granted, for the flesh-pots which we may enjoy in peace, we persuade ourselves, and others, that we are no longer Jews, but full-blooded citizens. Idle delusion! Though you prove yourselves patriots a thousand times, you will still be reminded at every opportunity of your Semitic descent. This fateful *memento mori*[10] will not prevent you, however, from accepting the extended hospitality, until some fine morning you find yourself crossing the border, and you are reminded by the mob that you are, after all, nothing but vagrants and parasites, without the protection of law.

But even humane treatment does not prove that we are welcome.

Indeed, what a pitiful figure we cut! We are not counted among the nations, neither have we a voice in their councils, even when the affairs concern us. Our fatherland—the other man's country; our unity—dispersion; our solidarity—the battle against us; our weapon—humility; our defense—flight; our individuality—adaptability; our future—the next day. What a miserable role for a nation which descends from the Maccabees!

Do you wonder that a people which allowed itself for dear life's sake to be trampled upon, and has learned to love these very feet that trample upon·them, should have fallen into the utmost contempt!

WE CAN NEITHER LIVE NOR DIE

Our tragedy is that we can neither live nor die. We cannot die despite the blows of our enemies, and we do not wish to die by our own hand, through apostasy or self-destruction. Neither can we live; our enemies have taken care of that. We will not recommence life as a nation and live like the other peoples, thanks to those over-zealous patriots, who think it is necessary to sacrifice every claim upon independent national life to their loyalty as citizens—which should be a matter of course. Such fanatical patriots deny their ancient national character for the sake of any other nationality, whatever it may be, of high rank or low. But they deceive no one. They do not see how glad one is to decline Jewish companionship.

Thus for eighteen centuries we have lived in disgrace, without a single earnest attempt to shake it off! . . .

WE MUST HAVE A HOME OF OUR OWN

Today, when our kinsmen in a small part of the earth are allowed to breathe freely and can feel more deeply for the sufferings of their brothers; today, when a number of other subject and oppressed nationalities have been allowed to regain their independence, we, too, must not sit a moment longer with folded hands, we must not consent to play forever the hopeless role of the "Wandering Jew." It is a truly hopeless one, leading to despair.

When an individual finds himself despised and rejected by society, no one wonders if he commits suicide. But where is the deadly weapon to give the *coup de grace*[11] to the scattered limbs of the Jewish nation, and then who would lend his hand to it? The destruction is neither possible nor desirable. Consequently, we are bound by duty to devote all our remaining moral force to re-establishing ourselves as a living nation, so that we may ultimately assume a more fitting and dignified role among the family of the nations.

If the basis of our argument is sound, if the prejudice of mankind against us rests upon anthropological and social principles, innate and ineradical, we must look no more to the slow progress of humanity. And we must learn to recognize that as long as we lack a home of our own, such as the other nations have, we must resign forever the noble hope of becoming the equals of our fellow-men. We must recognize that before the great idea of human brotherhood will unite all the peoples of the earth, milleniums must elapse; and that meanwhile a people which is at home everywhere and nowhere, must everywhere be regarded as alien. The time has come for a sober and dispassionate realization of our true position.

With unbiased eyes and without prejudice we must see in the mirror of the nations the tragi-comic figure of our people, which with distorted countenance and maimed limbs helps to make *universal* history without managing properly its *own* little history. We must reconcile ourselves once and for all to the idea that the other nations, by reason of their inherent *natural* antagonism, will forever reject us. We must not shut our eyes to this natural force which works like every other elemental force; we *must* not *complain* of it; on the contrary, we are in *duty bound* to take courage, to rise, and to see to it that we do not remain forever the Cinderella, the butt of the peoples.[12]

QUESTIONS AND TOPICS FOR DISCUSSION

1. *Do you agree with Pinsker's psychological analysis of our people?*
2. *Are Pinsker's arguments more or less valid to-day as they were in his time?*
3. *Are we justified in classifying Pinsker among the true prophets of Israel?*
4. *How were Pinsker's arguments borne out by what happened to our people in Europe fifty years later?*
5. *How have we become even more of a "shuttle-cock" in recent years?*
6. *How did Pinsker, the physician, help his people psychologically to accept themselves and to become wholesome?*

EXCERPTS FROM THE DIARIES
by Theodor Herzl

A GIGANTIC DREAM

Paris, 1895

I have been occupied for some time past with a work which is of immeasurable greatness. I cannot tell to-day whether I shall bring it to a close. It has the appearance of a gigantic dream. But for days and weeks it has filled me, saturated even my subconsciousness; it accompanies me wherever I go, broods above my ordinary daily conversations, looks over my shoulder at my petty, comical journalistic work, disturbs me and intoxicates me.

What it will lead to is impossible to surmise as yet. But my experience tells me that it is something marvelous, even as a dream, and that I should write it down—if not as a memorial for mankind, then for my own delight or meditation in after years. And perhaps for something between both these possibilities; for the enrichment of literature. If the romance does not become a fact, at least the fact can become a romance. *Title: The Promised Land!*

AN INTERVIEW WITH BARON DE HIRSCH[13]

JUNE 2, 1895

"You will consider parts of what I am going to tell you too simple and others too fantastic. But people are led by what is simple and fantastic. It is astonishing—and well-known—with what little understanding the world is governed.

"Now I never had the slightest inclination to occupy myself with the Jewish question. Nor did you ever think originally of becoming a patron of the Jews. You were a banker, engaged in important affairs; and now finally you are applying your time and your money to the cause of the Jews. And I also was by nature a writer and journalist, never giving a thought to the Jews. But my experience and observations, and the growing pressure of anti-Semitism forced me into the service of the cause.

"I shall not go into the history of the Jews, with which I wanted to begin. It is well-known. But I must emphasize one thing. Throughout our

two thousand years of dispersion we have never had any unified leadership in our political life. I regard this as our principal misfortune; that is
what has harmed us more than any persecution. That is what has ruined
us internally, and destroyed us. For there was no one who could train us
to be straight-forward men. We were pushed into every kind of vicious
trade, and held down in the Ghetto where we decayed among ourselves;
and when we were let out people wanted us to have the habits of freedom
all at once.

"But if we had a unified political leadership, whose necessity need
be proven no further, and which is by no means to represent a secret
society—if we had this leadership we could apply ourselves to the solution
of the Jewish problem. And do that from above and from below and
from all sides.

"And the end we shall wish to pursue, when we have such a center
or head, will determine the means.

"Two ends are possible. Either to remain or to emigrate.

"For either, the same kind of popular education will be necessary,
because even if we emigrate it will be a long time before we come into
the Promised Land. Moses needed forty years. We may need twenty or
thirty. In any case new generations will come up in the meantime, which
we shall have to train for ourselves.

"Now I wish to begin from the very outset with quite different
methods of training from yours.

"First of all there is the prinicple of philanthropy, which I consider
completely fallacious. You are breeding *Shnorrers*.[14] It is characteristic
that no other people has so much philanthropy and so much beggary as
the Jews. The impression is forced on one that there must be a connection
between the two phenomena, in such a way that the character of the
people is ruined by philanthropy."

He interrupted me: "You are quite right."

I continued:

"Years ago I heard that your experiments with the Jews in the
Argentine are producing no results or bad ones —

"But in any case the project should never have begun as you did it.
You drag these agricultural Jews all the way over there, and they must
think that they have a further right to your support, and it is just this
which doesn't help the will to work. Whatever such an export-Jew costs
you he's not worth it. And how many specimens can you send over there
anyhow? Fifteen, twenty thousand! More than that live in one alley of
the Leopoldstadt[15] in Vienna. No, direct means are quite inapplicable
for moving masses of people. You can only be effective with indirect ones.

"Even if your twenty thousand Argentinian Jews do well, you will not have proved anything. But if they fail, you will be furnishing terrible evidence against the Jews. . . .

"Enough of criticism. What is to be done?" . . .

Then he said in a benevolent tone of voice, as though I had asked him for an appointment in his banking house:

"I can see that you're an intelligent person."

I only smiled to myself. Such things as my project are beyond self-love. I shall yet see and hear a diversity of things.

And Hirsch finished off his praise: "But you have such fantastic notions."

At that I got up: "Well, didn't I tell you before that this would appear too simple or too fantastic to you? You have no idea what the fantastic is, and that people's great traits can only be observed from a height."

He said: "Emigration would be the only thing. There are enough countries to be bought."

I almost cried out: "Yes, but who has told you that I do not want emigration. Here it is, in these notes."

Hirsch said: "Where will you get the money? Rothschild will subscribe five hundred francs."

"The money?" I said, laughing and contrary. "I shall collect a national Jewish loan of ten billion marks."

"Fantasy!" the Baron smiled. "The rich Jews won't give a thing. The rich are bad, they have no interest in the sufferings of the poor."

"You are speaking like a socialist, Baron Hirsch!"

"And I am one. I'll be ready in a moment to give away everything if the others will have to do it too."

THE MOVEMENT MUST BE STEERED

MAY 12, 1896

Great things do not need to have a firm foundation. An apple must be put on the table so that it should not fall. The earth swims in space.

In the same way I may perhaps found and secure the Jewish State without a firm hold on anything.

The secret lies in movement. I believe that on this principle the steerable airship will ultimately be invented. Weight must be overcome by motion: not the ship, but the movement, must be steered.

AT BASLE[16] I FOUNDED THE JEWISH STATE

Vienna, SEPTEMBER 3, 1897

If I were to sum up the Basle Congress in one word—which I shall not do openly—it would be this: At Basle I founded the Jewish State.

If I were to say this to-day, I would be met by universal laughter. In five years, perhaps, and certainly in fifty, everyone will see it. A State is founded essentially on the will of the people for the State; yes, even on the will of one individual if he is powerful enough (the *"l'Etat c'est moi"* of Louis XIV). Territory is only the concrete manifestation: and even where it possesses a territory, the State is always something abstract. The Church State, too, exists without a territory, or else the Pope would not be sovereign.

In Basle I created this thing which is abstract and which is therefore invisible to the great majority of people. Actually with infinitesimal means. I gradually infused into people the mood of the State and inspired them with the feeling that they were the National Assembly.

MAN CAN CREATE ON THE MOST THANKLESS SOIL

The Hague, SEPTEMBER 30, 1898

Traveled again through the sweet-smelling landscape of Holland. But not as I did the first time. Then, in 1885, I was a young dreamer, void of content, seeing only the forms of things.

To-day the land says something else to me.

I see a city rise suddenly out of the plain, without hill, river, or sea—without any encouragement, so to speak. That is the Hague.

A proof that the will makes the city.

If I point with my finger to a certain place and say: Let a city rise here—then a city rises.

The whole of Holland is proof of what man can create on the most thankless soil.

When a young man is in love he sees his beloved under every bonnet. So everything I see reminds me of my idea.

ZIONISM WAS THE SABBATH OF MY LIFE

JANUARY 24, 1902

Zionism was the Sabbath of my life.

I believe that my influence as a leader is based on the fact that while as man and writer I had so many faults, and committed so many blunders and mistakes, as a leader in Zionism I have remained pure of heart and quite selfless.

It is marvelous how far my thoughts reach out when I awake too early in the morning. Then I solve many of the problems of the present, and glimpse some of the problems of eternity.[17]

QUESTIONS AND TOPICS FOR DISCUSSION

1. *Read about the life of Herzl up to 1895 and report on your findings to the class.*
2. *Tell about Herzl's "mysterious" transformation into the leader of his people.*
3. *What was the work referred to in the first excerpt? Tell about it.*
4. *Find out about the work of Baron de Hirsch. Tell about the projects which he established. Which are still in existence?*
5. *In the argument between Herzl and de Hirsch, who, in your opinion, was right?*
6. *Tell about the first Zionist Congress at Basle and of its achievements.*
7. *What does Herzl mean by his statement "Zionism was the Sabbath of my life"?*
8. *Tell how Tel Aviv and other cities in Eretz rose "suddenly out of the plain . . . without any encouragement, so to speak," like The Hague in Holland.*

THE FULL-STATURED JEW
by Ahad Ha-Am

[*In the following excerpt which is taken from Ahad Ha-Am's eulogy of Leo Pinsker, the author dreams a dream. He sees Jews living securely in every land. They are rapidly assimilating. No one, except, perhaps, a visionary here and there, thinks of the future of the Jews as a people. However —*]

MANY A HEART is uneasily stirred by the question of Judaism in its national aspect. The bond that has hitherto kept Israel a unit, has suffered considerable weakening, and there is nothing to fortify it, not even the distress which craves the help of brethren. The customs of religion and of daily life have assumed a form peculiar to each portion of the globe, accommodating themselves to the general spirit prevailing there. The Hebrew language and its literature have well-nigh vanished from the memory of Israel. Their last vestiges linger on in the liturgy for Sabbaths and festivals, and even that is not known everywhere. In short, being divided according to the lands and the nations of their sojourn, and each section of them having taken on a form corresponding to the spiritual make-up of the nation of which it is a division, the Jews have stripped themselves wholly of all the distinctiveness of a people animated by a common spirit. Most of them have long left off feeling the need of being distinctive. With tranquil mind they face the impending dissolution of their nationality.

Here and there, however, there are men of strong feeling whose heart is heavy with grief and sorrow as they view the death agony of their nation—a great nation by reason of length of life at least and a checkered history. They must needs seek to fit the dismembered limbs together again and breathe into them the breath of life. After trying various expedients and succeeding with none, and proving to their own satisfaction that it is impossible to create a "Young Palestine" in the heart of Europe by means of researches into the Jewish past, the idea occurs to them to try "Old Palestine," the land of Israel's youth, which the Jews, no less than the other nations, continue to acknowledge as holy, and which, because it enjoys the respect of the other nations, the Jews regard with a certain degree of national pride. This national bond, weak as it is, the nationalists consider a sufficiently strong basis for their efforts to establish national unity. It is a tangible reality, and it stands outside the circle of the civilized countries, so that all Jews are in a position to participate in the work which is to center about it, reciprocally exercising influence upon it and permitting themselves to be influenced by it. For this purpose they form an international alliance, and they call it the "Society for the Promotion of the Love of Zion."

The founders of the Society being men of dignity and knowledge, who have intelligence and skill and use all needful care and foresight, they succeed in attracting many members from among the Jews living in the various countries of the Dispersion, as well as in collecting considerable means. Without delay the Society proceeds to execute its plans. It begins by founding agricultural colonies, settling them with the best of the young native Palestinian Jews, who are joined by robust and experienced men from elsewhere; by founding also a number of schools, religious, secular, agricultural, and technical; and in general by giving intelligent attention to whatever scheme may result in the elevation of Judaism and its adherents in the Holy Land. . . .

Throughout the Diaspora the news spreads that there are true Jewish farmers in the Holy land — true farmers, who with their own hands plough and sow and reap, and true Jews, sterling men, who at eventide, when they come home from the fields, read and study, nor do they drink to excess. Jewish farmers in an age of complete emancipation! A rare, almost incredible phenomenon in the lands of the Diaspora! Is it remarkable, then, that a number of prominent Jews journey from their homes in the various countries of the Exile, and go to Palestine to witness the wonder with their own eyes? And when they see this and more that has been accomplished by the Palestinian Jews, their hearts swell with deep love for the land of their fathers and for their brethren there, who by their normal, healthy life are glorifying the name of Israel in the sight of the other nations. . . . The example set by the distinguished is followed by the rank and file, until it becomes customary for every Jew of any pretensions to respectability to consider it a duty and a privilege to be a member of the "Society for the Promotion of the Love of Zion," and now and then to pay visits to the Holy Land when he travels abroad for rest and diversion.

The young men who are raised in the schools of the Society take up temporary residence in the civilized countries, in accordance with its arrangement to send well-endowed pupils abroad to finish their education. And wonder of wonders! Here we have intelligent students, who are neither from Germany nor from France nor from any other European country, who are only Jews from Palestine, and care to be nothing else. They are masters of several languages, but their own language is the ancient Hebrew. . . . The Germans and French and other students of the Mosaic faith . . . gradually grow accustomed to the Hebrew, and in spite of themselves they begin to consider it a language the peer of other languages. When they see their Christian companions pay respect to the venerable tongue in which the Holy Scriptures were written, they, too, the students of Mosaic faith, begin to remember and remind others, that Hebrew was the language of their forefathers in ancient times, and they end by being proud of it. . . . Suddenly they even discover that its sound is sweet and pleasant, and they express a desire to study it. When this desire becomes general, there is no dearth of "native Hebrew teachers from Palestine," who are preferred to teachers of Hebrew hailing from other countries, as "native teachers" are preferred in the study of all living languages.

Seeing its work prosper, the Society resolves to extend the circle of its activities to include the field of language and letters. First of all it founds a great and respectable journal, edited by accomplished people. . . . The paper acquires an enviable reputation among all Jews, and even the prominent European journals know it well, and quote it with due respect. The increase in readers brings about an increase in writers, and with the increase in expert writers increases also the number of good books in the Hebrew language, which appear in Palestine and are read with avidity in all the lands of the Dispersion. So Hebrew literature grows in quantity and, what is more important, in quality, too.

But why should I continue? In this style we might lengthen out our dream indefinitely. To sum up the whole matter: in the measure in which the work in Palestine develops and ripens, the number of interested participants grows in the other countries; and in the measure in which the number of participants grows, the work develops and ripens, and the more effective becomes its influence upon the Jews of the Diaspora.

A movement like this, having its origin in the problem of Judaism and not in the problem of the Jew, hence not receiving its impetus from outward accidental circumstances, is not subject to feverish, convulsive changes. It is a well-ordered movement, directed by inner, rational considerations. . . . Finally, after the lapse of several generations, it attains to the desired end: In Palestine there exists a "national, spiritual center" for Judaism, a center beloved of all the people and dear to it, serving to unify the nation and fuse it into one body; a center for the law and the sciences, for language and literature, for physical labor and spiritual elevation; a miniature representation of what the Jewish people as a whole ought to be. All this accomplished, the Jew living in the

Diaspora deems himself fortunate if once in his life he is permitted to look upon "the center of Judaism" with his own eyes. When he returns to his home he says to his neighbor: "You desire to see the type of the full-statured Jew, be he rabbi, scholar, or writer; be he peasant, artisan, or tradesman? Then go to Palestine, there you will behold him." . . .

"But," I hear you object, "how long the road you tell of, how distant the hope you hold out!"

True, my brethren, "distant, very distant is the port our souls seek. But no road, however long, may seem too long to the wanderer of a thousand years."[18]

Questions and Topics for Discussion

1. *What is the difference between the problem of Judaism and the problem of the Jew?*
2. *To what extent has Ahad Ha-Am's dream been realized?*
3. *Were the factors that led to the realization of his dream the same or different from those described in the above selection?*
4. *What are some of the institutions that have helped in realizing this dream?*
5. *How has modern Hebrew become recognized as equal to other modern languages? Give instances.*
6. *Is the "full-statured Jew" of Eretz Yisrael different from that in the Diaspora? How? Why?*

THE *SHOMER*
by Lotta Levensohn

[*In 1909 a small group of Jewish farm workers of the Second Aliyah organized the Hashomer or the Jewish Watchmen organization. Their purpose was to guard the settlements against attack from Arab Bedouins, marauders and thieves. Eleven years later, its mission accomplished, Hashomer dissolved. It left behind, however, stories of achievement, valor and heroism which have inspired Palestinian youth with a superb sense of Jewish patriotism and bravery. Hashomer is the spiritual parent of the Haganah.*]

THE WATCHMAN'S duties in Palestine are performed in circumstances wholly different from those which prevail in most European countries. There theft, robbery, and murder are crimes not only in the sight of the law, but of public opinion, and are regarded as crimes by the lawbreakers themselves. But in Palestine the code of the desert is still extant, whatever legislators may have written into the criminal code. In the eyes of his fellows, the lawbreaker is in many instances not a criminal at all. On the contrary, the bolder the exploit, the greater his prestige. The stealthy chicken-thief is despised; but the cattle-raider, who operates in broad daylight and succeeds in spite of the herdsman is celebrated in song and story. A man who commits murder to avenge the death of a kinsman is not a murderer at all according to the code of the desert, which prescribes vengeance as his paramount duty. The kinsman avenged may have been killed while attacking a man on the roads or attempting to make off with his property. No matter! A life for a life, whatever the circumstances! When one man kills another, even in self-defense, he and his family and even his village become involved in a blood-feud. . . .

Every *Shomer* had to be a good shot. If he belonged to the mounted troop, he also had to be a skilled horseman. But presence of mind and coolness in the face of danger were rated quite as high as skill in riding and marksmanship. Weapons were to be used only when mortal danger threatened; mother-wit must always be exercised first, if possible. For every shot fired the watchman had to give an accounting to a jury of his peers. If his story was not satisfactory, suspension from duty or even expulsion from *Hashomer* might follow.

When conflicting codes meet, nothing eases the impact so much as a neighborly spirit. Desiring peace above all things, the Jewish watchmen set about cultivating friendly relations with Arabs and Bedouins wherever they were posted. As a rule this was not difficult because they spoke the Arabic language and their skill with mount and rifle was sufficient to gain the esteem of men well versed in those arts.

Often a band of Jewish watchmen might have been seen riding out on visits of courtesy to sheikhs, who received them with the stately etiquette which Arab hospitality prescribes. Coffee was ground and brewed in the presence of the guests and served in tiny cups. While they were being entertained a sheep was killed and roasted in their honor. At dinner they were seated in the most honorable places and otherwise made much of. Every detail of the complicated etiquette was carefully noted by the guests, so that they might acquit themselves properly when the visits were returned. In some settlements, the watchmen fitted up reception rooms for the entertainment of Arab guests.

The men kept their ears wide open for stray bits of information about inter-village and inter-tribal relationships. Many a useful hint, too, they gathered from casual conversation about the care of riding mares and of weapons. Defense tactics were often improved as a result of these visits, and no inconsiderable insight gained into folkways and superstitions. And, as men of the Western world, the *Shomrim* were not insensible to the glamor of the ancient tales and legends which were rehearsed in their presence. . . .

Stolen property could occasionally be recovered by exploiting the good relationship between the *Shomrim* and the local Bedouins. An amusing instance is told about a donkey and a rifle which once vanished from Mescha in broad daylight. To risk a breach with the Bedouins over such "trifles" would have been unwise; conversely, however, the matter could not be passed over in silence. On the morning after the theft the head watchman rode out with several of his men to call on the sheikh of the Bedouin tribe encamped hard by the village. Coffee was served as usual, and they talked of one thing and another. In the course of the conversation, the head *Shomer* inquired whether, perchance, the sheikh had heard anything about a donkey and a rifle that had been missed from Mescha? The sheikh raised his eyebrows and uttered an astonished disclaimer. His people could hardly have been guilty of such an act against their good neighbors, but he would make inquiries. The missing objects were returned the same afternoon, but the "finders" claimed a small reward. It was paid, but very unwillingly, blackmail being blackmail whatever the sum involved. Later in the day a fine bull disappeared from the Bedouin herd grazing near Mescha. At daybreak the next morning two Bedouins on horseback called to inquire whether a stray bull had been found. No, but it probably would be! In case it were found, a reward (naming the exact sum paid the previous day) would be asked. The men tried to haggle, but the head *Shomer* laughingly cut them short. "You know well," he admonished them, "that we desire neither your bull nor your money, but such things as you did are not seemly between neighbors. We meant only to teach you a lesson!" The lesson was taken to heart, and for a time nothing more vanished from Mescha village. . . .

Meir Hasanowitz's success in certain cases was due as much to his humorous insight as to his bluff courage. One day he found Arab herdsmen calmly pasturing their flock on Jewish land in Emek Jezreel. He rode out to them accompanied by Giladi, whom all the Arabs called the "sheikh of the Jews." "Ya, ye shepherds," he shouted, "do you not see that I come with our great sheikh?" The men had been ready to fight, but awe of the "sheikh" stayed their hands. They wavered. Hasanowitz quickly followed up his advantage. "Where are your manners, O shepherds?" he jibed. "Will ye not render even so much as a ewe to the sheikh?" The ewe was handed over with a shamefaced mien, and the crestfallen men silently drove off their flocks.[19]

QUESTIONS AND TOPICS FOR DISCUSSION

1. *Why was the* Hashomer *organization needed?*
2. *What skills and abilities were required of the* Shomer?
3. *From this selection describe some of the problems and difficulties encountered by the pioneers during the early days of the* Yishuv.
4. *Compare the* Shomer *organization of old with the* Haganah.
5. *Tell what you have learned or read in books or newspapers about Arab life.*

THE HEBREW UNIVERSITY
by Chaim Weizmann

[*On July 24, 1918, when the Allied and Turkish armies were still locked in battle and the sound of cannons was still heard in the distance, Dr. Chaim Weizmann laid the cornerstone of what was to be the world renowned Hebrew University. Following are excerpts of his address on that historic occasion.*]

IT SEEMS AT first sight paradoxical that in a land with so sparse a population, in a land where everything still remains to be done, in a land crying out for such simple things as plows, roads, and harbors, we should begin by creating a center of spiritual and intellectual development. But it is no paradox for those who know the soul of the Jew. . . . We Jews know that when the mind is given fullest play, when we have a center for the development of Jewish consciousness, then coincidentally we shall attain the fulfillment of our material needs. In the darkest ages of our existence we found protection and shelter within the walls of our schools and colleges, and in devoted study of Jewish science the tormented Jew found relief and consolation. Amid all the sordid squalor of the Ghetto there stood schools of learning where numbers of young Jews sat at the feet of our rabbis and teachers. Those schools and colleges served as large reservoirs where there was stored up during the long ages of persecution an intellectual and spiritual energy which on the one hand helped to maintain our national existence, and on the other hand blossomed forth for the benefit of mankind when once the walls of the Ghetto fell. The sages of Babylon and Jerusalem, Maimonides and the Gaon of Wilna, the lens polisher of Amsterdam[20] and Karl Marx, Heinrich Heine and Paul Ehrlich, are some of the links in the long, unbroken chain of intellectual development. . . .

A Hebrew University! I do not suppose that there is any one here who can conceive of a university in Jerusalem being other than a Hebrew one. The claim that the university should be a Hebrew one rests upon the values the Jews have transmitted to the world from this land. Here in the presence of adherents of the three great religions of the world, which amid many diversities built their faith upon the Lord who made

Himself known unto Moses, before this world which has founded itself on Jewish law, has paid reverence to Hebrew seers, has acknowledged the great mental and spiritual values the Jewish people have given to it, the question is answered. The university is to stimulate the Jewish people to reach further truth. Am I too bold if, here today in this place among the hills of Ephraim and Judah, I state my conviction that the seers of Israel have not utterly perished, that under the aegis of this university there will be a renaissance of the Divine power of prophetic wisdom that once was ours? The university will be the focus of the rehabilitation of our Jewish consciousness now so tenuous, because it has become so world-diffused. Under the atmospheric pressure of this Mount our Jewish consciousness can become diffused without becoming feeble, our consciousness will be rekindled and our Jewish youth will be reinvigorated from Jewish sources. . . .

The Hebrew University, though intended primarily for Jews, will, of course, give an affectionate welcome to the members of every race and creed. "For my house will be called a house of prayer for all the nations." Besides the usual schools and institutions which go to form a modern university, there will be certain branches of science which it will be peculiarly appropriate to associate with our university. Archeological research, which has revealed so much of the mysterious past of Egypt and Greece, has a harvest still to be reaped in Palestine, and our university is destined to play an important part in this field of knowledge. . . .

Side by side with scientific research the humanities will occupy a distinguished place. Ancient Jewish learning, the accumulated, half-hidden treasures of our ancient philosophical, religious, and juridic literature, are to be brought to light again and freed from the dust of ages. They will be incorporated in the new life now about to develop in this country, and so our past will be linked up with the present.

May I be allowed, before concluding, to point to one very important aspect of our university? The university, while trying to maintain the highest scientific level must, at the same time, be rendered accessible to all classes of the people. The Jewish workman and farm laborer must be enabled to find there a possibility of continuing and completing their education in their free hours. The doors of our libraries, lecture rooms, and laboratories must be opened widely to them all. Thus the university will exercise its beneficial influence on the nation as a whole. . . .

Manifold are the preparations yet to be made. Some of them are already in progress; some, like the actual building, must necessarily be postponed until the happy day of peace arrives. But from this day the Hebrew University is a reality. Our university, formed by Jewish learning and Jewish energy, will mold itself into an integral part of our national structure which is in process of erection. It will have a centripetal force, attracting all that is noblest in Jewry throughout the world; a unifying center for our scattered elements. There will go forth, too, inspiration and strength, that shall revivify the powers now latent in our scattered communities. Here the wandering soul of Israel shall reach its haven, its strength no longer consumed in restless and vain wanderings. Israel shall at last remain at peace within itself and with the world. There is a Talmudic legend that tells of the Jewish soul deprived of its body, hovering between heaven and earth. Such is our soul today; tomorrow it shall come to rest, in this our sanctuary. That is our faith.[21]

QUESTIONS AND TOPICS FOR DISCUSSION

1. *Write to the American Friends of the Hebrew University and obtain the latest report of the activities of the University. Bring in a digest of it to class.*
2. *What contributions has the Hebrew University been making to Eretz, to the Middle East, to the world?*
3. *Consult the* Universal Jewish Encyclopedia *or some other source and then tell about the dedication of the Hebrew University on April 1, 1925.*
4. *Would you be interested in attending the Hebrew University as an undergraduate or graduate student? Why?*

LABOR ALONE WILL HEAL US
by Aaron David Gordon

A PEOPLE WHICH has completely been cut off from nature and for thousands of years penned in between walls, a people that has become accustomed to every mode of life, save a natural one, a life of labor, self-conscious and self-supporting—such a people will never be able to become again a living, natural, laboring people unless it strain every nerve of its will power to attain this goal. . . . Now it is true that among other nations, too, not all the people are working. Even among them there are many who disdain a life of labor and look for ways of living by the fruits of other people's labor. But, as far as a living nation is concerned, its organism functions in a normal way, and labor too is one of its organic functions performed in a normal manner. A living nation consists always of a large majority of people, to whom labor is their second nature. Such is not our case. We all disdain a life of labor, and even those who are working, work only because of compelling circumstances and out of an ever-present hope to be able in the long run to get out of it and make a "good living." Let us not deceive ourselves. Let us with open eyes recognize how much we lack in this respect, and how estranged our minds, not only as individuals, but also as a nation, have become to a life of labor. In this respect it is sufficient to recall the characteristic saying: "As long as Israel will comply with the law of God, their labor will be done by other people." This is not a mere saying. The idea expressed in it has, consciously or unconsciously, become an instinctive feeling within us and our second nature. . . .

All we look for in Palestine is an opportunity to make with our own two hands all those things that constitute life, to do with our own two hands every kind of labor, of craft, of work, every job; to begin with the most intelligent, the cleanest and the most comfortable ones down to the crudest, the most difficult and disfavored ones, to feel whatever the man who works at these various kinds of work may feel, to think whatever he thinks, to experience whatever he experiences, in accordance with our own concepts. Then we shall possess a civilization, for then we shall possess life.

What is the moral to be derived from all this?

Obviously the matter is clear and plain enough. The moral to be derived from all this is that henceforward our supreme ideal ought to be: labor. Our shortcoming—I do not say "our sin," because it was not our fault that brought it about—was with regard to labor. Labor alone will heal us. We have to make labor the center of all our endeavor, to base on it our whole undertaking. Only when raising labor as such to the height of an ideal—or to put it more correctly—when revealing the ideal contained in labor, shall we be healed from the disease with which we have been stricken, shall we be able to bridge the gulf which divides us from nature. Labor is a great human ideal, the ideal of the future. And a great ideal—in this sense—is like a healing sun. . . .

We need fanatics of labor—fanatics, in the most exalted sense of the term. To those who give their whole lives to this ideal I need not explain how hard the thing is, but neither have I to argue with them the necessity of doing it.[22]

QUESTIONS AND TOPICS FOR DISCUSSION

1. *Relate this essay to Fishkin's monologue in the selection from Yehuda on page 173.*
2. *How has the stress on labor influenced Jewish life in Eretz?*
3. *Expain the underlying philosophy of the Jewish labor movement in Eretz.*
4. *What are the chief occupations of American Jews? Why are we not sufficiently represented in certain types of labor? Why the difference in Eretz?*
5. *What arguments can our achievements in Eretz provide against those who accuse us of being capable only as professionals and businessmen?*

FISHKIN PERSUADES MR. PALEY TO STAY
IN THE *KIBBUTZ*
by Meyer Levin

[*Near the river Kishon, in the farm commune called "Carmel" (Yagur)
lived a group of* Halutzim, *most of them immigrants from Poland. They
were a very interesting lot—Yehuda, artist-violinist, "Doc" Pinsker, once
a medical student, now a ploughman, Chaim-Trask, intellectual, and
many others, including women. They were the vanguard of a people,
"trying to build something clean." To this commune came enterprising
Mr. Paley, an insurance agent from St. Louis, who crossed "half the
world" in order to see for himself, "if there really was such a place where
Jews were building for themselves a homeland with the sweat of their
muscles." Very soon Mr. Paley was absorbed in the commune where "a
man was a man again," where you had the feeling of doing something
real, and where the worries, taken off the individual, "belonged to the
whole commune." Mr. Paley would have liked to stay on, but it was too
late in life for him to make the change. . . .*]

THEY RODE HOME in the wagon from work. In the wagon many comrades were bunched squatting, sprawling, perching on the last sacks of
corn. Yehuda was there. . . .

Mr. Paley and Fishkin sat on the end of the rick, swinging their feet.

"Well, Mr. Paley," said Fishkin, "look at you now. Would any of
your businessmen in America recognize you?"

Mr. Paley pulled a delighted face, and then a worried face. Ah, but
he would soon have to be going back. In his pocket was a letter from
his wife. Maybe he was crazy, she said; and their daughter going and
getting herself engaged, and his partner doing God knows what with the
business. "Ah, for you young fellows it is all very easy, but for me—"

"Why must you go back?" said Fishkin. "Stay with us. You have a
daughter! You see how we are in need of young girls here! Oho, how
the *Halutzim* will run after her! Bring your daughter, bring your wife,
settle here. Be our business man from America!"

"Oho-ho!" said Mr. Paley, shaking his head sadly, sighing.

"But what do you think," said Fishkin, "that we will always be like

this: beggars and paupers? Look, here too there is work to be done! Here
you can be even busier than in America! Here too we want to make
everything modern, up to the minute, we want to work with great ma-
chines, to do everything with the power of engines! In many ways we
are fools, yes; there you see Pinsker ploughing a field with mules instead
of a tractor; and in the kitchen we have a stove that eats up ten pounds
worth of wood a month, when for fifty pounds we could buy a stove that
would do both the cooking and the baking with half that much fuel.
Well, we haven't the fifty pounds to lay out, but that will come, everything will come; see, we have many things to work for. Stay here, Mr.
Paley, be our power from America! You will see what will be done here
on this plain! Look, right on this line across our lands the cables of
Rutenberg's electric power will be carried, the spots have already been
marked out on which the cable-towers will stand; then electric power will
be cheap, we will have electric lights in our cabins, our yard will be as
bright as an American street; an electric motor will pump our water, and
we will have all the water we want; we will be able to plant a greater
field with bananas; bananas yield a profit of twenty pounds a dunam,
next year these banana trees that Shimshon has already been raising will
bear fruit, we will sell the bananas at high prices, with the profit we will
enlarge our plantation; next year, too, the vines you see on the hill
will begin to yield grapes, we will sell the grapes, and the year after that
the second vineyard will give fruit and we will make wine for ourselves,
we will drink wine in the commune, Mr. Paley! Look, here by the
Kishon[23] the government had promised to help us make improvements so
that malaria will disappear from this district, we will dig a narrow ditch
for the Kishon, and we will pour cement walls along the ditch, the
Kishon will run in banks of concrete, yes, that is already planned, not
many years now and that work will begin! Look how our forest grows,
Mr. Paley! When we came here there wasn't a tree to be seen! Now our
bees feed on the eucalyptus and give honey; in two years we will begin
to cut down wood and sell the wood, but that's a kind of a tree, the
eucalyptus, when you cut it down it grows again! Every year we'll have
more wood, more honey too as our bees increase! Now you see us living
in shacks, yes, but when we came here we lived in tents; we have already
built a house of concrete for the children; stay this winter, Mr. Paley,
and you will work with us putting the roof on our cow-stable, do you see
the rows of cows that are waiting to go into it! We started with twelve
cows, now we have fifty, next year we will have seventy! Then we'll begin
to keep milk for ourselves to drink! And when we have finished with the
cow-stable, we'll begin to build the barn; then another hennery has to be
built, the newest kind, with one side all of glass; after that we'll build a

grain storehouse, and then we will put up concrete houses for ourselves to live in! We will have a whole street of little houses, and a great mess-hall, and there will even be a stage in the mess-hall, that's all in the plans! We will have a radio, too, we will listen to the music from America, Mr. Paley, when Rutenberg comes along with his electric power! . . .

"Here we are going over this little wooden bridge over the Kishon, the *Hasidim* built this bridge, and we laugh about it because planks are always breaking out of it. The paper bridge we call it, because you know there is a story that the Messiah will come riding on his white horse over a bridge of paper; but never mind, we will not wait for the Messiah! Someday we together with the *Hasidim* will build a great road here, and we will throw a bridge from one high bank to the other." . . .

And as Fishkin talked, queer feelings as smiling mixed with tears lifted in the throat of Mr. Paley, for this was sloppy Fishkin, the little peanut whose feet were always sloshing in mud, whose pants always sagged from his hips, whose shirt was blotted with patches, and whose girl went off with *Hayim Trask!* What wild imaginings, what foolish dreams! And yet how filled with vigor, how filled with song!

"The towers for Rutenberg's cables will march across our field charging our land with power, driving the water through our soil, bursting the crops from under; the Kishon will flow in banks of concrete, the dry cracks in the earth will grow together; tractors will ride over the stickler weeds; the sunburst flowers will give place to waving grain; the obnoxious mosquitoes will find no weed for refuge, they will come no more; our bees will make honey, our cows will give milk, our hens will give eggs; the Kishon will flow in banks of concrete, and eucalyptus will stand high all along her length; those who are afflicted will become strong, there will be no more fever among us; the Kishon will draw in from her marshes and seep away from her muddy places, the Kishon will flow in banks of concrete—!"[24]

QUESTIONS AND TOPICS FOR DISCUSSION

1. *The colony described in the book is Yagur. Look up the story of Yagur and report how Fishkin's prophecies have been realized.*
2. *Find out about some of the achievements of the* Halutzim *in Eretz and report on them to class.*
3. *Do the same for the story of Rutenberg and how he made possible the electrification of Eretz.*
4. *For a breathtaking vision and prophecy read parts of Walter C. Lowdermilk's book,* Palestine, Land of Promise, *Harper, 1944.*

5. *For a vivid, colorful description of the miraculous achievements of
the Jews in Eretz read Ellen Thorbecke's* Promised Land, *Harper,
1947, Sections II, III, and IV.*

SABBATH IN MERHAVIAH
by Jessie Sampter

"I wish," he said, "you could be here this Sabbath,
To see how beautiful it is."
            I remembered
Nehama and her horror of their Sabbath.
I told him. "Is it true you wash and cook
And ride upon the Sabbath?"
            He's a "radical,"
Makes no pretense at what is called "religion."
"It's true, the women cook as much as they find needful;
There is no formalism. But the washing
Is never done on Sabbath. No, we rest
With all our might. Yet if a girl should care
To wash her blouse or rinse some handkerchief,
We make no inquisition. As for riding,
We sometimes take our wagons out on Sabbaths
To pay calls at the neighbouring settlements,
And singing, whistling, trundle down the roads.
But once there came a tourist, very urgent —
A Jew — and begged on Sabbath for the hire
Of a wagon to take him on to Ein Harod.
No, Sir, we said, we don't do business
on Sabbath. No, Sir, we are not *Goyim.*"

On Friday evening there is singing, chanting
of Hebrew ecstasies about our God
That would in other lands be called a prayer.
Here it is not a prayer, here it is re-creation.
Hands join in circle, feet begin to beat,
The circle sways, the feet and hands

And heads and bodies sing and dance,
The Hora turns now right now left,
With swaying, praying, playing forms,
Faster and faster, lighter, lighter,
Leaping, laughing, clapping, chanting,
Circle within the circle panting,
Dancing with passion, dancing with power,
With love and joy till the midnight hour.

Long sleep and tender rest
While the fields rest, and the beasts;
Singing again, and books and quiet talk,
And time for courtship and gay visiting,
And time for thought and speechless thanksgiving,
The mystic ease of muscles taut and tired. . . .[25]

QUESTIONS AND TOPICS FOR DISCUSSION

1. *Tell about the newer forms of Jewish ceremonial and festival life created by our people in Eretz, such as the* Hanukah Maccabiad, *the* Purim Adloyoda, *the* Shavuot Bikkurim *Festival, and the* Oneg Shabbat.

2. *Which of the above have been transplanted in America? In which have you participated?*

3. *Compare this poem with the one on the same theme on page 101.*

4. *Have you ever danced the* Hora? *How many different* Hora *dances do you know? Explain the steps.*

LATIFA
by Moshe Smilansky

"If you never saw Latifa's eyes—you don't know how beautiful eyes can be."

So I used to say when I was still a lad and Latifa a young Arab girl, hardly more than a child.

And I still say so, for all the many years that have passed.

It was January, the rainy season.

I was in the fields with a group of Arabs, preparing the ground for planting my first vineyard. My heart was in a festive mood, which seemed to be shared by all my surroundings. It was a fine bright day. The air was clear and calm, warm and invigorating. The sun stood in the east, shedding a reddish early morning radiance over all things; it was a pleasure to breathe, to fill the lungs to their utmost capacity. Everything around was green, and graceful and beautiful wild flowers nodded on the untilled hills.

Among the Arab women clearing stones I saw a fresh face. It was that of a young girl of about fourteen, upright and agile, in a blue dress. One end of a white kerchief covered her head, while the other end fell onto her shoulders.

"What is your name?" I asked her, wishing to note it down.

A small face, brunette and coy, turned to me, while two black eyes sparkled.

"Latifa."

Her eyes were lovely—large, black, flaming. The pupils sparkled with happiness and the joy of life.

"The daughter of Sheikh Surbaji," added Atala, a young Arab who was at that moment shifting a big stone. His remark was flung into the air as though casually.

"Like two stars in a fine summer night. . . ." Atala began lilting in his rich strong voice, glancing mischievously at me as he sang.

Henceforth my work acquired a fresh interest for me. When I felt heavy or dejected I would look at Latifa, and my depression and melancholy would vanish as at a magic touch.

Often I would feel the gaze of Latifa as she watched me. Often I would feel the flashing of her eyes, and sometimes her gaze was sad.

Once I was riding to the field on my small grey donkey. At the well I met Latifa, a pitcher of water on her head. She was bringing water for the laborers.

"How are you, Latifa?"

"My father will not permit me to go on working. . . ."

The words came pouring from her lips, as though she were emptying her heart of something that had long been oppressing it. Her voice was sad, as though some misfortune had befallen her.

"Would you not rather stay at home than work?"

Latifa looked at me, her eyes becoming dim as though a shadow passed over them. For a few seconds she remained silent.

"My father wants to give me to the Sheikh of Agar's son."

"And you?"

"Sooner would I die. . . ."

She was silent once again. Then she asked:

"Hawaja, is it true that your folk take but one?"

"But one, Latifa."

"And your folk do not beat your women?"

"Nay. How shall one beat the woman whom he loves and who loves him?"

"Among you the maidens take those they love?"

"Assuredly."

"While us they sell like beasts of burden. . . ."

During those moments Latifa's eyes were even more beautiful, deeper and blacker.

"My father says," she added a moment later, "that he would give me to you, if you would become a Moslem. . . ."

"To me?"

I burst out laughing in spite of myself. Latifa gazed at me, her eyes full of anguish.

"Latifa," I said, "become a Jewess and I will take you."

"My father would slay me, and you too."

Next day Sheikh Surbaji came to my vineyard.

He was an old man with a fine white beard, a tall tarbush on his head, riding on a spirited white mare that pranced and curveted beneath him.

He gave greeting to the laborers, who on their side all bowed to him with great humility and became silent. At me he threw an ill-tempered look, and he greeted me with a snarl in his voice: I responded with equal coolness. There was no love lost between the Colony and the Sheikh, who bore a fanatic hatred toward the Jews.

When the Sheikh saw his daughter his anger grew to fury.

"Did I not order you to cease going to the Jew?" he stormed.

And to the laborers he said:

"Shame upon you, Moslems, who sell your toil to the unbelievers!"

The stick in his hand fell several times on the head and shoulders of Latifa. Thoroughly angered, I made a motion toward him, but the sad, black, tear-filled eyes of Latifa looked at me as though entreating me to be still.

The Sheikh and his daughter departed. The laborers breathed more freely.

"Sheikh Surbaji is pitiless," said one.

"He is furious because he can no longer get his laborers at half the wages, and make them toil from morning to night. The Jews compete," said a second.

"And I know why he is in a rage today," said Atala, a cunning smile hovering about his lips.

Latifa did not return to work.

One afternoon a few weeks later, when I left the house where I was accustomed to take my meals, I met her. She sat on the ground outside offering chickens for sale. When she saw me she rose. Her eyes were more beautiful and more sad than ever.

"How are you, Latifa?"

"Thank you, Hawaja."

Her voice shook.

And Latifa often brought chickens for sale, and always at the noon hour. . . .

One day Atala said to me:

"Hawaja, Latifa has gone to Agar; the Sheikh's son has taken her— a small and ugly fellow. . . ."

To me his words were like a stab in the heart.

Afterwards I heard that the house of Latifa's husband had been destroyed by fire, that Latifa had fled to her father's house, and that they had taken her back to her husband against her will.

Some years passed. I was living in the house which I had built for myself. Other black eyes had made me forget the eyes of Latifa.

One morning I went out and found two old Arab women holding chickens.

"What do you want?"

One of the women rose from the ground and gazed at me.

"Hawaja Musa?"

"Latifa!"

Ay, this was Latifa; this old woman with her seamed and wrinkled face. She had grown old, but her eyes still retained traces of their former brightness.

"You have a beard—how changed—" she whispered, not moving her eyes from me.

"How are you? Why have you changed so?"

"All things come from Allah, Hawaja!"

She was silent. Then:

"Hawaja Musa has taken a wife?"

"Yes, Latifa."

"I would like to see her. . . ."

I called my wife out.

Latifa looked at her for a long time.

There were tears in her eyes. . . .

I have not seen Latifa since then.[26]

QUESTIONS AND TOPICS FOR DISCUSSION

1. *What are the undercurrents in the story "Latifa"? Point out the incidents which lead you to this conclusion.*
2. *What is the attitude of the Arabs to their women?*
3. *How does this story alone suggest that the Yishuv has influenced the life of our Arab cousins? Illustrate by quoting from the story.*
4. *Describe certain Arab folkways and customs which are brought out in this story.*
5. *"Latifa" points up some of the antagonisms the Arabs feel toward the Jews. What are they?*
6. *Can you suggest how Jew and Arab can learn to live together in peace in Eretz?*

WE ARE BROTHERS
by J. H. Brenner

[*The following selection is of special significance because it was among Brenner's last written words. It was composed at the end of April, 1921, a few days before he was murdered by Arab assassins.*]

TOWARDS EVENING I had been straying along the paths of the Arab groves just below the city of Jaffa. I happened to pass an effendi's house. On the doorstep there sat an effendi in the company of two elderly neighbors and a young fellow of about twenty in a cap. I greeted them; they did not answer. So I went on. As I happened to glance back I noticed by their looks that their silence was a purposeful and mean one. The young fellow had already stretched himself upon the ground and cast about a triumphant expression, as if to say: We didn't answer that *Yahud*.

I went on. Suddenly, from one of the groves an Arab jumped out, dressed in a short tattered topcoat, with a spade slung across his shoulder.

"*Hawaja!*" he exclaimed upon overtaking me.

I noticed that he was not as old as he seemed at first, but only a lad of 13 years. He asked me something in a small, shrill voice, emphasizing each and every word. Unfortunately, since I didn't know any Arabic, I couldn't answer him. I replied with only one word:

"From Selima?" (i.e., From the nearby town Selima?)

He replied: "No, I come from this neighborhood, from the grove."

Then he went on with his story. I asked him, pointing my finger:

"Effendi?" (i.e., Does the grove where you're coming from and where you seemingly work belong to that effendi sitting there on the doorstep?)

He nodded with his head, "yes" and then continued to tell me his story in the same manner. From a few of his words and more from his movements and gesticulations I gathered that his parents had died during the war and that he was an orphan. He also understood my next question:

"*Khadesh?*" (i.e., How much do you earn a day?)

He answered in a dignified manner: "Eight grush."

"That's not so good," I told him. For a moment he was puzzled and did not know what I had meant by "no good." Was it too much or too little? Then he went on to tell me that there were workers in the grove who received fifteen grush a day, and some even got twenty a day. But these were the big workers . . . and he had a younger sister . . . they had to eat and live . . . and he only made eight grush. Allah deemed it so.

Just then I reproached myself, rather severely, for not having learned to speak Arabic. Oh, if I could only have conversed with you better—my orphan worker! My young comrade, whether it is true or not what the scholars say about your being my blood relation, I feel responsible for you. I should have opened your eyes and let you enjoy some human kindness. No! Not only revolutionary machinations in the Near East, not on one foot, not at the command of some committee or agents of some socialist politics. No, not any politics! Maybe this isn't even any of our business. We'd probably have to do this by force, out of despair or the lack of an alternative! No, we don't want this! We want only a soulful relationship . . . today . . . for centuries to come . . . for many, many days . . . with the meaning to be brothers, comrades.

"Farewell, *Hawaja!*" the young Arab bid me, as we took leave of each other, noticing how absorbed I was over our conversation. His farewell greeting imparted a feeling of satisfaction over his having had a chance to speak to a grown-up expertly and manlike.

"*Shalom,* my brother!" I whispered through my lips, my heart beating for both myself and him.[27]

QUESTIONS AND TOPICS FOR DISCUSSION

1. *What are the relations between the effendi and the fellahen in Arab Palestine? Between them and the Jews?*
2. *How have our people helped in improving the conditions of Arab life?*
3. *How have they helped in improving Arab labor conditions?*
4. *Why is it vital for our people in Eretz Yisrael to learn to live in peace with the Arabs?*

A COMMON RESPONSIBILITY
(EXCERPTS FROM HER LETTERS)
by Henrietta Szold

[*The first newcomers of the Youth Aliyah immigration, who were 15-17 years of age, arrived in February, 1934. Their training program, set up by Miss Szold, provided for instruction in practical work on the farm, in the stables and the workshop, as well as Hebrew and general academic studies in school, excursions into the country, and the like.*

Miss Szold took care of every detail of the program from the first moment of their arrival. She was in constant touch with their parents overseas. All this, when she was already in her 75th year!]

Jerusalem, MARCH 2, 1934

AT THIS HOUR a week ago I returned to Jerusalem after four days spent in Haifa, Ain Harod, and Kfar Giladi. It took me two hours and a half to remove mud from my shoes, my overshoes, my coat, my dress, my unders — for from the moment on Monday morning when the train reached the environs of Haifa until the moment on Friday when I escaped from the environs of Kfar Giladi, it rained and hailed and blew and stormed and then began all over again. Such depths of mud as I trudged through! Every time I took a step I dug up great clods, and by the time I approached any destination I was bound for — dining room or my bedroom in the *Kevutzot*—I was dragging with me a mountain of earth.

What was it all about? The first group of boys and girls arrived from Germany at Haifa, the detachment of forty-three destined for Ain Harod. I went up to meet them, and then traveled to Ain Harod with them and stayed with them there for two days. It was a great experience for me. I am going to send you an account I have written of their arrival and their reception at Ain Harod as soon as it is stencilled. The account is intended for the committees that are raising funds for the Youth Aliyah. I did not succeed in conveying in the account the beautiful attitude of the Ain Harod community toward the young people, and how solemnly and yet joyously they assumed the responsibility for them. The way they introduce them into the *kevutzah* life is a religious poem. I don't mean a ceremonial. They worked out a plan of gradual adjustment that is of the

essence of delicacy and tact. The boys and girls felt the forethought instinctively. I wish I might have stayed with them a month.

Jerusalem, DECEMBER 28, 1934

Two weeks ago eighty-six children arrived from Germany. I met
seventy-five of them at Haifa and escorted them to the *Emek Ha-Yarden*
settlements. I remained with them until the next day, saw them well
bestowed, assured myself of the presence of screens, mosquito nets, and
sanitary installations; I celebrated a charming reception with them, at
which there was feasting, singing, dancing, and speech-making, and
for which the settlers of five neighboring *kevutzot* had come together at
Deganiah Aleph. The *kevutzot* were naturally not established as educational institutions, but they might have been if one was to judge by the
way they make these fugitive youths at home and prepare for their
training.

My pessimism regularly vanishes when I spend a few hours in a
kevutzah — I forget that I am a cynic. It's a life of hardship, but not of
strain. And the hardship has its compensation in the form of achievement,
and the consciousness that both the hardship and the success are a common responsibility and a common advantage.[28]

QUESTIONS AND TOPICS FOR DISCUSSION

1. *Read Elma Ehrlich Levinger's* The Fighting Angel *(Behrman) and
   report on Henrietta Szold's life and work.*
2. *Write to the Hadassah office in New York City for information as to
   its history and activities, and report on your findings.*
3. *Write to Hadassah to send you information on its Youth Aliyah program and report on this magnificent story.*
4. *Find out what your community has done for Youth Aliyah.*

THE POWER AND THE CHARM OF ERETZ
by Moshe Mosenson

FEBRUARY 22, 1941

IT IS THE Sabbath Eve. All of us have gathered in the half-shattered hall to take part in the Sabbath festivity. I was surprised to get a letter from you after several weeks of waiting without one. The boys are singing here and I sit in a corner, reading and re-reading your letter and trying to feel myself at home with you. And my home seems far away, though I can see the lights of the Sabbath in it. It seems far away, not merely because hundreds of kilometers separate us, or because the frontiers of four countries lie between us, or because merely of the distance in time, for it is only a few months since I left you—but because things have happened to me in the space of these few months that make me feel as though they were decades. And everything that I have left behind me seems so distant and inaccessible. If only you knew how good it is to receive a letter from home. If only you could see how it changes them all, so that they seem to be radiant with goodness. . . .

There are some among us who never receive any letters at all. These are "illegal" immigrants, lonely, solitary souls, without friends; their parents have remained in the Diaspora, a prey to the hazards of war and persecution, and there is no one to write to them. They seem so pitiful at a moment like this. In comparison with them, there are well-fed, well-rooted boys who receive an abundance of good things, letters and packages of money. The contrast between them and between the boys who don't receive anything, not even a letter or a newspaper, is shocking to see. There is also the member of a *Kibutz* who has received nothing at all, not a single letter, not even the "diary" of his village. There were tears in his eyes. At that moment I saw quite clearly how a man's ties with his group and with the whole movement can be destroyed by his sense of pain and disgrace. Is there no way of avoiding this? If the volunteer does not have relatives or close friends he is left forsaken and alone, in most cases.

I had an experience today that was very touching. There is an "illegal" immigrant from Germany among us, a man with a wife and son. He is very embittered. In Palestine he had some bad experiences with "connections" and "pull"—and he was crushed by them. Now he is in the army, and most of our boys, instead of teaching him Hebrew, have been grumbling about his German. They use every opportunity to call him *Yekeh*. He, in his bitterness, threatens that he will return to Germany again, after the war, "when it becomes democratic again." Today he came to me pleadingly: *"Bitte,* read this letter to me." I sat down, with a letter in childish handwriting in my hands, and read to him: "Dear Father, Mother cries every evening and says, 'Hansi, let's pray to God so that father will come home safely.' I want you to come home already and I want you to bring me a bicycle. I had a birthday party at school. I am ten years old already. When you come home we'll make another party and mother will fix the coffee the way you like it. I am studying well. When I am big I will work in a *Kibutz* and you will drink coffee and rest from the war. Only come home soon!" I read the letter slowly and translated each word into my broken German, and he, the father, sat there weeping. Then I realized what had happened. The son had taken root in the country, and his father, for his son's sake, would take root in it too. When I finished reading the letter I said to him that we would teach him Hebrew so that he would be able to read his son's letters himself. He was very moved by this offer and almost kissed me. Such is the power of children. . . .

I had another interesting encounter with an Australian Jew. I was standing next to the store-room with my machine when an Australian came up to me and asked me to help him. I went over to his truck to help him load a heavy crate on it. It didn't "go." The boy took a pencil out of his pocket, drew a Star of David and said: "This time it will work." I wondered at this, but I didn't say anything. We tried again, and this time it "worked." When the crate was settled on top he explained:

"Listen, boy, if ever you have trouble loading, make this drawing on it and then it will be all right."

I asked him in English: "What does that mean?"

Luckily he didn't notice anything wrong with my English and he explained further: "I am a Jew, and this is a Jewish religious symbol and it helps."

I asked: "Do you speak Hebrew?"

"Yes," he said, "I learned how in my new homeland, in Palestine; I was there for about a year."

"Do you like Palestine?" I asked, still in English.

"The way you love England, and the way I love Australia." Then he turned to me excitedly and said: "Listen, have you ever been in Palestine? No? Listen to me, then. Go there on your next leave. You will see labor groups there such as you never saw in your life." And he went on to tell me, the "Englishman," about the *Kibutz* and about the country. He talked like this for about a quarter of an hour. I couldn't understand everything he said, but I understood the tone. After the war, he said, he would go back to Palestine and join a *Kibutz*. His father is a landowner in Australia, but he said that he would persuade him to come to settle in Palestine.

After this I couldn't restrain myself any longer and told him who I was. He was very amused at my little trick and embraced me. He is a handsome, broad-shouldered boy whose name is Billy Gorsch. We laughed a long time together. Finally he took a bottle out of a crate in the truck and together we drank to Palestine and to the *Kibutz*. He promised to come and visit our Sabbath festivities, but this morning he came to tell me that he has to push on, and we parted affectionately. I hope to meet him again one of these days and some time I will bring him to Naan. He left me his picture and a tremendous box of cigarettes.[29]

QUESTIONS AND TOPICS FOR DISCUSSION

1. *The Jewish Brigade Group was not the first to fight in recent times as a distinctly Jewish army unit. Tell about the organization and campaign of the Jewish Legion. Who were among its leaders?*

2. *Investigate and report on the life and work of General Kisch, head of the Jewish Brigade.*

3. *Read about some of the exploits of the Jewish Brigade in Lewis Rabinowitz's* Soldiers from Judea *(American Zionist Emergency Council) and in Pierre Van Paassen's* The Forgotten Ally *(Dial Press) and tell your class about them.*

LANDING IN ERETZ YISRAEL
by M. B. Stein

[*The following account of the successful landing of the passengers of the* Shabtai Lazinsky *was related to M. B. Stein, in Jerusalem, and printed by him in the* Yiddisher Kemfer, *April 18, 1947. It was later translated and published in the* Jewish Frontier, *May, 1947, from which the following is reprinted.*]

DURING the whole ten, fourteen or sixteen days of our journey on the boat—I lost count of the days and nights—it somehow seemed to us that we were under constant watch, that the English were only biding their time to attack us with all their force. Many times we were certain that we heard close at hand the pounding motors of British battleships that were tracking us. We were mortally afraid of a new internment camp—whatever name it might be given. After the Hitler inferno, after so much pain, persecution and humiliation, the blood froze in our veins at the mere idea of a new camp, at the very thought of barbed wire. And if not for the hope of Eretz Yisrael, we would surely not have been able to stand it. Surely not.

After days and nights of weary travel, we approached in fear and trembling the shore of Palestine. Our joy at being so close to the goal was almost enough to set us dancing, in spite of everything. But we also knew we were approaching the lion's jaws. No child dared to weep, no man to whisper lest our ship be betrayed. If throughout our trip we thought we heard the throbbing motors, now in the dark night we thought that the cannons of the British fleet are swung over upon us; soon they will bar our way. But, miraculously, the sea was stormy. Great foaming waves leapt like mad dogs upon our little ship to overwhelm it. Above roared a strong wind, whistling and whirling, so that many of us imagined that it was the souls of our martyred fathers and mothers, our brethren, bemoaning their lives cut off by Hitler before their time. Or perhaps they were bewailing the lives which Hitler's new disciples were now bent on forcing upon us. But we were ready for anything, if it led towards our goal of reaching Eretz Yisrael; and in mingled fear and hope we sat beneath the deck until —

Suddenly our ship shuddered, the motors went dead, and a deathly silence fell all around us. What had happened? Had the British caught us and made us stop? Catastrophe so close to our goal? We looked at one another mutely, and our limbs grew heavy.

What happened to us then, you probably know from the newspapers. Two hundred meters from the shore, our ship ran upon a sand bar and was stuck. Well, two hundred meters, even though it was quite deep, is not far. That distance could easily be covered in small boats. But the sea would not calm. The foaming waves beat at us incessantly; furiously one rose above the other as though to swallow it. There could be no question of lowering a lifeboat. We were helpless. What now? To sit with folded arms and wait for the British to remove us? To escape them till the very shores of Eretz Yisrael and now submit to them and ask their aid? It was a bitter thing. Thoughts, each more gloomy and wicked than the other, tormented us. The wind roared, whistled and howled, and the dark coast was dumb.

I don't know how long it lasted. Such moments are hours—eternities. Suddenly it seemed as if a voice called to us out of the darkness. A light showed at the shoreline. Before we could think what we had to do, three young fellows, one after another, were climbing up the side of our ship. Then something very queer happened. We couldn't understand what these Palestinians meant, what they intended, whether they weren't mocking us and laughing at our plight. Only at daybreak did we begin to grasp the wonderful pedagogical lesson those Palestinians had given us. But let me tell it as it happened.

First the Palestinians lowered one of our rubber lifeboats, but it was seized by the waves, tossed and crushed, and two of our men who dropped into it were flung into the sea. It was lucky that we suffered nothing more than fright. The Palestinians dived in, swimming like fish, and dragged them back more dead than alive. Then the Palestinians began fastening a heavy rope which they sent ashore so that we could hold it while swimming. But the rope did not avail either, for the sea and the wind were too wild. That too was given up, for they said it may cost lives. We will have to wait until dawn.

Until dawn they played at diving from our ship into the sea. They dove once and again, as in sport. They began to jeer at us, because we were afraid to dive. They demonstrated how to stretch out one's arms, how to place one's feet, then plunged into the water and were right back on board once more. Just as though it were not a refugee ship, surrounded with sorrow and peril, but a pleasure boat. And the older ones began to grumble: A fine time to show us stunts!

Even we, the younger ones, had to admit that the Palestinians were not behaving decently towards us. They shouldn't be showing off their skill in this critical hour. It meant mocking us in our despair. But they continued to dive, as though we did not concern them at all, and to talk about diving, and from one remark to another, to stretch forth their hands and leap into the sea. Among us there were a few boys who were considered good swimmers in Europe. The Palestinians teased our swimmers, egged them on to competition, to emulation, to an argument in which we all soon became participants. And in the end, even the older ones grew excited and it became a disgrace to say one was afraid to dive, just as though it were a slight thing to jump eight meters from the ship into the stormy sea.

At daybreak, as though upon command, there were more than 150 bronzed, healthy Palestinians ranged around our ship. They made a chain around the ship, with its end anchored upon the shore. Then quite spontaneously our young people began to jump into the sea. Palestinians below caught them up like so many balls. Each passed the swimmer to the next, the second to the third, until he reached land. Danger and fear seemed entirely forgotten.

And those hours of pedagogy even worked with the older people. The middle-aged jumped, women jumped, children jumped into the sea. One middle-aged couple with an eight year old child did not wish to jump because of the child, but the child jumped first and the parents had to follow. Even pregnant women jumped, and one woman, in her fifth month, became hysterical when she came to shore and realized how much she had risked. It took more than an hour to calm her.

On shore it was even more marvelous. A plan no less heroic, no less wise, and no less precisely calculated than the first. At night, in unrelieved darkness, when they heard in the labor settlements and the villages of our coming, the whole community set out for the seashore. Whole families, young people and old, everybody ran out as one man. They left their doors ajar and their homes unguarded, their lamps lit. Mothers and fathers left their children untended and ran. They say that one woman, who was in the midst of ironing clothes, left the plug in the socket and went forth. Thousands trudged over the sand dunes, in a storm that tore the breath from one's mouth. They risked the danger of traversing Arab villages, where a wakeful dog or rooster might warn the police or Arab informers. There is no need to speak of doctors, nurses, bus-drivers— they were all there. And they all streamed in the dark night to the boat.

Every refugee brought to shore by the young Palestinians, wet, hungry, chilled, and often half-drowned with sea water was cared for by the doctors and nurses. Dried, their lungs cleared, warmly dressed, fed, the refugees merged with the multitude, wearing the clothing of Palestinians, so that the police could not distinguish the newcomers from those long resident in the country.

The greatest thing which the mass of Palestinians did, however, came when the police arrived in the morning, armed with guns and rubber truncheons, with fury in their eyes and blazoned on their red, inflamed faces. They were keyed up for their piece of work, for the kind of policing Jews know only too well from Palestine itself, as well as from their former countries. But what the police found was a bonfire in which all the documents of hundreds of Palestinian Jews were burning, the documents which attested their long residence in the country and their Palestinian citizenship. The police were helpless. They had nothing to start with, nothing to show who had come on the boat and who was a Palestinian. And if the people were to be moved, all had to be moved.

The police began their search by examining our clothing, scrutinizing faces, but they could see nothing more than the exhaustion common to all of us, refugees and Palestinians alike, after that wild night. We were all dressed alike in khaki trousers and sweaters, and neither we nor the Palestinians had any papers.

One elderly woman from a nearby village was recognized by a local policeman. "What are you doing here? Go home!" he said.

"My husband and sons are here, and I won't leave without them," the old lady answered.

"Find your husband and sons and go home!"

"All right," said the woman, and chose a "husband" and two "sons" from among the newcomers, and departed.

The police were even more confused by the young people who surrounded our ship. They all climbed aboard. The police, taking them for refugees, and seeing so many people on the ship, concluded that none had escaped. . . .[30]

QUESTIONS AND TOPICS FOR DISCUSSION

1. *Why was the British White Paper of 1939 an act of great injustice? How did it help in the extermination of many of our European brothers and sisters?*

2. *What steps did we take to overcome the evil effects of the White Paper? What role did the Haganah play in this struggle?*

3. *How did the entire Jewish world, and especially our people in Eretz aid in the so-called "illegal" immigration into Eretz?*

4. *Why has the name "Cyprus" assumed a tragic meaning to our people in the so-called post-war years?*

TO THE CAPTAIN OF THE HANNAH SENESCH
by Nathan Alterman
(ABRIDGED)

[*This poem was stimulated by the reception given to the Italian captain of the ship Hannah Senesch when he safely ran the British blockade and brought his cargo of unauthorized immigrants to the shore of Eretz Yisrael.*]

The wind lashed the sea, and the sea lashed the ship;
You steered through the tempest's commotion.
We drink to you, Captain, and lift the glass high;
We'll meet again on this ocean.

This frail, hidden fleet, grey and silent, will be
The subject of song and story;
And many a captain who hears of the tale
Will envy you, Captain, your glory.

The night hid the battle with wave and with tide,
But our lads than the storm-wind were stronger;
Oh, Captain, you saw how from ship to the shore
Each swam with a man on his shoulder.

Years to come—you'll be sipping a glass of mulled wine,
Or quaffing a draught that is stronger;
Then you'll smile, draw your pipe, and shake your grey head,
And think of the days you were younger.[31]

QUESTIONS AND TOPICS FOR DISCUSSION
1. *Read the story of Hannah Senesch in Dorothy and Pesach Bar Adon's* Seven Who Fell *(Palestine Pioneer Library, 1947) and in Marie Syrkin's* Blessed Is the Match *(J.P.S., 1947).*

SONG OF THE HAGANAH BLOCKADE RUNNERS
by Nathan Alterman

I.

We do not ask you whence you came or wherefore,
You step aboard the ship on which we sail;
If firm your heart about the way we're heading
Then, comrade, mount the deck; we bid you hail!

II.

From deepest hold up to the highest smoke-stack
She bears no cannon nor machine-guns now;
But though her cargo holds no bomb nor armor
This boat's a battle-ship from stern to prow.

III.

She carries stalwart, resolute battalions
An army with no weapons in its hand
But with the will to build and firmly fashion
A future for our people and its land![31]

QUESTIONS AND TOPICS FOR DISCUSSION

1. Read I. F. Stone's Underground to Palestine *(Boni and Gaer, 1946)* *for the gripping story of the "underground movement" organized by the Haganah to bring our European brethren to Eretz.*
2. *Find out the stories of such boats as the* Patria, *the* Struma, *the* Exodus, 1947.

A PRAYER FOR MASADAH
by Yitzhak Lamdan

Of those escaped from foreign gallows
Who reached the fortress walls —
Let their feet not slip, O God,
Let them not fall —
Too wearied, they are groping still.

The seven suns in the seven heavens of the world
For them are already black.
Light up, Almighty God of warmth,
Their last sun in the sky above Masadah.
For if that sun too is darkened
How will they find the way?

Lord, give to those who tore themselves
From strange banners of seventy nations
And came — naked —
Give them, O Lord, a single garment
To warm them, to cover their nakedness.

And those with lips still moist with mothers' milk
And cheeks still glowing with caress of fathers
Ease Thou, O God, their lonely burden;
Be Thou their Father
Protect their bitter sorrow against
The crush of armor.

Some have wandered throughout the world
Their head still covered with destruction's ash,
And sackcloth on their shoulders —
Atop the fortress seeking solace —
God grant patience;
Give them still more patience, if solace be denied.

To those whom our nation's *Shekhinah*[32]
Oppressed with the riddle of our fate,
Driven to find answer
In abnegation
Give them, O God, strength to carry their burden,
To the goal ordained.

Weary the defenders of Masadah,
Heavy the burden of the few
Who braved every slaughter,
Bared their breast against attack,
Where they were found worthy.

Let not the flames of their revolt be extinguished
Like the candle lights on the Holy Sabbath
In the twilight of the world.
Let not those fires die out;
How much longer will our people's
Frail hand grope with blind fingers for comfort?

See Thou, Lord, the hand outstretched—
Outstretched from sea and desert —
And in it lies the last dream
Snatched from a sleepless, eternal light
Masadah.

In the hands of this little fortress
Lie dream and solution
Hast not, God, this last proof of justice
To make the dream reality
And wilt Thou not — not even now —
Give courage to those groping dreamers?
O God, defend *Masadah.*[33]

Questions and Topics for Discussion

1. *What is the symbol of* Masadah *as used by Lamdan? Why is* Masadah
   hallowed in Jewish tradition and history?
2. *This poem, written more than twenty years ago, has become one of
   the great prophetic utterances of modern times. Explain why.*

CONTINUE THE PEACEFUL WORK
by Albert Einstein

[*Address delivered in 1939 when the infamous White Paper was issued by the British Government.*]

ENGLAND HAS, in part, ignored its sacred pledge. She gave her word in a dire hour and she is acting now, too, in a dire hour.

Remember, however, that in the life of a people, and especially in times of need, there can be only one source of security, namely: confidence in one's own strength and steadfastness. We are justified in this feeling of confidence. For, what the Jewish nation has achieved in Palestine through the self-sacrificing efforts of the pioneers and through the unselfish voluntary aid of Jews in other lands, bears witness to an extraordinary productive force.

I remember vividly the time when the all-too-wise and all-too-cautious people among us were wont to say: "It is futile to invest energies and to attach hopes to this wasteland!" Today we find large sections of this wasteland converted into flourishing gardens, and close to a half-million of our brethren, including a considerable number of former sceptics and opponents as well as their children, have found a new home in the old homeland. . . .

We must strive, therefore, that in our ranks, reason should prevail over disappointment and embitterment. The Arabs have been led into their suicidal uprisings by terror and foreign agitation. But they, too, will after a while recognize the logic of facts, especially when we will have learned that our own future depends on our ability to arrive at a modus of honest cooperation with them. There could be no greater calamity than a permanent discord between us and the Arab people. Despite the great wrong that has been done us, we must strive for a just and lasting compromise with the Arab people. In the face of the common foe that confronts us both, this goal must be accessible. Let us recall that in former times no people lived in greater friendship with us than the ancestors of these same Arabs.

On the other hand, let us not always fix our gaze on England and passively await the determination of our fate from there. Undaunted by the events of recent days, we must continue our peaceful work with re-doubled effort. We know that the path of least resistance leads to ruin as surely as does the path of conquering force; but we are certainly not in a position to persuade others of this truth. We can only stand firm and not lose courage for a single moment.

This spirit of faith carried our forefathers through times of greatest distress, so that our productive force—unbroken through millenia—contributed to the enrichment of human culture. Let us be steadfast, so that future generations may be justified to say the same of us.[34]

Questions and Topics for Discussion

1. *Translate Einstein's advice to "continue with our peaceful work with redoubled effort" into concrete illustrations.*
2. *What is Einstein's attitude to the problem of Jewish-Arab relations?*
3. *Do you think Einstein would have been of the same mind in this matter during 1946 as he was in 1939?*
4. *What injustices did England commit against the Jewish people in 1939, in 1945 and succeeding years?*
5. *How did the Jews respond to these injustices?*

OUR UNIQUE DESTINY AS A NATION
by Chaim Weizmann
(ABRIDGED)

[*Text of Dr. Chaim Weizmann's address before the Ad Hoc Committee on the Palestine Question at Lake Success on October 18, 1947.*]

Mr. Chairman and Gentlemen:

It is a moving experience for me to come before this committee of the United Nations for the purpose of summarizing the views and sentiments of the Jewish people at this turning point of its fortunes.

My mind goes back a quarter of a century to the previous assembly of nations which solemnly endorsed our program for the reconstitution in Palestine of our National Home. I came from the council room in which the mandate was ratified with the feeling that the most cherished ideals of our own history had been sanctioned by the conscience of all mankind.

Our ancient civilization, which had enriched the thought and spirit of the world, was to be given a free abode in the very cradle of its birth. Our people were to find a home—not a refuge, not an asylum, not a mere shelter, but a home with which their past memory and future hope were inseparably bound up. The Jewish people was to fashion its own political and social institutions in the image of its own character and tradition, on a level of equality with all other nations in the human family.

I can testify here that the establishment of the Jews as a nation amongst the nations of the world was the real purpose and motive of that international covenant endorsed by the League of Nations. In the light of this knowledge, I cannot fail to be amused by such frivolous assertions as that made by an Arab delegate here to the effect that the motive of the mandate was to reward me for alleged discoveries of poison gas. I cannot avoid the conclusion that those who made these assertions must have been equally unversed in the political and chemical literature of the time. . . .

LEADERS INSPIRED BY HIGH PURPOSES

The mandate was inspired by high purposes, worthy of all the exertion and sacrifice which we could bring. Our achievements in Palestine, where our people have created new social and cultural values and opened new economic opportunities for themselves and their neighbors, were carried out under the sanction of this international treaty.

Times have changed; new situations, new conflicts have arisen; and new conditions must now be sought to enable us to fulfill our unique destiny as a nation in Palestine. But I cannot turn to the consideration of these new conditions without paying tribute to the vision, the courage and the universal equity which animated the fifty-two signatories of the Palestine mandate in enabling our people to approach the threshold of independence, where I believe it now stands.

It is no coincidence that the statesmen who developed the idea of organized international cooperation were prominently identified with the struggle for Jewish national equality as well. Wilson and Balfour, Lloyd George, Smuts and Masaryk and Cecil as well as the leaders in the creation of the United Nations found time, amid their universal preoccupations, to plan for the Jewish State. . . .

PARTITION NOT AN EASY COMPROMISE

For several years I have consistently believed and advocated that the idea of partition . . . represents the only practical compromise which faces the hard facts and offers an escape from deadlock and frustration.

It is not an easy compromise to envisage—least of all to one like myself who knows that the original purpose of the mandate involved no such limitation as is now proposed. Nobody dreamed in those days that the processes of Jewish immigration and development would have to be confined in one-eighth of the area in which the national home was to be established by international consent. . . .

THE THREE ALTERNATIVES

Consider the position. Here is a community of 700,000 with its language, its religion, its cultural traditions and movements, its distinctive social outlook, its industrial and agricultural projects, its scientific spirit, its art and its music, its universities and schools.

Here, likewise, is a community with a great democratic spirit and a thoroughgoing democratic structure, confronting another group which is in a different stage of development, but is numerically superior. The institutions of the Jewish homeland are in some way distinctive to itself and to the Jewish people of which it is the core. The strongest solidarity of this community is with its kindred in Europe, the battered remnants of ancient communities, survivors who linger amidst the memories of the past and the graveyards of the present.

Not one of these characteristics which marks this community is shared by its Arab neighbors. The question before the Assembly is how and by whom shall this Jewish community be governed? By whom shall its development and growth be determined?

Shall it be governed by a trustee? By the Arabs? By itself? These three alternatives cover all the variations of Palestinian solutions and the simplest analysis of them must lead this committee inevitably to the conclusions of the majority report. . . .

SUBJECTION IS NOT ACCEPTABLE

Now subjection of the Jews as a minority under Arab rule is a solution which all impartial commissions and tribunals have rejected and must reject. On moral grounds it is impossible to take the only community in the world which expresses the national identity of the Jewish people and to place it under the domination of the Arab Higher Committee. It is not only that the chairman and members of the Arab Higher Committee cannot be regarded as having anything but a hostile attitude to Jewish national ideals.

The subjection of the Jews as a minority to them is unacceptable in all conditions. Those of us Jews who, on the strength of international promise and under the impulse of our own history, made our homes in Palestine did not do so with the object of becoming Arab citizens of Jewish persuasion. . . It is not the purpose for which under international auspices we were encouraged to come to Palestine. The idea that a national home can ever be equated with a minority position in an Arab state deserves no consideration at all. It would burst out of such an unnatural subjection.

It should be obvious by now that a distinct national unit cannot be subjected by force to another nation in the name of majority rule. The distinguished delegate of Canada uttered a profound truth when he said that "unity cannot be imposed without consent." . . .

EQUALITY IS ESSENTIAL

If we discard the mandate and emphatically reject minority status in an Arab state, we are left with partition and Jewish statehood as the only possible condition for the future government of Palestine. It is the only solution which promises finality—a clear definition of the limits within which Jews and Arabs are free to develop their national wills.

Above all it offers equality which is the essential precondition of Arab-Jewish cooperation. When the Jews face the Arabs, as equals, members of this Assembly, and of the family of nations, only then will the prospect of a real partnership open out.

A Jewish State in Palestine will in its own interests, as well as by its own ideals, seek close cooperation with the Arab states on its borders. The majority report in a moving passage refers to the results which can ensue from such equal cooperation between the two Semitic peoples. . . .

The area of Arab independence stretches far and wide. Independence is not the exclusive right of the Arabs. We Jews have an equal claim to it. This Assembly cannot possibly decree that the desire of the Arabs to possess an eighth state must obliterate the right of the Jews to possess a single centre of independent national life.

Gentlemen: Despite some of the things that have been said in this debate, I retain my belief in the prospect of Arab-Jewish cooperation once a solution based on finality and equality has received the sanction of international consent. The Jewish State in Palestine may become a pilot plant for processes and examples which may have a constructive message for its neighbors as well.

The smallness of the state will be no bar to its full intellectual achievement. Athens was only one small city and the whole world is still its debtor. . . .

STATE WILL SOLVE TWO PROBLEMS

Life in Palestine offers our people not only a refuge amongst their kinsmen but also a chance of contributing to the rebirth of a nation and the development of its institutions. In this way the immigrant achieves a unity between himself and the society in which he lives.

Our remnants in Europe, who have before their eyes their 6,000,000 slaughtered kinsmen, cannot stand the thought of another dispersion. They do not throw themselves on the mercy of the world. They are not suppliant, they are not beggars. They wish to be citizens of a Jewish society in which their capacities and ideals will be fully at home. . . .

Therefore, in establishing Jewish equality and nationhood, the United Nations can both solve the problem of Palestine's political future and relieve the darkest human tragedy of our time. In bringing so many countries together on a basis of agreement, the majority report has already done some service to the cause of international harmony. . . .

CONSIDERATIONS OF JUSTICE AND HUMANITY

Mr. Chairman and Gentlemen: When this committee comes to plan the creation of a Jewish State, it will be fulfilling a proud historic mission. Despite its small scope, this enterprise stands high in the esteem of liberal thought. So many considerations of justice and humanity are involved.

There is redress for a persecuted people; equality for the Jewish people amongst the nations; the redemption of desert soil by cultivation; the creation of a new economy and society; the embodiment of progressive social ideas in an area that has fallen behind the best standards of modern life; the revival of one of the oldest cultures of mankind. . . .

I cannot allow this statement of the Jewish case to conclude without a word of appeal at this great bar of the world's conscience. A world which does not hear us in this moment of our agony would be deaf to the voice of justice and human feeling which must be raised loud and clear if the moral foundations of our society are to survive.

If you follow the impartial judgment of your own qualified committee and admit us to your honored table, we shall enter your company with a sense of the spiritual and intellectual challenge which the idea of the United Nations makes to the conscience of man. In giving us this opportunity you will be faithful to the noblest ideals which have been conceived by our ancestors and transmitted by them to the common heritage of the world.

"The Lord shall set His hand again the second time to recover the remnants of His people. And He shall set up an ensign for the nations, and shall assemble the outcast of Israel and gather together the depressed of Judah from the four corners of the earth" (Isa. XI: 11-12).

QUESTIONS AND TOPICS FOR DISCUSSION

1. *Why is November 29, 1947, an historic day in Jewish life? What are the steps that led up to the Partition Plan?*
2. *What are the elements of the Plan?*
3. *What has happened since November 29, 1947?*
4. *What has been Weizmann's role in the Zionist Movement in the last 50 years?*
5. *How do you feel about the Jewish State?*
6. *How will the Jewish State affect the Jews of America and other lands?*
7. *Who are the statesmen, mentioned by Weizmann, who developed the idea of organized international cooperation?*

ISRAEL'S DECLARATION OF INDEPENDENCE

[Friday, May 14, 1948 (Iyar 5, 5708), 10:05 A.M. —
To the tune of the melancholy "Minstrel Boy" played on a bagpipe, General Alan Cunningham, British High Commissioner for Palestine, steps aboard an English naval launch at Haifa. The thirty-year-old British mandate over Eretz Yisrael is ended. After 1878 years the DAY has finally come . . .
Erev Shabbat, May 14, a few minutes before 4:00 P.M.
At the Tel Aviv Museum, under the careful guard and watchful eyes of the Haganah, thirteen men sit down at a long table. Around them 400 people, standing under the blue-white flags, begin to sing the Hatikvah. White-haired David Ben Gurion, first Prime Minister of the new state about to be born, arises and reads the Proclamation. As his words ring out to the world, Jews everywhere dance in the streets, parade with blue and white streamers and flags . . .

In Washington amidst weeping and cheering the blue-white flag with the Star of David is hoisted in front of the Jewish Agency Building, and a short time later President Truman issues the announcement: "The United States Government recognizes the Provisional Government as the de facto authority of the new State of Israel."
The Proclamation of the new State of Israel reads:]

THE LAND OF ISRAEL was the birthplace of the Jewish people. Here their spiritual, religious and national identity was formed. Here they achieved independence and created a culture of national and universal significance. Here they wrote and gave the Bible to the world.

Exiled from the Land of Israel the Jewish people remained faithful to it in all the countries of their dispersion, never ceasing to pray and hope for their return and the restoration of their national freedom.

Impelled by this historic association, Jews strove throughout the centuries to go back to the land of their fathers and regain their statehood. In recent decades they returned in their masses. They reclaimed the wilderness, revived their language, built cities and villages, and established a vigorous and ever-growing community, with its own economic and cultural life. They sought peace yet were prepared to defend themselves.

They brought the blessings of progress to all inhabitants of the country and looked forward to sovereign independence.

In the year 1897 the First Zionist Congress, inspired by Theodor Herzl's vision of the Jewish State, proclaimed the right of the Jewish people to national revival in their own country.

This right was acknowledged by the Balfour Declaration of November 2, 1917, and reaffirmed by the Mandate of the League of Nations, which gave explicit international recognition to the historic connection of the Jewish people with Palestine and their right to reconstitute their National Home.

The recent holocaust, which engulfed millions of Jews in Europe, proved anew the need to solve the problem of the homelessness and lack of independence of the Jewish people by means of the reestablishment of the Jewish State, which would open the gates to all Jews and endow the Jewish people with equality of status among the family of nations.

The survivors of the disastrous slaughter in Europe, and also Jews from other lands, have not desisted from their efforts to reach Eretz-Yisrael, in face of difficulties, obstacles and perils; and have not ceased to urge their right to a life of dignity, freedom and honest toil in their ancestral land.

In the Second World War the Jewish people in Palestine made their full contribution to the struggle of the freedom-loving nations against the Nazi evil. The sacrifices of their soldiers and their war effort gained them the right to rank with the nations which founded the United Nations.

On November 29, 1947, the General Assembly of the United Nations adopted a Resolution requiring the establishment of a Jewish State in Palestine. The General Assembly called upon the inhabitants of the country to take all the necessary steps on their part to put the plan into effect. This recognition by the United Nations of the right of the Jewish people to establish their independent State is unassailable.

It is the natural right of the Jewish people to lead, as do all other nations, an independent existence in its sovereign State.

ACCORDINGLY WE, the members of the National Council, representing the Jewish people in Palestine and the World Zionist Movement, are met together in solemn assembly today, the day of termination of the British Mandate for Palestine; and by virtue of the natural and historic right of the Jewish people and of the Resolution of the General Assembly of the United Nations,

WE HEREBY PROCLAIM the establishment of the Jewish State in Palestine, to be called Medinat Yisrael (The State of Israel).

WE HEREBY DECLARE that, as from the termination of the Mandate at midnight, the 14th-15th May, 1948, and pending the setting up of the duly elected bodies of the State in accordance with a Constitution, to be drawn up by the Constituent Assembly not later than the 1st October, 1948, the National Council shall act as the Provisional State Council, and that the National Administration shall constitute the Provisional Government of the Jewish State, which shall be known as Israel.

THE STATE OF ISRAEL will be open to the immigration of Jews from all countries of their dispersion; will promote the development of the country for the benefit of all its inhabitants; will be based on the principles of liberty, justice and peace as conceived by the Prophets of Israel; will uphold the full social and political equality of all its citizens, without distinction of religion, race, or sex; will guarantee freedom of religion, conscience, education and culture; will safeguard the Holy Places of all religions; and will loyally uphold the principles of the United Nations Charter.

THE STATE OF ISRAEL will be ready to cooperate with the organs and representatives of the United Nations in the implementation of the Resolution of the Assembly of November 29, 1947, and will take steps to bring about the Economic Union over the whole of Palestine.

We appeal to the United Nations to assist the Jewish people in the building of its State and to admit Israel into the family of nations.

In the midst of wanton aggression, we yet call upon the Arab inhabitants of the State of Israel to preserve the ways of peace and play their part in the development of the State, on the basis of full and equal citizenship and due representation in all its bodies and institutions—provisional and permanent.

We extend our hand in peace and neighbourliness to all the neighbouring states and their peoples, and invite them to cooperate with the independent Jewish nation for the common good of all. The State of Israel is prepared to make its contribution to the progress of the Middle East as a whole.

Our call goes out to the Jewish people all over the world to rally to our side in the task of immigration and development and to stand by us in the great struggle for the fulfillment of the dream of generations for the redemption of Israel.

With trust in Almighty God, we set our hand to this Declaration, at this Session of the Provisional State Council, on the soil of the Homeland, in the city of Tel Aviv, on this Sabbath eve, the fifth of Iyar, 5708, the fourteenth day of May, 1948.

QUESTIONS AND TOPICS FOR DISCUSSION

1. *Draw a time chart showing the important dates in the history of the Zionist Movement.*

2. *Compare this Proclamation with that of Cyrus, king of Persia (Ezra I, 2-4).*

3. *The Proclamation states: "The Jewish people remained faithful to it (Eretz Yisrael) in all countries of their dispersion." Give examples supporting this statement.*

4. *Who are some of the men on the Provisional Governing Council of 13, and what offices do they hold?*

5. *"The State of Israel," reads the Proclamation, "is ready to contribute its full share to the peaceful progress . . . of the Middle East." Explain how Israel has achieved and can further achieve this aim.*

6. *Tell about the events in Israel after May 14, 1948.*

SUGGESTED BIBLIOGRAPHY FOR ADDITIONAL READING

Bein, Alex, *Theodore Herzl*, Jewish Publication Society, 1940
Ben Shalom, *Deep Furrows, Pioneer Life in the Collective*,
     Hashomer Hatzair, 1937
DeHaas, Jacob, *Theodore Herzl*, Leonard Co., 1927
Edidin, Ben M., *Rebuilding Palestine*, Behrman, 1939
Einstein, Albert, *About Zionism*, Macmillan, 1939
Frankenstein, Ernst, *Justice for My People*, Dial, 1944
Gottheil, Richard J., *Zionism*, Jewish Publication Society, 1914
Herzl, Theodore, *The Jewish State*,
     American Zionist Emergency Council, 1946
Herzl, Theodore, *Old-New Land*, Bloch, 1941
Hess, Moses, *Rome and Jerusalem*, Bloch, 1918
Kahn, Dorothy, *Spring Up, Oh Well*, Holt, 1936
Katzenelson-Rubashov, Rachel (ed.), *The Plough Woman*,
     Nicholas L. Brown, 1932
Kurland, Samuel, *Biluim, Pioneers of Zionist Colonization*, Scopus, 1943
Levensohn, Lotta, *Outline of Zionist History*, Scopus Publishing Co., 1941
Levin, Meyer, *My Father's House*, Viking Press, 1947
Levinger, Elma E., *Fighting Angel*, Behrman, 1946
Lewisohn, Ludwig, *Israel*, Liveright, 1925
Lewisohn, Ludwig (ed.), *Rebirth*, Harper, 1935
Rabinowitz, Lewis Isaac, *Soldiers From Judaea*,
     American Zionist Emergency Council, 1945
Revusky, Abraham, *Jews in Palestine*, Vanguard, 1947 (rev.)
Rubinstein, Marion, *Adventuring in Palestine*, Knopf, 1935
Samuel, Maurice, *Harvest in the Desert*, Jewish Publication Society, 1944
Sankowsky, Shoshanna H., *A Short History of Zionism*, Bloch, 1947
Thorbecke, Ellen, *Promised Land*, Harper & Bro., 1947
Van Paassen, Pierre, *The Forgotten Ally*, Dial, 1943
Weisgal, Meyer W., *Chaim Weizmann*, Dial, 1944
Yaari, Yehuda, *When the Candle Was Burning*, Gollancz, London, 1947
Yehoash, *The Feet of the Messenger*, Jewish Publication Society, 1923
Zeligs, Dorothy, *The Story of Modern Palestine*, Bloch, 1944

PART FIVE

Looking Forward

I want you to know, my dear colleagues and friends, that
none is left in these hard times to bear the standard of Moses
and to engage in Talmudic studies but you and those near you.
I know that you are continually establishing places of learning
and that you are men of understanding and wisdom. Everywhere
else the Torah has disappeared. Most of the great communities
are spiritually dead, while some are in decline. . . There is no
help left unto us but you, our brethren, from whom salvation
will come. Be strong and of good courage. Act valiantly on
behalf of our people . . . since you are courageous and men of
power. Everything depends on you; the decision rests in your
hands.

May the Lord, blessed be He, help you in your work and
make you known, praised and blessed. . . Amen!

FROM MAIMONIDES' LETTER TO THE JEWISH
COMMUNITY OF LUNEL[1]

Introduction: LOOKING FORWARD

AND SO WE stand at the threshold of tomorrow. Tomorrow rests chiefly with us. The sad, cruel hand of history has closed the long, rich chapter of European Jewry. Venerable Dr. Leo Baeck, former Chief Rabbi of Berlin, put it succinctly when he said, "The great epoch of American Jews is beginning. The burden of the Jewish task . . . is laid on the Jews of America." But this selfsame hand has also opened for us new vistas in the miracles of our day, the Third Jewish Commonwealth and the American Jewish Community.

The scholars and men of letters included in this book are almost all of European origin. This was neither by design nor accident. We, the Jews of America, have been living on the spiritual deposits made largely by European Jewry. Now we must begin to look to ourselves if we are to survive as a people and if we are to live wholesomely as Jews.

Looking back into our past for guidance, we find that there were several factors which helped us survive. We had faith in ourselves and in our tradition. Voluntarily and gladly did we accept the disciplines of our Torah and the Jewish way of life. Our inspired men of vision, our seers and prophets, gave vitality, purpose and meaning to our lives. In terms of life tomorrow, the lesson of yesterday teaches us that to make us worthy of the Jewish name and of our immortal past, we must live up to the time-tested ideals in which there are profound meaning, poetry and melody.

Many misguided and erring persons, in their desire to be at one with humanity at large, wish to "emancipate" themselves from the "yoke" and "confines" of Judaism. They do not realize that humanity is you and I, and that the way to serve mankind best is to serve one's people well. We can be all the better and richer American citizens if we cultivate our own culture deeply. Here we are offered the challenging opportunity of becoming Americans "plus." The cultivation of this "plus" will make it possible for us to live happily and with dignity, and to continue to enrich world civilization in general and American culture in particular.

The men whom you have already met and will meet in this last section hold out high hopes for American Jewry. Possessing historical perspective and intimate knowledge of other Jewries, they have been impressed with the possibilities of American Jewry. America has produced a new type of Jew, energetic, self-assertive, successful and endowed with a sense of democracy and organization. Although successor to immortal cultural centers, our Jewry is still a young community. It is groping to express itself and to make its contribution to Jewish life and culture. In this effort, Conservative Jewry, with its emphasis on the synthesis of historical tradition, Jewish scholarship and Hebraic learning, has a very significant and unique role to play in the future of Judaism.

Since World War I we have seen telescoped in a brief span of years incredible changes to the good and to the bad. On the one hand we have seen the fulfillment of an age-old dream and prayer, and the unparalleled growth of American Jewry. On the other hand, we have seen the liquidation of European Jewry and the snuffing out of Judaism in Russia—the two vital mainsprings of our recent past. No people can point to losses like our losses and to sorrows like our sorrows. Yet we have lived on, courageous and hopeful. We have had the privilege of seeing with our eyes the miraculous third rebirth of our people and our land. From here on Jewish survival, Jewish culture and tradition, Jewish idealism, American Israel, Eretz Yisrael mean YOU. Tomorrow rests with you!

EVERY JEW MUST FEEL THAT HE IS THE TRUSTEE OF WHAT IS BEST IN JEWISH HISTORY
by Louis D. Brandeis

WHAT IS BEING achieved in Palestine can perhaps be achieved only there in the fullest degree; but the lesson applies to the Jews all over the world. We have our obligations, the same *noblesse oblige*.[2] Our traditions are the same. They have been transmitted also to us. We have not applied them in the same degree as those of our people who have returned to our ancestral home. But the ages of sacrifice have left us with the sense of brotherhood. That brotherhood has given us the feeling of solidarity which makes each one of us ready and anxious to fulfill his obligations. And we know, from the lesson of history, that the traditions we cherish depend for their life upon the conduct of every single one of us.

It is not wealth, it is not station, it is not social standing and ambition, which makes us worthy of the Jewish name, of the Jewish heritage. To be worthy of them, we must live up to and with them. We must regard ourselves their custodians. Every young man here must feel that he is the trustee of what is best in Jewish history. We cannot go as far as the pioneers in Palestine, but we must make their example to radiate in our lives. We must sense our solidarity to such an extent that even an unconscious departure from our noble traditions will make us feel guilty of a breach of a most sacred trust.

Here then is the task before you. . . . It is to promote the ideals which the Jews have carried forward through thousands of years of persecution and by much sacrifice. We must learn to realize that our sacrifices have enhanced the quality of our achievements, and that the overcoming of obstacles is part of our attainments.

Men differ in ability, however great the average ability of the Jews is, but every single Jew can make his own contribution to the Jewish way of life. Every single one of us can do that for himself. Every one of us can declare: "What is mean is not for us." We bespeak what is best, what is noblest and finest in all civilization. This is our heritage. We have survived persecution because of the virtues and sacrifices of our ancestors. It is for us to follow in that path. It is the Jewish tradition, and the Jewish law, and the Jewish spirit which prepare us for the lessons of life.[3]

QUESTIONS AND TOPICS FOR DISCUSSION

1. *Show how Brandeis lived his life in accordance with the ideals expressed by him.*
2. *Can you visualize possible conflicts between Americanism and Judaism? Have you experienced any in your life?*
3. *Give concrete illustrations of some of the ideals which, according to Brandeis, we should promote.*
4. *What in your opinion brought back to us such personalities as Emma Lazarus, Herzl, Brandeis, Jessie Sampter and others?*

WE ALONE SURVIVED
by Solomon Goldman

OF THE WHOLE welter of ancient peoples we alone survived. . . Dispersed, broken into fragments . . . multi-colored and diversified, black and yellow and white, occidental and oriental but withal one people.

We survived, I should like to believe, because we were inveterate optimists. No obstacle stopped us, no crisis dismayed us, no catastrophe crushed us. We swallowed the bitterness of life and pursued the sweet thereof. Aye, we loved life—this very thing of living. "Be fruitful and multiply," we urged unashamed, unapologetic. . . "Remember us unto life, O King, that delightest in life." . . Israel wanted life abundantly, clung to it and lived.

We survived because of Torah. We loved life and our sages knew that life needs direction, norms, discipline. We denied ourselves that we might live. . . We placed ourselves under the yoke of the Torah and rejoiced that we had *Mitzvot.* . . The Prophets, the Scribes, the Pharisees fashioned Torah—the blending of thought with resolution—thought that leads to action. The Torah is teaching and living. Our greatest intellects concerned themselves with "everyday things." Even the trifles that "man treads under his heel" were the concern of a Hillel, an Akiba, a Rashi, or a Maimonides.

We survived because ours was a genuine democracy. No caste system was permitted to develop, no autocrat went unchallenged. The lowly and the mighty were the children of Abraham, Isaac and Jacob. Smiths, peddlers, shoemakers could become great teachers and be hearkened to by the whole people. The son of a carpenter could believe himself a Messiah and humble fishermen might become the founders of a new religion.

At the end of the eighteenth century it could be maintained in civilized England that "everyone but an idiot knows that the lower classes must be kept poor," and that it were folly to educate the poor for they might become "insolent to their superiors." In Israel it was hoped in the remotest past, "Would God that all the Lord's people become prophets." We could say to every man, *"Bishvilkha Nivra Ha-Olam,"* for thy sake the world was created. . . .

We survived, I believe, above all, because of the prophetic voices that broke out in Israel from time to time. We were blessed with men that never made peace with the foibles of the people or the whims of the rulers. We were compelled to listen to denunciations that "cried aloud like a trumpet." We could not allow ourselves to sink into the sweet lassitude of dissipation and degeneracy which led so many peoples to despair and death. We were shaken by a mighty hand and outstretched arm. Israel, we were warned, . . . "Wash ye, make you clean . . . cease to do evil; learn to do well; seek judgment, relieve the oppressed, judge the fatherless, plead for the widow."[4]

QUESTIONS AND TOPICS FOR DISCUSSION

1. *According to Solomon Goldman what factors helped us survive?*
2. *What do you think has helped us survive as a people?*
3. *Utilizing the author's arguments, what are the possibilities for our future survival?*
4. *What is the attitude of our people in these days to this "very thing of living"? To Torah? To democracy in Jewish life?*
5. *What factors in our present Jewish life will help us in our survival in the future?*

AMERICAN ISRAEL, A COMMUNITY SUCH AS THE PROPHET OF THE EXILE SAW IN HIS VISION
by Israel Friedlaender

HE WHO FEELS the pulse of American Jewish life can detect . . . the beginnings of a Jewish renaissance, the budding forth of a new spirit. The Jews of America, as represented in their noblest and best . . . are fully alive to the future of their country as a center of Jewish culture. They build not only hospitals and infirmaries, but also schools and colleges; they welcome not only immigrants, but also libraries; not only tradesmen and laborers, but also scholars and writers. Everywhere we perceive the evidence of a new life.

To be sure, we are only at the beginning. Gigantic and complicated tasks confront us in the future. The enormous stores of latent Jewish energy that are formlessly piled up in this country will have to be transformed into living power. The dead capital which we constantly draw from the Ghetto will have to be made into a working capital to produce new values. We first of all have to lay our foundation: to rescue the Jewish education of our future generations from the chaos in which it is now entangled. But we are on the right road. . . The American Jews will work and live for a Judaism which will encompass all phases of Jewish life and thought; which will not be a faint sickly hot-house plant, but, as it was in the days of old, "a tree of life for those who hold it fast, bestowing happiness on those who cling to it." . . .

When we try to penetrate the mist that encircles the horizon of the present, a vision unfolds itself before our mind's eye, presenting a picture of the future American Israel. We perceive a community great in numbers, mighty in power, enjoying life, liberty and the pursuit of happiness: true life, not mere breathing space; full liberty, not mere elbow room; real happiness, not that of pasture beasts; actively participating in the civic, social and economic progress of the country, fully sharing and increasing its spiritual possessions and acquisitions, doubling its joys, halving its sorrows; yet deeply rooted in the soil of Judaism, clinging to its past, working for its future, true to its traditions, faithful to its aspirations, one in sentiment with their brethren wherever they are, attached to the land of their fathers as the cradle and resting place of the Jewish spirit; men with straight backs and raised heads, with big hearts and strong minds, with no conviction crippled, with no emotion stifled, with souls harmoniously developed, self-centered and self-reliant; receiving and resisting, not yielding like wax to every impress from the outside, but blending the best they possess with the best they encounter; not a horde of individuals, but a set of individualities, adding a new note to the richness of American life, leading a new current into the stream of American civilization; not a formless crowd of taxpayers and voters, but a sharply marked community, distinct and distinguished, trusted for its loyalty, respected for its dignity, esteemed for its traditions, valued for its aspirations, a community such as the Prophet of the Exile saw it in his vision: "And marked will be their seed among the nations, and their offspring among the peoples. Everyone that will see them will point to them as a community blessed by the Lord."[5]

Questions and Topics for Discussion

1. *Do you agree with the author's optimism about the future of American Jewry?*
2. *Relate the contents of this selection to those of Brandeis on p. 213.*
3. *Describe the ideal American Jew as seen by Friedlaender.*
4. *What American Jewish institutions do you know which demonstrate "the budding forth of a new spirit"?*
5. *What contributions have the Jews made to American life? What further contributions can me make?*

THE SEMINARY AIMS TO PRESERVE
THE KNOWLEDGE AND PRACTICE
OF HISTORICAL JUDAISM
by Cyrus Adler

JUDAISM IS, unquestionably, a way of life. This is not peculiar to Judaism, for it is the purpose of any religion to make good people, right living people, people who are trained to carry on the work of the world with a high spirit. Judaism has developed for this purpose a code of law, and under this code there are definite and positive acts to be done. A religious Jew believes that he must act in accordance with the Jewish law. The reform movement held that this Jewish law was in effect abrogated. It was as a protest against this philosophy that the Seminary was founded.

The Seminary therefore . . . has not modified the prayer book, it has not changed the calendar, it has not altered the dietary laws, it has not abolished the second day of the holidays, and although some of its founders and some of its graduates have, without protest from the Seminary, attempted changes in the ritual, the Seminary itself has never adopted any of these changes. . . .

The Seminary aims to teach a form of Judaism to which all people could come so far as fundamental values are concerned. A common language, the understanding of a common history and a common literature, are the strongest factors for keeping together the Synagogue— stronger in our opinion than any set of resolutions or platforms. . . .

I cannot wholly deplore the fact that there are differences among us. When have there not been? The differences which have arisen among the Jewish people in the past have not proved a wholly unmixed evil. It is to the Karaite heresy that Judaism owes a careful study of the Bible, Hebrew grammar and a reasonable exegesis. Probably the most distinguished works of the great Gaon Saadyah were written under its inspiration. The philosophy of Maimonides was, as you all know, followed by the most bitter quarrel that medieval Jewry developed, and those that came after him actually destroyed his books, holding that such rationalism undermined the foundations of Judaism. This view the Seminary has never held. We welcome legalists, rationalists, mystics, always provided that they recognize the validity of the Jewish tradition and the Jewish law and are willing to live under it even though their explanation thereof may be different. . . .

The Seminary is an institution of Jewish learning designed for the purpose of creating an educated Jewish rabbinate in the United States. . . The Seminary aims to open up the entire domain of Jewish knowledge to its students, by which it will best serve the purpose for which it was founded—to preserve in America the knowledge and practice of historical Judaism as contained in the laws of Moses and expounded by the prophets and sages in Israel in Biblical and Talmudical writings.[7]

QUESTIONS AND TOPICS FOR DISCUSSION

1. *What does the statement mean: "Judaism is a way of life"? Give examples of what this means.*
2. *How do Orthodox, Conservative and Reform Jews differ from each other in synagogue and home observances? In other matters?*
3. *What are the fundamental principles of Conservative Judaism according to Adler? How are they being lived up to by the members of your congregation?*
4. *Describe the activities of the Seminary and the United Synagogue. Make a diagram illustrating these activities.*

IT IS "A WORK OF HEAVEN" TO WHICH YOU ARE INVITED
by Solomon Schechter
(ABRIDGED)

[The date is February 23, 1913, and the place is the old building of the Jewish Theological Seminary on West 123rd Street, New York. The flood of Jewish immigration to America is at its very crest. The teeming Jewish ghettoes in the large cosmopolitan centers are in their heyday, when Solomon Schechter convened the first meeting of what was to become the United Synagogue of America.]

"BLESSED BE HE that cometh in the name of the Lord." It is in the name of the Lord that we have invited you to join the United Synagogue of America, which is entering upon its existence this day. It is a real "work of Heaven," for which I invite your attention and participation—a work on which, in my humble opinion, depends the continuance and the survival of traditional Judaism in this country. . . .

Let me premise that this United Synagogue has not been called into life with any purpose of creating a new division. While it will, as its name implies, unite us for certain purposes, which we deem sacred and indispensable to the welfare of Judaism, it is not our intention to enter into a feud with the existing parties. Life is too short for feuds, and the task before us is so great and so manifold, that we must spare all our faculties and save all our strength for the work of a positive nature, which I will outline presently. Moreover, feuds and controversies are only productive of bitterness and strife, which we are anxious to avoid. They would result in mere negative work, whilst the work before us, as already indicated, is of a distinctive, positive nature.

Indeed, what we intend to accomplish is not to create a new party, but to consolidate an old one, which has always existed in this country, but was never conscious of its own strength, nor perhaps realized the need of organization. I refer to the large number of Jews who, thoroughly American in habits of life and mode of thinking and, in many cases, imbued with the best culture of the day, have always maintained conservative principles and remained aloof from the Reform movement. . .

They are sometimes stigmatized as the Neo-Orthodox. This is not correct. Their Orthodoxy is not new. It is as old as the hills, and the taunt "new" can only be accounted for by the ignorance of those who took it into their heads, that an observant Jew, who has taken a degree in a college, is a new phenomenon, representing a mere paradox. A better knowledge of Jewish history would have taught them that culture combined with religion was the rule of the Jew; culture without religion was the exception. . . .

This conservative, or if you prefer so to call it, this Orthodox tendency, represented by some of the noblest minds of American Jewry, to which several of the oldest synagogues bear witness, received a fresh impetus by the immigration from the Eastern part of Europe, begun some thirty years ago. This immigration brought hundreds and thousands, mostly from countries which were never touched by the Reform movement that had its birth in Germany. Their presence brought to the consciousness of even some of the most thorough-going Reformers that the large majority of Israel still sought their spiritual salvation in the Torah and the Talmud and the Jewish Codes. The authority of various Synods[6] in Germany were never recognized by these immigrants, if indeed they ever heard of them, and whatever the excesses of the individual may have been in the one case or the other, they have never been allowed any innovation in their synagogues or any alteration in their liturgy. If they were scolded as medievalists, they could point with pride to their prayer-book, which was the same in its main features as that from which Rashi and Rabenu Tam, on the one side, and Ibn Gabirol and Maimonides, on the other, said their prayers. They not only erected any number of synagogues, in which they worshiped entirely in conformity with the old Jewish ritual, but by the mere virtue of their numbers again brought the conservative tendency into prominence. Contemporary with this immigration, a Conservative Seminary was erected by the greatest leader of traditional Judaism in this country, Dr. Sabato Morais, the Rabbi of Congregation Mikveh Israel of Philadelphia, who, with a chosen band of friends, which included the late Marcus Jastrow and Benjamin Szold, labored in it for many years. . . .

I am very reluctant to denounce any party in existence. But close observation for ten years and more has convinced me that, unless we succeed in effecting an organization which, while loyal to the Torah, to the teachings of our Sages, to the traditions of our fathers, to the usages and customs of Israel, shall at the same time introduce the English sermon, and adopt scientific methods in our seminaries, in our training of rabbis and schoolmasters for our synagogues and Talmud Torahs, and bring order and decorum into our synagogues,—unless this is done, I declare unhesitatingly that traditional Judaism will not survive another generation in this country. . . .

I do not belong to those who despair of Judaism, even in my moments of greatest depression. I thoroughly believe with the old Rabbi that a general apostasy is impossible, the freedom of choosing another religion or no religion being granted only to the individual and not to the bulk of Israel. But I believe also, at the same time, in the homily of the Rabbis regarding man's efforts in the material life. God promises Israel His blessing (Deut. 15:18). But the condition is that He will withhold His blessing from them if they are mere lazy onlookers. We must labor and work. And it is for this purpose that this United Synagogue has been created. . . .

Our work, however, must not remain confined to the Synagogue. We want synagogue extension, but this in the sense our ancients understood it. The first place to which the influence of the Synagogue should be extended is the home, becoming thereby a Jewish home. But the Jewishness must be something visible and tangible. A Jewish home without symbols, such as, for instance, the *Mezuzah*, is an anomaly, and is mere sentimental talk. A Jewish home, again, in which the dietary laws are not observed, is, more properly speaking, a non-Jewish home. . . .

It is a "work of Heaven," to which you have been invited. And thus may the blessing of Heaven come upon all of you, so that the Divine Presence shall dwell in the work of your hands, which blessing alone can give it permanence and efficiency.

QUESTIONS AND TOPICS FOR DISCUSSION

1. *What are the aims and purposes of the United Synagogue according to Schechter?*

2. *Wherein do they differ from those of the Union of American Hebrew Congregations, which is the synagogue organization of the Reform wing?*

3. *What were the conditions of Jewish life a generation ago, as reflected in this address?*

4. *What are the activities and functions of the United Synagogue? What are its brother and sister organizations?*

THE JEWISH COMMUNITY MUST ENABLE THE
JEW TO EXPERIENCE THE REALITY OF
JEWISH FELLOWSHIP
by Mordecai M. Kaplan

TO ENABLE THE Jewish community to function . . . it is necessary that Jews create a social structure which will insure the coordination of all Jewish efforts. The exact form of such Jewish communal organization would have to vary in detail in accordance with differences in local conditions. But, in its general outlines, it would probably be similar in all considerable centers of Jewish population. The structural pattern here proposed may be taken as the norm. Differences in local conditions will suggest adaptive modification of that norm.

Every organized Jewish community will have a general membership, a democratically representative governing council that shall determine its policies, an administrative committee and executive officers to supervise the execution of these policies, various functional bureaus to direct the day-to-day activities of the community under the control of the council, and organizations for specific Jewish purposes such as already exist— synagogues, schools, community centers, charitable institutions and the like.

The general membership of the community organization will have to be open to every adult Jew who wishes to be registered. Registration in the community must be accompanied by payment of nominal dues, with special provision to be made for the registration of dependents on the community. A vigorous campaign should be conducted for the registration of all who are eligible. Although membership would have to be on a voluntary basis, the community must not hesitate to apply social pressure by denying such services as Jewish marriage and Jewish burial to all who keep aloof from affiliation with it.

The governing council of the Jewish community organization should consist of representatives elected by the various Jewish organizations whose members are enrolled in the Jewish community. Special provision should be made also for participation in the election of registered members of the community who are not affiliated with any of its constituent organizations. Although such elections by organizations would give an individual who is a member of more than one organization more than one vote, no harm can come from this practice. The important principle is not that every man have an equal voice in determining Jewish policy, regardless of the extent of his Jewish interests, but that every Jewish interest or tendency which is manifest in the community be adequately and proportionately represented.

The governing council should elect all the executive officers of the Jewish community organization and its administrative committee. It should hold title to and administer all communal properties such as synagogues, schools, hospitals, etc. In all matters of policy other than the administration of their properties and the allocation of their share of the communal budget, these organizations should continue to enjoy full autonomy. Although this measure of autonomy may at times impede the unification of the communal program, this risk must be run in order to avoid the greater danger of unwise regimentation. The opportunity must at all times be open for groups of Jews who are interested in particular phases of Jewish activity to give full expression to this interest. . . .

The governing council should employ all communal functionaries such as rabbis, teachers, social workers and the like. This does not mean that their selection should not be left to the particular institutions to which their immediate services are to be rendered. It means that their salaries should be paid from a general fund and that the amount of their salaries, their technical qualifications, their tenure of office, the general definition of their duties and other conditions of their employment should be determined by the governing council. This procedure will have the effect of insuring uniform standards of communal services to all elements of the Jewish community. . . .

In order to be able to regulate the affairs of the Jewish community, the governing council must have full control over the communal budget and the allocation of funds for all communal purposes. This prerogative carries with it the responsibility for raising the necessary funds. Although it would lack the power to impose taxes for Jewish community purposes, it might lay down standards for voluntary self-taxation on the same lines as prevailing income taxes. . . .

In order to correlate the work of the many communal institutions and promote their efficient functioning, the governing council would have to create a number of bureaus, each assigned to the supervision and stimulation of some important function of the community. Thus there should be a bureau of vital statistics, an economic bureau, a bureau of education, a bureau of religion and a social service bureau. The bureau of vital statistics would provide for the registration of all Jewish marriages and divorces, births and deaths, and the collection of statistical data of demographic interest. The economic bureau would study the economic problems of the Jewish people, and devise and apply ways and means for enabling the human and material resources of the Jewish community to contribute to the economic security and welfare of the individual Jew. The bureau of education would function along lines similar to the functioning of such bureaus where they exist. Without interfering with the right of parents in respect to the content of the Jewish education which their children should receive, it would offer planning, guidance and supervision, would establish professional standards of teaching, would provide educational facilities where needed and would do all in its power to develop the kind of Jewish education which is essential to a worthy and satisfactory Jewish life. The bureau of religion would provide facilities for public worship wherever needed, would co-ordinate the religious activities of the different congregations, would interest itself in such activities as the development of liturgic music and religious architecture, would seek the perfection of the ritual to make it most expressive of the actual religious point of view of the congregation, would stimulate the study of religion, would seek ways for promoting religious observance in the home, and would provide for the administration of *kashrut* and other ritual practices that need communal supervision. The social service bureau would co-ordinate and supervise the social service activities of the Jewish community much in the same way that the offices of the federated charities now do.

The above may serve as a brief sketch of the organization of local Jewish communities. To be sure, if Jewish community organization is to satisfy the psychological need of Jews for status, self-respect and spiritual adjustment, Jewry must be integrated not alone locally but also nationally and internationally. But local organization must be the basis of the entire structure, for it is the local community that mediates the relation of the individual Jew to the Jewish people. Without such local organization to enable the Jew to experience the reality of Jewish fellowship, the Jewish people becomes a mere name, and Jewish national and international organizations impinge on the life of the individual only on the sporadic occasions when they appeal for financial support.[8]

Questions and Topics for Discussion

1. *Find out from your rabbi or better still from your Jewish community organization how the community Federation and Welfare Fund Boards are made up, how they function and in what areas.*
2. *Explain Kaplan's blueprint for Jewish communal organization.*

3. *Wherein does it differ from your Jewish community structure and functions?*

4. *Discuss with your class which type of community organization you think is better. Which is more practical?*

5. *If you are in favor of Kaplan's plan, what changes in your community organization would be necessary if that plan were applied to your city?*

VISION FOR OUR DAY
by Milton Steinberg

[*Rabbi Milton Steinberg (b. Rochester 1903; d. New York City 1950) was one of America's distinguished rabbis, authors and leaders. His books,* A Partisan Guide to the Jewish Problem, The Making of the Modern Jew, As a Driven Leaf, Basic Judaism, *and* A Believing Jew, *have already become classics. The following excerpt is taken from* A Partisan Guide to the Jewish Problem.]

I SEE in Palestine a Jewish Commonwealth where the homeless Jews of the world have found rest, where the Jewish spirit has been reborn, whence flow to the dispersion inspiration and the stuffs on which it feeds.

I see the Jewries of the world, each at ease and firmly rooted in the land of its residence, each unswervingly devoted to the polity and culture of that land and at the same time the bearer and transmitter of a living Hebraism, significant to itself, its environment and the world.

Most specifically, I see an American Jewry, emancipated along with all other Americans from the restraints of prejudice, secure against violence, free to fulfill itself without hindrance.

An American Jewry alight with a religious faith hallowed by antiquity and responsive to the mystery of all things, yet sanctioned by the best in modern thought and clean with reasonableness.

An American Jewry standing four square by Judaism's great moral ideals, sharpening them into the keenest contemporaneousness, applying them boldly, imaginatively—so that the name Jew is a synonym for the practice and advocacy of justice, compassion, freedom and peace.

An American Jewry literate in both its heritages, the American and

Hebraic, creative in both, cross-blending and fertilizing the two until all devotion to one shall connote blessing for the other as well.

An American Jewry that in its observances is both reverential of the tradition and awake to current needs, so that the precious freightage of the past is enriched by new gifts in each generation.

An American Jewry whose household is set in order.

An American Jewry which, having labored that Zion be rebuilt, now draws waters in joy from the fountainhead of the Jewish spirit.

I see in sum a Jewry which in its inner life has made of Judaism what it is intended to be, what it. is now in some measure, and what it can become in infinitely greater degree—that is to say, a source of blessing.

And I see all this set in a new, brave and free world which Jews, together with all men of good will, have helped to set free, laboring as individuals but also as Jews, as members of a fellowship consecrated from the womb to the ideal of a new, brave and free world. . . .

Shall not Jewish dreams and ideals, hands and hearts, blood and anguish have contributed to this end so long desired and prayed for? Will it then be a little thing—will it not rather be accounted a very great thing —to have played a part, not the largest perhaps but not the meanest either, in the building of the Kingdom of God on earth?

Questions and Topics for Discussion

1. *Compare Steinberg's vision to that of Friedlander's on pp. 216-17 and Brandeis' on pp. 213-14. What does each one stress?*
2. *How do visions like these help you set up goals for your daily life?*
3. *State some of Judaism's great moral ideals which Steinberg enjoins us to stand by "four square"?*
4. *Can you point to and describe the lives of certain people of your acquaintance who are already fulfilling Steinberg's vision?*
5. *The book from which this selection is taken was written several years before Israel became an independent state. Show how Steinberg's prophecy concerning Israel has already been fulfilled.*
6. *What does the author mean by "An American Jewry whose household is set in order"? Give particulars. What is required "to set our household in order"?*
7. *How does Conservative Jewry try to be both "reverential of the tradition and awake to current needs"? Cite examples.*

I LIVE IN YOU, IN EACH OF YOU, IN ALL OF YOU
by Abraham Isaac Kook

Hearken, O my people!
From the very depths of my soul
I speak unto you;
From the core of life where lies the tie
That binds us one to the other,
With devotion, deep and profound,
I declare unto you
That you, each one of you,
All of you, the whole of you,
Your very souls, your generations, —
Only you are the essence of my life.
I live in you, in each of you, in all of you;
In your life, my life has deeper, truer meaning;
Without you I am as naught.
Hope, aspiration and life's intrinsic worth, —
All this I find only when I am with you.
I am bound up inextricably
With the soul of all of you,
And I love you with infinite love;
I cannot feel otherwise.
All life's loves, small and great,
Are treasured in my love of you,
In my love of all of you,
Each one of you, each individual soul
Is a glowing spark of that torch eternal,
Kindling the light of life for me.
You give meaning to life, to labor,
To learning, to prayer, song and hope;
Through the channel of your being, life pulsates in me;
On the wings of your love I rise to the love of God.

Everything becomes crystal-clear to me, unequivocal,
Like a flame in my heart purifying my thoughts.
With you, O my people, my kin-folk, my mother,
Source of my life,
With you I soar the wide spaces of the world;
In your eternity I have life eternal.
In your glory I am honored, in your sorrow I am grieved,
In your affliction, I suffer anguish,
In your knowledge and understanding,
Behold, I am filled with knowledge and understanding.
Every footstep, wherever you have trod, is a treasure of life.
Your land, the land of your hope, is sacred to me;
Its heavens a source of beauty, of eternal splendor;
Its Carmel[9] and Sharon[10] are the spring of hope,
The fountain of blessing, the source of life's joy.
Even its thorns and thistles are garbed in glory,
In deathless beauty![11]

QUESTIONS AND TOPICS FOR DISCUSSION

1. *What does Rabbi Kook say of his relations with our people? With Eretz Yisrael?*
2. *Paraphrase Kook's poetic words in your own.*
3. *How can one "rise to the love of God" through love of one's people?*
4. *If a Jew were to feel toward his people as Rabbi Kook, how would his feelings express themselves in his daily life?*

CREDO
by Saul Tchernikhowsky

Laugh at all my dreams, my dearest;
    Laugh, and I repeat anew
That I still believe in man—
    As I still believe in you.

For my soul is not yet unsold
    To the golden calf of scorn
And I still believe in man
    And the spirit in him born.

By the passion of his spirit
    Shall his ancient bonds be shed.
Let the soul be given freedom,
    Let the body have its bread!

Laugh, for I believe in friendship,
    And in one I still believe,
One whose heart shall beat with my heart
    And with mine rejoice and grieve.

Let the time be dark with hatred,
    I believe in years beyond,
Love at last shall bind the peoples
    In an everlasting bond.

In that day shall my own people
    Rooted in its soil arise,
Shake the yoke from off its shoulders
    And the darkness from its eyes.

Life and love and strength and action
In their heart and blood shall beat,
And their hopes shall be both heaven
And the earth beneath their feet.

Then a new song shall be lifted
To the young, the free, the brave,
And the wreath to crown the singer
Shall be gathered from my grave.[12]

Questions and Topics for Discussion

1. *This popular poem, called in Hebrew "Sahaki," has been set to music. It is found in many song books. Look it up in* Songs of Zion *by Harry Coopersmith and learn it.*
2. *What notes of hope and optimism are struck in this poem?*
3. *Do you entertain the same hopes as the poet?*
4. *Could we have existed as a people if we had not hoped and striven for the day of the "good life" and the "Kingdom of Heaven on earth"?*

SUGGESTED BIBLIOGRAPHY FOR ADDITIONAL READING

Adler, Cyrus, *I Have Considered the Days*,
    Jewish Publication Society, 1941
Bentwich, Norman, *Solomon Schechter*, Jewish Publication Society, 1938
De Haas, Jacob, *Louis D. Brandeis*, Bloch, 1929
Eisenstein, Ira, *Creative Judaism*, Behrman, 1936
Feuer, Leon, *Why a Jewish State?*, Richard Smith, 1942
Fleg, Edmond, *Why I Am a Jew*, Bloch, 1929
Gordis, Robert, *Conservative Judaism*, Behrman, 1945
Gordis, Robert, *The Jew Faces a New World*, Behrman, 1941
Greenberg, Simon, *Living As a Jew Today*, Behrman, 1940
Kaplan, Mordecai M., *The Future of the American Jew*, Macmillan, 1948
Kohn, Eugene, *Future of Judaism in America*, Liberal Press, 1934
Neuman, Abraham A., *Cyrus Adler*, American Jewish Committee, 1942
Pilch, Judah, *Jewish Life in Our Times*, Behrman, 1944
Ruppin, Arthur, *The Jewish Fate and Future*, Macmillan, 1940
Samuel, Maurice, *The Great Hatred*, Knopf, 1940
Silver, A. H., *The World Crisis and Jewish Survival*,
    Richard R. Smith, 1941
Steinberg, Milton, *The Making of the Modern Jew*, Behrman, 1933
Steinberg, Milton, *A Partisan Guide to the Jewish Problem*,
    Bobbs-Merrill Co., 1945

BIOGRAPHIES

ADLER, CYRUS: Builder of American Jewry and especially of Conservative Judaism, Cyrus Adler (b. Van Buren, Ark., 1863; d. Philadelphia, 1940) after completing his studies at the Universities of Pennsylvania and Johns Hopkins, began his career as teacher, librarian and museum curator in the field of Semitic and Oriental studies. He achieved distinction in these professions and in 1908 he was appointed president of Dropsie College in Philadelphia, a school of higher learning in Hebrew and related subjects.

The story of Cyrus Adler's life reads like a history of American Jewry in the last 50 years. As early as 1888, he participated in the founding of the Jewish Publication Society which has enriched the English-speaking world with Jewish classics and countless works of significance and interest. He was chairman of the group of scholars who translated the authorized Jewish version of the Bible in English. In 1899 he began editing the *American Jewish Year Book*, which has been appearing annually ever since.

He was the leading spirit in the organization of the American Jewish Historical Society, Gratz College of Philadelphia, the Jewish Theological Seminary of America, the United Synagogue of America, the American Jewish Committee, the Jewish Agency for Palestine, and many other important organizations. When Schechter died, Adler succeeded him first as acting president of the Seminary and then as president. Cyrus Adler was a pillar of Congregation Mikveh Israel, the Spanish-Portuguese Congregation of Philadelphia and was universally acknowledged as the leader of Conservative Jewry.

In addition to all the above-mentioned activities, Cyrus Adler was active in civic and national affairs. He served on the Philadelphia Board of Education and that of the Free Library. He was active in scientific societies, the Boy Scouts of America, the Jewish Welfare Board, and many others. In 1919 he, together with Louis Marshall, represented the American Jewish Committee at the Versailles Peace Conference, where he fought for the rights of minorities and the abolition of anti-Semitism. He was awarded honorary degrees and distinctions by leading universities and institutions in America and abroad.

Withal Adler found time to write. He was author of *Jacob H. Schiff, His Life and Letters; The Voice of America on Kishineff; Oriental Studies; Turkish Folk Tales* and many articles and lectures. His autobiography, *I Have Considered the Days*, was published after his death. A biography of him by Dr. Abraham A. Neuman, his successor at Dropsie College, appeared in 1942.

AHAD HA-AM ("One of the People"), the pen name of Asher Ginzberg (b. near Kiev, Russia, 1856; d. Tel Aviv, 1927), was one of the foremost philosophers and moulders of Zionist thought in the last generation. Brought up in a traditional Hasidic environment, he showed signs of genius at an early age. As soon as he grew to maturity, he began to master European literature and philosophy. He studied in prominent European universities though without intention of obtaining a degree. In 1886, at the age of thirty, he settled in Odessa where he became active in the movement known as *Lovers of Zion* which was led by Dr. Leo Pinsker. He soon emerged as a leader of first rank. In 1889, he organized an exclusive society called *Bnai Moshe*, which proved influential in shaping Zionist thought and action. He visited Eretz in 1891 and returned to it repeatedly until he finally settled in Tel Aviv in 1921. Throughout his early years Ahad Ha-Am was employed by a famous Jewish tea firm. His literary and communal work was avocational. In 1896, however, he became the director of a Hebrew publishing house, Ahiasaf, and editor of *Ha-Shiloah*, one of the most influential magazines in Hebrew literary history. His painstaking devotion to his task as editor set a high standard for a generation of Hebrew writers, and helped raise Hebrew literature to a high level.

Ahad Ha-Am's contribution to Zionism was his stress on its cultural aspects. He emphasized the idea of Eretz Yisrael as a "spiritual center" for world Jewry, and the value of Hebrew as the medium of expression for our people. Championing these ideas, he often found himself in conflict with Herzl and the political Zionists who viewed Eretz Yisrael as the solution of Jewish political and economic problems. Ahad Ha-Am did not write books. His essays and addresses, models of clear thinking eloquently and precisely expressed, have been collected in four volumes entitled *Al Parashat Derakhim* (At the Cross Roads or Parting of the Ways). They constitute a first-rate modern classic.

Ahad Ha-Am was the teacher of an entire generation of Hebrew writers, thinkers and Zionist leaders, from Bialik and Shemarya Levin to Chaim Weizmann, Israel Friedlaender and Mordecai M. Kaplan, His ideas have had a profound effect on the thinking Jewish world. He was the creator of the Hebrew essay. He freed the modern Hebrew style from artificiality and verbosity. He taught his disciples—many of whom have become luminaries in the Jewish world—how to think and how to express themselves as Europeans. And above all he inspired his generation with vision, faith and confidence in the creative powers of the Jewish people.

In addition to *Al Parashat Derakhim*, six Hebrew volumes of his letters are available. Two volumes of his essays have been translated into English by Sir Leon Simon.

ALTERMAN, NATHAN: (b. Warsaw, 1910) is one of the young popular poets of Palestine. His light verse and satires which deal with timely topics are widely read. One of the poems reprinted in this book was stimulated by the reception given to the Italian captain of the *Hannah Senesch* when he safely ran the British blockade and brought his cargo of unauthorized immigrants to the shores of Eretz Yisrael.

BIALIK, HAYIM NAHMAN: (b. Volhynia, 1872; d. Vienna, 1934) is recognized as the greatest Hebrew poet of modern times. He was born into a very poor family. When he was a young child, his father died. He went to live with his grandfather. Bialik's youth was spent in an atmosphere of Jewish tradition. He received a thorough Hebrew education, including the study of Bible, Talmud and Rabbinic literature. He began writing early in life and his reputation as a poet soon spread throughout the Jewish world. He became active in the Zionist movement and was soon recognized as one of its intellectual leaders. In 1905 Bialik founded Moriah, a Hebrew publishing house which exerted great influence on Hebrew education and culture. When Moriah was dissolved, he founded Dvir, one of the leading publishing houses in Eretz Yisrael.

In order to realize his ambition to make a fundamental contribution toward the rebuilding of Eretz, he made his home in Tel Aviv in 1924. In 1926, he visited the United States where he was acclaimed by the American Jewish community, and was awarded honorary degrees by two Jewish seminaries in New York. During the last years of his life he wrote very little poetry but devoted himself to the practical work of editing and publishing both ancient and modern Hebrew classics, and of encouraging the work of young Hebrew writers. His work has undoubtedly been one of the great factors in developing modern Hebrew as a living language.

Bialik was greatly influenced in his poetry by the Bible. Many of his poems read like Prophetic selections. Although he wrote beautifully of nature, of yearning for Zion and love, he is best known for his poems describing his early experiences as an orphan, a child of dire poverty and a diligent student of the Talmud. Nowhere in Hebrew poetry is there a finer expression reflecting the upbringing of the average Jew of Eastern Europe than in his poems, "The *Matmid*," "My Song," "My Father," "The Source of Strength," "On My Return," and many others. "The *Matmid*," included in this book, is an exemplary poetic outpouring describing the Rabbinic scholar, who was the ideal, the "hero" of the Jewish "pale."

Fortunately, many of Bialik's works are available in English. His beautiful folk tales will be found in *And It Came to Pass*, translated by the Christian Hebrew student, Canon Danby. His children's poems will be found in *Far Over the Sea*, translated by Jessie Sampter, and in *Knight of Onions and Knight of Garlic*, translated by Canon Danby. His poems have been translated by Maurice Samuel of the United States, by Abraham M. Klein of Canada, by L. V. Snowman of England, by Bertha Beinkinstadt of South Africa, and others. His stories were translated by I. M. Lask in *Aftergrowth*. Both in Hebrew and Yiddish there is a voluminous literature on Bialik, which is growing larger with the passing of time. The name of Bialik has become a legend in Jewish life. Indeed it may be said that he has joined the family of the revered sages and seers of Israel.

BRANDEIS, LOUIS DEMBITZ: (b. Louisville, Ky., 1856; d. Washington, D. C., 1941) was perhaps the outstanding American Jew of his generation. His family had fled from Germany after the failure of the liberal-inspired revolution of 1848. Graduating first in his class at Harvard Law School, he settled in Boston where he soon acquired a nationwide reputation. He became known as the "people's attorney." He fought the tyranny of the big corporations, the large railroad systems, the giant insurance companies. In 1916 he was nominated by President Wilson to the Supreme Court, and after a heated battle in the Senate, a battle which stirred the entire nation, his name was finally confirmed. For 22 years, until his retirement in 1939, Brandeis served our highest court with distinction. Together with Justice Oliver Wendell Holmes, he helped greatly in moulding the American way of living and thinking as it is reflected in the law.

At the height of his career, Brandeis, a "typical American assimilationist," discovered his people and Zionism. It happened in 1910, while he was involved in arbitrating a strike for the International

Ladies Garment Workers, a union in which Jews played a leading role. Brandeis, already in his fifties, became interested in the Jewish problem. Prior to that time no one had known him as Jew or Gentile. He had been accepted simply as a New England American who had no connection whatsoever with Jewish causes or interests.

In 1912 he joined the Zionist movement and unhesitatingly threw in his lot with his people. Immediately he rose to national leadership. He came to Zionism at the beginning of a new era and brought to it his keen mind and passionate zeal. In 1914, when the World War broke out, Brandeis became virtually leader of the American Zionist Organization. From then on his services to the movement were varied and valuable. He guided the creation and formation of many Zionist activities. He attracted influential friends to the Zionist cause and he was instrumental in winning President Wilson's approval of the Balfour Declaration.

When he was appointed to the Supreme Court, tradition dictated his official resignation from formal responsible Zionist offices. But he remained, in fact, the silent leader of the movement.

Brandeis became a beloved name throughout the Jewish world including Eretz Yisrael, which he visited. In Eretz a colony was named after him, and in America a recently founded university in Waltham (near Boston) bears his name.

BRENNER, J. H.: Saint and martyr of the early pioneering period in Eretz, Brenner (b. Ukraine, 1881; d. Jaffa, 1921) came of a very poor family and all his life lived in poverty. He never ceased to be the spokesman for the hungry, the down-trodden and the inarticulate. Early in his career he became active in the Bund, the Jewish Socialist Party in Russia. Later he left it to become active in the Labor Zionist movement.

After a year's service in the hateful Russian army, Brenner fled to London. Later he went to Austria, and finally settled in Eretz. In 1906, when the pogroms and persecutions in Czarist Russia had almost paralyzed Jewish life and Hebrew literature, Brenner roused the Hebrew world with his *Ha-Meorer* (The Awakener), a small journal which he published in London. Together with a few devoted colleagues, he edited, set type, printed, bound, delivered and mailed the one and only Hebrew periodical of the time. It was written with "flame and fire" and struck a spark in the Hebrew world which in time flared into a radiant flame. Indeed, his devotion to Hebrew literature knew no bounds. Unhesitatingly and unstintingly he gave to it his all, mentally and physically.

In his delineations of character, Brenner probed deeply into his own self for material. All of his heroes depict facets of his own complex personality. They are serious, critical, argumentative; they demand much from themselves and from others; they are frustrated and tragic.

A pioneer of the Second *Aliyah* (1904-1914), Brenner became its spiritual leader. He edited several periodicals and headed publishing houses established by the Labor Zionist movement. Although he worked as laborer and teacher, he served his people best with his pen.

Because he was born in the year during which the Russian pogroms began, Brenner often called himself the "son of pogroms." His life came to an abrupt end during the Arab pogroms of 1921. An automobile was sent to Jaffa in order to remove him to safety. He refused to go and met his death at the hands of Arab assassins. An ever-growing stock of legends now surrounds the personality of Brenner.

The selection chosen for this book is of special significance since it was among Brenner's very last written words. It was composed at the end of April, 1921, a few days before he was killed.

CAHAN, ABRAHAM: Socialist leader and editor of the *Jewish Daily Forward*, Abraham Cahan (b. near Vilna, 1860) was originally a student at the Rabbinical Seminary in Vilna and a Hebrew teacher by profession. A member of the revolutionary movement in 1882, he was informed on and was forced to flee Czarist Russia. He came to New York City and has lived there ever since.

Cahan has contributed profoundly to the Americanization of the Jewish immigrant working class and to the organization of the Socialist Party. He served these causes as journalist, organizer and editor. He represented the American Socialist movement at international conferences. Under his direction and editorship the *Jewish Daily Forward* has become the Yiddish newspaper with the largest circulation in America. Cahan has played a twofold role in American Jewish life. He has interpreted American life and letters to the immigrant Jew and has depicted the life of the immigrant to the American world. He is the author of *The Rise of David Levinsky*, *Yekl*, and other works.

COHEN, HYMAN and LESTER: are father and son. Dr. Hyman Cohen is a physician residing in Chicago. He is also the author of *The Tents of Jacob*, and has written a great deal in the field of medicine and public health. He has been a pioneer in infant welfare work and such public health projects as the free distribution of antitoxin, establishment of quarantine regulations, and the like.

Lester Cohen, co-author, has written such "best sellers" as *Coming Home, Sweepings,* and other works.

DWORZECKI, MARK: was born in Vilna and is one of the few who escaped from the horror of Nazi ghettos and concentration camps. He is a leader of the Labor Zionist movement in Europe and, in 1946, was a delegate to the 22nd Zionist Congress at Basle, Switzerland. He is a correspondent for *The Jewish Morning Journal* of New York.

EINSTEIN, ALBERT: (b. Germany, 1879) is the greatest intellect of our times. As a child he was slow of speech, shy, and rather poor in his studies except for mathematics. In this he showed marks of genius. He studied in Germany and Switzerland. At the early age of 26, he published the thirty-page mathematical equation known as the "Special Theory of Relativity." He worked out this theory while employed as a patent-examiner in Berne, Switzerland.

He was offered professorships first at the University of Zurich and at the University of Prague. Later, he was accorded the unusual honor—for a Jew—of directing the distinguished Prussian Academy of Science.

Einstein's Theory of Relativity, changing the conception of the universe as established by Newton, was successfully tested during a total solar eclipse (Gulf of Guiana, May 29, 1919). After the confirmation of his theory, Einstein became a by-word for genius. In 1922 he received the Nobel Prize in Physics.

During World War I, Einstein was the only one of Germany's 93 greatest men of science and letters who refused to sign the declaration laying the guilt of the war on England. With the rise of Hitlerism (1933), Einstein renounced his German citizenship and settled in Princeton, New Jersey, where he is continuing his mathematical research.

Einstein has been and still is one of the greatest champions of his people and of the Zionist cause. He has declared proudly, "that the pursuit of knowledge for its own sake, an almost fanatical love of justice, and the desire for personal independence are the features of the Jewish tradition, which make me thank my stars that I belong to it."

Einstein has been active on behalf of the Hebrew University, and in many other Jewish causes. He is universally beloved and admired for his utter simplicity and modesty, and for his great charm and courage.

FERBER, EDNA: A leading figure in modern American literature, Edna Ferber (b. Kalamazoo, Mich., 1887) is well known for her short stories, novels, plays, movies, radio programs, musical comedies, etc. She started out as a reporter in the mid-western cities of Appleton and Milwaukee, Wisconsin. Later her family settled in Chicago, where she became a contributor to short story magazines. Her rise to fame was rapid. The collections of her short stories alone number more than ten volumes.

In 1925, Edna Ferber became nationally famous for her book, *So Big*, which was awarded the Pulitzer Prize. The book sold in hundreds of thousands of copies and was filmed first as a silent movie and then as a talkie. Most of her literary career has been devoted to depicting the story of pioneering America. Her books, some of which were filmed and some reworked for the radio, are *Show Boat*, which deals with life in the South; *Cimarron*, which depicts the early days of Oklahoma and the mad rush of 1889; *American Beauty*, a story about the lumber men of Wisconsin and Michigan; *Fanny Herself*, the story of a Jewish girl; *Saratoga Trunk*, which has also been filmed; and many others. She also collaborated with the celebrated playwright, George S. Kaufman, in three noteworthy plays, *The Royal Family*, *Dinner at Eight*, and *Stage Door*. These have enjoyed successful runs on the legitimate stage and were seen by millions on the cinema screen.

The selection in the book is taken from the author's autobiography, *A Peculiar Treasure*.

FEUCHTWANGER, LION: (b. Munich, Germany, 1884) is one of the outstanding novelists of Europe and America. His books have been best sellers for many years. Some of his better known works (especially recommended to the attention of the Jewish reading public) are *Power* and the trilogy *Josephus, Jew of Rome*, and *Josephus and the Emperor*.

Early in his career Feuchtwanger rebelled against the Prussian military spirit. During World War I he wrote revolutionary works which were suppressed by the reactionaries. When Hitler deprived him of his citizenship, he settled in France. When the Nazis invaded France, he narrowly escaped capture. In 1940 he fled to America, where he now resides.

FINEMAN, IRVING: (b. New York City, 1893) began his career as an engineer. He later turned to writing and to the teaching of English literature. In 1930 he was awarded a substantial prize for his first novel, *This Pure Young Man*. Since then he has written several well-known books such as *Hear Ye Sons, Jacob, Doctor Addams,* and others. *Hear Ye Sons,* from which the excerpt in this anthology is taken, is a book describing with great warmth the life of the small town in Poland at the end of the nineteenth century. *Jacob* is a very interesting attempt at an autobiography, as it were, of the Patriarch Jacob in which he addresses himself to his son Joseph.

FRIEDLAENDER, ISRAEL: (b. Poland, 1876; d. Ukraine, 1920) was a martyr who died for his people. His childhood and youth were typical of the promising scholar described elsewhere in this book. He received his doctorate in Semitic studies at a German university. In 1903 he accepted an invitation from Dr. Solomon Schechter to join the distinguished staff of the Jewish Theological Seminary of America.

In this country Friedlaender soon rose to eminence in Jewish communal and educational circles. He assumed positions of leadership in the New York Bureau of Jewish Education, Young Judea, and the Menorah Society.

At the height of his career, he was murdered in the Ukraine. This happened during the tragic era following World War I. He and a colleague, Rabbi Kantor, volunteered to tour the afflicted Jewish communities of the Ukraine in order to bring food, medicine and clothing to our suffering brethren. His death shocked American Jewry and especially the thousands of young people who revered him as guide and mentor. His loss was felt keenly. To honor his memory, the Seminary has named its extension department "The Israel Friedlaender Classes."

FRISHMAN, DAVID: (b. near Lodz, Poland, 1860; d. Berlin, 1922) was the first modern Hebrew critic. He began to write at the early age of eight and even as a child showed outstanding talent. His first work, *Chaos,* "upset the apple-cart" of Hebrew literature of his day because of its sharp criticism. He opposed the involved style used by the writers of his time and urged clarity and simplicity. He wrote so prodigiously that as early as 1914 the published collection of his volumes numbered sixteen. He was a master of the short story in Hebrew. Especially is he known for his collection of Biblical stories entitled *Ba-Midbar* (In the Desert). He also wrote poetry, critical essays, and light satires.

An outstanding achievement of Frishman's was his translation of world classics into Hebrew, including Andersen's and Grimm's fairy tales. He undertook this task in order to teach his generation the best of modern European literature. Frishman was also the first editor of

Stybel Publications, a publishing house which has enriched Hebrew literature with hundreds of valuable books in all fields. He succeeded in helping to modernize the content and style of Hebrew literature and to inspire a generation of Hebrew writers.

GOLDMAN, SOLOMON: (b. Volhynia, 1893) was brought to the United States as a child of seven. He is a graduate of the Jewish Theological Seminary and has studied in leading universities. He has served in the ministry of leading synagogues in Brooklyn, Cleveland and Chicago (since 1929), and is regarded as one of the most scholarly and distinguished men in the Conservative Rabbinate.

Active in communal, Hebrew, cultural, and Zionist activities, Rabbi Goldman was at one time president of the Zionist Organization of America. He has travelled extensively for Zionist and Hebraic causes and has made important contributions to Jewish literature. His books, which command wide interest, are *A Rabbi Takes Stock, Crisis and Decision, The Jew and the Universe.* The last has been translated into Hebrew and Spanish. He has also edited and written text materials for Hebrew schools and adult institutes.

GORDON, A. D.: (b. in Podolya, Russia, 1850; d. Dagania, Eretz, 1922) was born into a family of well-to-do Orthodox parents. Although reared in a traditional atmosphere Gordon was permitted to study modern European languages and literature. Related to the most prominent Russian Jewish family of the time, that of Baron Gunzberg, Gordon was employed as an overseer of one of the Baron's estates, a post which he held for twenty-three years. When the estate was sold in 1903, Gordon left for Eretz where he began life anew. Aleph Dalet (as he was popularly known) underwent a complete transformation which marked him as the Grand Old Man of the labor movement. He became the philosopher of manual labor and the theorist of the working class. Living as a laborer with three other men in one room, digging and tilling the ground like the rest, shunning special privileges, joining with the young in song and dance, Gordon became the living symbol of the *Yishuv.* In the last years of his life he bore the fearful burden of personal tragedy (he had lost six of his seven children!) and the crushing burden of the tragedy of his people during the war years. His spirit, however, was not broken. He labored on in the fields up to a few months before his death. Is it any wonder that in Eretz Gordon has become an inspired legend to young and old!

Selections of A. D. Gordon's works translated into English are available in a one-volume edition published by the League for Labor Palestine, entitled *Selected Essays.*

GRINDELL, ELLEN: (b. New York, 1913) studied at the University of Wisconsin, New York University, and the Women's Medical College of Philadelphia. She also spent three years studying Hebrew and Jewish history at the Israel Friedlaender Classes of the Jewish Theological Seminary of America. Her literary interests are of necessity subordinated to her work as a physician.

HERZL, THEODOR: (b. Budapest, Hungary, 1860; d. Austria, 1904) was born into a well-to-do, nearly assimilated family. While still a student in the secondary school at Budapest, he began to write poetry and light satire, at first in Hungarian and later in German. His adult life may be divided into three parts: 1878 to 1890, when he was a student at the University of Vienna; 1891 to 1895, when he was appointed Paris correspondent of the Viennese *New Free Press*; 1895 to 1904, when he literally consumed himself in his zeal for his people as creator and leader of Political Zionism.

It was while he was in Paris covering the Dreyfus Affair for his newspaper, that he was shocked into an awareness of the Jewish problem. This was almost a mystic experience, for Herzl, an assimilated Western Jew, was transformed overnight into a Jewish leader of first rank.

Herzl's solution of the Jewish problem, a solution embodied in his book, *The Jewish State,* led to the Zionist Movement and to the miracle of modern Eretz Yisrael. Receiving no salary from the Zionist Organization—in fact he helped finance it with his own slender means—Herzl continued to write his articles for his paper while he travelled indefatigably through the countries of Europe and the Near East. He met with several of the kings and rulers of Europe and endeavored to enlist their support. Although he bore heroically the crushing burdens of the new organization which he had brought into life, he nevertheless found time to write *The Jewish State, Old-New Land* and his *Diaries.*

Like Moses, Herzl did not live to see his dream fulfilled. But in the few short years during which he shone like a bright star on the dark Jewish horizon, Herzl accomplished wonders. He created a national movement; he inspired his people with a new ideal, a new faith and a new hope. Herzl made Zionism a dynamic force and Eretz Yisrael a tangible reality. Only fifty years after the Congress of Basle (1897) when modern Zionism was born, Eretz Yisrael was recognized as an independent, sovereign state in the family of nations.

KAHAN, JACOB: (b. State of Minsk, Russia, 1881) is one of the three greatest living Hebrew poets. Like many of his colleagues, he studied in Switzerland where he received a doctorate in philosophy. In 1905, he was aroused by Joseph Hayim Brenner's *Ha-Meorer* (The Awakener), famous Hebrew periodical in London, and became an enthusiastic champion of Hebrew literature. He organized a Hebrew cultural society in Berlin and served as its director for a number of years. In 1916 he returned to Poland to occupy a prominent position in the field of Hebrew education. For a while he was president of the Hebrew Writers' Club. In 1934 he settled in Palestine, where he has lived ever since. Since 1903, when his first collection of poems appeared, Jacob Kahan has been in the forefront of Hebrew literature as poet, editor, dramatist and translator. He received awards and prizes from the Jewish communities of Warsaw and Tel Aviv.

KAPLAN, MORDECAI M.: Religious leader, philosopher and educator, Mordecai M. Kaplan (b. Lithuania, 1881) came to the United States at the age of eight. He went through the usual academic course of study, completing his post-graduate work at Columbia University. He was graduated as Rabbi from the Jewish Theological Seminary in 1902. In 1909 he was invited by Dr. Schechter to head the Hebrew teacher training program of the Seminary. He accepted and thus founded the Teachers' Institute which he conducted until his retirement in 1946.

Kaplan's greatest contribution to American Jewish life and culture is the Reconstructionist movement, "dedicated to the advancement of Judaism as a religious civilization, to the upbuilding of Israel's ancient homeland, and to the furtherance of universal freedom, justice and peace." He began this movement by founding the Society for the Advancement of Judaism. Among his activities on behalf of Reconstructionism are the editorship of *The Reconstructionist* magazine and the writing of such profound and challenging books as *Judaism as a Civilization, Judaism in Transition, The Meaning of God in Modern Jewish Life* and others. He has travelled and lectured extensively on behalf of this movement.

Under his leadership the Reconstructionist Foundation has published *The New Hagadah* or *Service for the Passover Seder*, a *Sabbath Prayer Book* and *Supplementary Readings and Prayers* for various occasions.

Dr. Kaplan has also served as Professor of Homiletics at the Jewish Theological Seminary, as guest professor at the Hebrew University in Jerusalem and as lecturer in other schools of higher Jewish learning.

He has been a distinguished leader in Zionist, Hebrew, cultural and communal activities.

KATZ, H. W.: (b. Galicia, 1906) made his mark as the youngest editor, in Germany, of a famous weekly. He fled from Berlin in 1922 and has resided in the United States since 1941. For his book, *The Fishmans*, from which the selection is taken, the author was awarded the Heinrich Heine Prize by a committee consisting of such men as Thomas Mann, Lion Feuchtwanger and others.

KLEIN, ABRAHAM M.: (b. Montreal, Canada, 1909) is a Canadian attorney and lecturer on English literature at McGill University. According to the celebrated literary critic, Ludwig Lewisohn, Klein is the "first contributor of authentic Jewish poetry to the English language." Klein is an artist of the pen. He sings of Montreal Jews in his "Portraits of a *Minyan*," of historical characters in his "Design for Medieval Tapestry," "Baal Shem Tov," "Elijah" and "Yehuda Halevi," and of his child in the poems quoted in the book. Jewish life is part of him, meaningful and vibrant. Klein's verse, consisting of original works and translations, have appeared in many periodicals. Thus far, three collections of his poetry on Jewish themes have been published: *Hath Not a Jew*, *The Hitleriad* and *Poems*.

KOBRIN, LEON: (b. Vitebsk, Russia, 1872; d. New York City, 1946) is well known to two generations of readers of the Yiddish press in America. In this country since 1892, Kobrin, perhaps more than anyone else, depicted the Russian Jewish immigrant's struggles and trials during the period of his Americanization, emphasizing particularly Jewish life in New York City. He wrote numerous plays and novels (which were printed originally in the Yiddish press as serials) and he translated many works from Russian and French novelists for the benefit of the Yiddish reading public. The only translation of Kobrin extant in English is *A Lithuanian Village*. Several of his works, however, have been translated into German and Russian.

KOOK, ABRAHAM ISAAC: Outstanding leader of Orthodox Judaism and Chief Rabbi of Eretz Yisrael, Rabbi Kook (b. Latvia, 1864; d. Jerusalem, 1935) was a scion of a famous scholarly family. At the tender age of nine he became known as an *Iluy* or Talmudical prodigy. His memory and diligence were phenomenal. He studied in the greatest rabbinical schools of Russia, including Volozhin, probably the foremost *Yeshivah* of its time. During his youth, he joined the *Musar* movement (led by Rabbi Israel Salanter) which stressed piety, self-examination and deep meditation leading to personal perfection. He occupied rabbinic positions in a number of cities. Distinguished from his colleagues in his emphasis on Hebrew as a spoken language, and on Zionism, he became known as the Orthodox Ahad Ha-Am.

In 1903 he accepted the call to minister in Jaffa where he lived until 1914. Stranded in Europe by the outbreak of World War I while attending a conference, he took a position in London, where he was among those instrumental in helping to bring about the Balfour Declaration.

In 1919, he returned to Eretz Yisrael where he became Chief Rabbi and the acknowledged leader of the world Mizrachi or Orthodox Zionists. He established a *Yeshivah* in which the language of instruction was Hebrew. He wrote articles and books on various phases of philosophy, law, legend and modern problems. In his writings Kook emerges as a mystic and profound religious personality. He was deeply beloved by all groups of the *Yishuv*, including the large number of unobservant and untraditional *Halutzim* whom he defended and protected from attack by fanatic opponents.

After his death, the Mizrachi established the Kook Foundation which has published many of his works and the works of other Orthodox scholars. Also founded in his memory was a fund for the promotion of *Yeshivah* education in Eretz Yisrael.

The story of the life and works of Rabbi Kook is contained in a book, *Banner of Jerusalem*, by Rabbi Jacob Agus (Bloch, 1947).

LAMDAN, YITZHAK: If Yitzhak Lamdan (b. Volhynia, Russia, 1899) had written nothing more than *Masadah*, he would have earned immortality in modern Hebrew literature. A refugee during World War I, Lamdan lived through the horrors of the war, of the Bolshevik Revolution and of the massacres of the Jews in the Ukraine. After untold suffering and dangers which are reflected in his epic poem, Lamdan finally reached Eretz. For years he worked as road builder and farm laborer. When his health broke down he devoted himself solely to literary pursuits. Lamdan has been in the forefront of contemporary Hebrew literature. He has published poems, essays, and translations from German, English, and other languages. He is universally known as the editor of *Gilyonot* (Leaves), a Hebrew monthly of high literary caliber. His poetry reflects the blood and tears of the war years, the toil and sweat of the *Halutz*, and the religious faith in the eternity of Israel.

LEVENSOHN, LOTTA: was born in Syracuse, N. Y., and became active in Zionism at an early age. She is the author of *Outline of Zionist History* and many articles and brochures dealing with Zionism and Eretz Yisrael. She translated Herzl's *Old-New Land* from German into English. Miss Levensohn is now residing in Jerusalem.

LEVIN, MEYER: (b. Chicago, 1905) is one of the well-known American Jewish writers of our generation. Although he has studied painting and has written several plays, he is best known as a novelist, editor and reporter. In his novels, *The Old Bunch* and *Citizens*, he depicts the American scene and reflects the life of the large metropolis. His *Golden Mountain* is a splendid contribution to Hasidic literature in English. His *Yehuda* is the first attempt of its kind to sketch the complex new forms of living in the Jewish collective, or commune, in Eretz. To a number of young American Jews who settled in Ain Hashofet (a colony named after Brandeis) *Yehuda* became "their torah for *Kibbutz* life."

In recent years, Levin was popularly known as the movie editor of *Esquire*, and later as a staff member of the Office of War Information, and as the Jewish Telegraphic Agency reporter of war-ravaged European Jewry. He was among the first correspondents to enter and to report on the horror camps of Dachau and Buchenwald.

More recently Levin has gained prominence as one of the founders of an American-Palestine film company and as a reporter and photographer of the Haganah boats which have run the British blockade.

LEVIN, SHEMARYA: (b. State of Minsk, Russia; d. Haifa, 1935) was a great Zionist leader, a renowned orator and a prominent writer of memoirs and essays in Hebrew, Yiddish and Russian. Like many of his illustrious contemporaries, he received a traditional Hebrew education which was followed by an academic education in German universities. After graduation he returned to Russia where he played a leading role as a contributor to famous Hebrew periodicals. He edited a Russian Jewish daily in Vilna, and served as the government Rabbi and spiritual leader of three large Jewish cities including Vilna, "the Jerusalem of Lithuania." In 1906 he was elected delegate by his district to the Russian *Duma* (Parliament) where he became known as a courageous champion of Israel and of liberal causes.

Early in his career Levin associated himself actively with the famed Zionist leader Ahad Ha-Am, and with the builder of the Jewish Commonwealth, Chaim Weizmann. During his lifetime, he participated in almost all of the world Zionist Congresses. The years of the first

World War he spent in America where he took a leading part in vitalizing the Zionist and Hebraic movements of this country.

In 1920 he became connected with the *Keren Hayesod* (Palestine Foundation Fund) which he helped establish. Together with Bialik he founded and headed Dvir, a famous publishing house in Eretz.

A gifted orator, blessed with a creative imagination and vast learning, Shemarya Levin toured world Jewish communities on behalf of Zionist and Hebraic causes. His truly charming personality fascinated all who met him. He was greatly beloved by the masses for his learning, idealism and wit. His stories and anecdotes are quoted widely to this day.

His three-volume autobiography entitled *Childhood in Exile, Youth in Revolt* and *The Arena*, mirrors the stormy period between the latter half of the nineteenth century and the early part of the twentieth, a period which saw the birth of Zionism, the revival of Hebrew, the break-up of the Russian Empire and the rebuilding of Zion.

LEWISOHN, LUDWIG: Outstanding critic and novelist, Ludwig Lewisohn (b. Berlin, 1882) came to this country as a child of eight. His family settled in South Carolina where Lewisohn was raised in an assimilated home and in a non-Jewish environment. As a young man of less than 20, he became acquainted with discrimination and the mild anti-Semitism existing in certain sections of America. These experiences made a deep impression on his sensitive, poetic soul.

In the years 1911-1919, Lewisohn taught German at the Universities of Wisconsin and Ohio State. When German became an unpopular language during World War I, Lewisohn turned to the writing of critical essays on literature and the theatre. He contributed chiefly to *The Nation*, famous liberal weekly.

For about a decade (1924-1934), Lewisohn lived in Paris where he wrote several novels and critical works. Since his return to America in 1934, he has become the great champion and exponent of Zionism. His novels, *The Island Within, Last Days of Shylock, Renegade, Breathe Upon These* and *The Romantic* are permeated with the passionate conviction that the modern Jew, to be wholesome and happy, must affirm his faith, and live deeply and richly as a Jew. In his essays, *Israel, Upstream* and *Mid-Channel*, he depicts masterfully the problems of modern Jewish life in the Twentieth Century. His critical works, such as *Creative Expression in America* and *History of American Literature* have earned Lewisohn a permanent place in American literature. His translations from Hauptmann, Wasserman, Werfel and others helped bring to the American reading public the

best in modern German literature. His Zionist anthology *Rebirth*
ranks as a classic in the field. His novels of American life, *Stephen
Escott, The Case of Mr. Crump, The Golden Vase* and others have
placed him in the forefront of American literature.

His brilliant pen is now at the service of the Zionist ideal and the
upbuilding of Palestine as a Jewish National Homeland. He is the
editor of the *New Palestine*, the publication of the Zionist Organization of America. He is a regular contributor to Jewish magazines and
is also well known as a lecturer and speaker on Jewish and literary
subjects. He has addressed numerous audiences from the platforms
of Jewish and non-Jewish institutions. Lewisohn is one of the leading
Zionists of the present day and is wholly consecrated to the service
of his people.

MENDELE MOKHER SEFARIM: Mendele was the first part of a pen name
which in full was known to all of Russian Jewry as Mendele Mokher
Sefarim (Mendele the Bookseller). His real name was Shalom Jacob
Abramovitsch (b. Lithuania, about 1836; d. Odessa, Russia, 1917).

The childhood and youth of Mendele were spent like most of his
contemporaries. He attended *heder* and continued his studies in various *yeshivot*. At the age of 17, however, he took to vagabonding with
a hobo band. His experiences during these wandering years are described in *Fishke the Lame* and in certain other works.

At the age of 20, Mendele obtained a position as Hebrew teacher.
Thereafter, much of his life was spent in the field of Jewish education,
as teacher and author. From 1881 to the end of his life he was principal of the celebrated Talmud Torah of Odessa. In this capacity he
played a significant role in the development of modern Hebrew
education. Indeed, his literary career began with a Hebrew essay on
Jewish education. When in 1864, he entered the literary world, he
took a bold step by writing in Yiddish, then disparaged as a jargon
fit only for the kitchen and market place. He chose this medium
because he felt that in Yiddish he could make his creations real and
because of its popular appeal. The works which followed portrayed
realistically and sympathetically the unworldliness and the pathetic
idealism of the Russian ghetto. He became its exponent and its most
eloquent interpreter.

After the Zionist Movement and the Hebrew Revival had created a
Hebrew reading public, Mendele began to translate his works into
Hebrew. He also wrote original works in Hebrew which he later
translated into Yiddish. His works in both languages were acclaimed
universally. He freed the Hebrew language from the chains of the

Biblical idiom. He synthesized Mishnaic, Talmudic and medieval Hebrew with classical Biblical Hebrew, and thus created the modern Hebraic style. During his lifetime there gathered around him a school of "spiritual grandchildren." They were the men who made modern Hebrew and Yiddish literature. They called him "*Zeide*" or "Grandfather," a fond title which has become immortalized in both literatures.

MOSENSON, MOSHE: was born in Palestine. He was a member of the immortal Jewish Brigade and emerged from the obscurity of a farmer's life in a small Judaean colony into fame in Eretz Yisrael and in America with his *Letters From the Desert.* They were written to family and friends during the three years of the war. He was one of the 30,000 Palestinians who joined voluntarily and fought bravely on the Mediterranean, Middle Eastern and European fronts from Italy to Abyssinia, from Syria to Tripoli, and from Sicily to Germany.

The story of the exploits and adventures of the Jewish Brigade is yet to be written. Only a fragment of the story has been told by Pierre van Paassen, in *The Forgotten Ally* (Dial Press, 1943). In Mosenson's letters there is an occasional glimpse into the truly magnificent devotion and sacrifice shown by members of the Jewish Brigade to our brethren in the ravaged Jewish communities of North Africa and Europe.

The book, made available by Sharon Books, an organization devoted to the publication of books of Zionist interest, was awarded the Louis LaMed Prize of 1946, a prize given annually to the best books in Hebrew, Yiddish and English.

PERETZ, ISAAC LEIB: (b. Zamosch, Poland, 1852; d. Warsaw, 1915) laid the foundation of modern Yiddish literature and became its central pillar. He was a poet, an essayist and a dramatist. He achieved immortality, however, as a writer of magnificent short stories. He was the creator of Jewish folk and Hasidic tales—literary gems which are unmatched to this day.

Beginning his career in business, in which he was not a success, Peretz turned to the practice of law. He prospered in this profession for ten years until he was compelled to abandon it because the Russian government had turned viciously anti-Semitic. Thereupon he settled in Warsaw where he obtained the position of secretary to the Jewish community. This job gave him some leisure to devote his talents and energies to writing. As an official of the Jewish community, he had opportunities to travel throughout the "pale of Jewish settlement" where he became acquainted first-hand with Jewish life. This information greatly benefited him in his work.

For some 25 years Peretz was the leader of the Warsaw group of Hebrew and Yiddish writers. He taught his disciples how to recreate the Jewish spiritual heritage. He edited libraries of books in Yiddish, books which included literary masterpieces as well as articles in the general and social sciences. He translated his own works from Yiddish into Hebrew and vice versa. His collected writings in Yiddish number 18 volumes while his collected works in Hebrew number 10 volumes.

Peretz was the poet of Hasidism. His style is terse and folksy. Some of his stories are enveloped in mystery, leaving much to the imagination of the reader. All of his works are brief, except for his long narrative poems.

Evidence of his influence on the world of Yiddish letters is the fact that many clubs of Yiddish writers are named after him. The largest of these is the I. L. Peretz Society of New York, which is universally recognized as the most distinguished body of its kind in the world.

Peretz has been translated into many languages. In English there are at least three books (translated by Helena Frank, a non-Jewess who was the first to introduce him to the English reading public, by A. S. Rappoport, and by Solomon Liptzin).

PINSKER, LEO: (b. Tomashov, Poland, 1821; d. Odessa, 1891) was the son of a distinguished Hebrew scholar, and a practicing physician of eminence. He had been active in the Society for the Dissemination of Culture, an organization dedicated to the spreading of assimilation. The pogroms against the Jews, instigated by the Czar during the 80's, led him to a re-evaluation of his former principles. He reversed his point of view and became an advocate of Jewish nationhood.

Interestingly enough, at the outset both Pinsker and Herzl sought a territory for the Jews other than Eretz Yisrael. *Auto-Emancipation,* published in 1882 in German and signed anonymously "A Russian Jew," mentions this fact specifically. Later, however, Pinsker came around to the Zionist ideal and in 1880 organized the *Hovevei Zion* (Lovers of Zion). He was its president until a few years before his death. In this endeavor he was helped especially by Baron Edmond Rothschild of Paris, patron of the early settlers. His *Auto-Emancipation* and his *Hovevei Zion* movement became vital forces in the rebirth of our people.

Auto-Emancipation is a source book of Zionism, a primer whose words and phrases have inspired Zionist ideas and ideals. It was the first forthright call to the Jews to take their fate into their own hands.

It gave new interpretation to Hillel's slogan: "If I do nothing for myself, who will?" Pinsker demanded of his people self-respect, self-aid, and self-determination. Herzl, it is told, said that had he known of Pinsker's *Auto-Emancipation*, he would not have written his book, *Old-New Land*. Both books, however, made distinct contributions. While Herzl's book views the problem from a political and economic angle, Pinsker's book views it from the psychological point of view.

ROSENFELD, MORRIS: (b. State of Suvalk, Russia, 1862; d. New York City, 1923) was the first poet of the toiling Jewish masses and of the sweat-shop. In his lifetime he worked as a diamond cutter in Amsterdam and as a tailor in London and New York. His poems and songs were declaimed and sung in the sweatshops, in the teeming tenements, at workers' meetings on the East Side of New York and in other metro-politan centers. His poetry was simple, direct and unadorned. It was charged with anger and hatred of the ugliness and squalor of the immigrant ghetto.

It was Prof. Leo Wiener of Harvard, early historian of Yiddish literature in America, who made Rosenfeld known to the non-Jewish world. In 1898 he published a translation of Rosenfeld's poems entitled *Songs of the Ghetto*. Acclaimed for his rare talent, Rosenfeld was invited to read his verse at such leading universities as Harvard, Chicago, Wellesley, Radcliffe. He went on a tour of Europe, visiting Cracow, Vienna, Budapest, London, and other large centers. In spite of his popularity and fame, however, he made his living for the greater part of his life as a poor tailor, sickly, embittered, and unhappy. His poetry was translated into many tongues, including the Japanese. His works, which also included essays and biography, were collected and published in many volumes. Many of his poems were set to music by celebrated composers and may be found in numerous songsters.

ROTH, HENRY: (b. Austria, 1906) was brought to New York City as an infant. He was graduated from the College of the City of New York. His first and only novel, *Call It Sleep*, from which this selection is taken, was received with great approval. It bears the marks of auto-biographical material.

SACHS, ABRAHAM S.: (b. Lithuania, 1879; d. Hoboken, N. J., 1931) por-trayed the life of Russian Jewry in his five-volume Yiddish work en-titled *Worlds That Passed*. A condensation of this work has appeared in one volume in English translation. He was editor of Yiddish periodicals and contributed to the Yiddish daily, *Der Tog* (The Day).

SAMPTER, JESSIE: Like Emma Lazarus, Jessie Sampter (b. New York City, 1883; d. Eretz Yisrael, 1939) was originally far removed from Jewish life. Her intense interest in the Bible, however, brought her back to her people. She studied Jewish history and Hebrew literature at Columbia University. When she came under the influence of that mother in Israel and Zion, Henrietta Szold, her life work became clearly defined. With Miss Szold she labored in laying the foundation of Hadassah, the American Women's Zionist Organization. After World War I, she went to Eretz Yisrael where she took active part in relief activities for the Yemenite Jews and later founded, with her own money, a convalescent home in Givat Brenner. All her life she was a semi-invalid, having been afflicted with infantile paralysis in childhood. Jessie Sampter is widely known for her collections of poems, *Around the Year in Rhymes*, *The Emek* and *Brand Plucked From the Fire*; also for her translation of Bialik's poems for children entitled *Far Over the Sea*, and for her articles in Jewish and general periodicals.

SCHECHTER, SOLOMON: (b. Roumania, about 1847; d. New York City, 1915) began his climb to fame as a result of his acquaintance with Claude G. Montefiore. Montefiore, member of an Anglo-Jewish aristocratic family, was a prominent English scholar, and a leader of Liberal Judaism. He met Schechter in Berlin and invited him to come to England as his tutor in Rabbinic literature. Prior to that, Schechter had studied at the Jewish Theological Seminary of Vienna and the University of Vienna.

In England, Solomon Schechter wrote a series of essays, explaining and clarifying traditional Judaism to the English-speaking world. His writings have been collected in many books, the most famous being *Studies in Judaism* (First, Second and Third Series), *Aspects of Jewish Theology* and others.

Schechter achieved world fame by discovering a veritable treasure of some 100,000 ancient, valuable Hebrew manuscripts in old Cairo. The thrilling story of the discovery of the *Genizah*, told by Norman Bentwich in his interesting biography of Schechter, is well worth reading by young and old. This collection has given stimulus to many studies in Jewish history, philosophy and literature. It will take many years before it becomes fully available in printed form.

Schechter, who was teaching at Cambridge at the time, was invited, in 1902, to become the president of the reorganized Jewish Theological Seminary of America. In this new role, he left a permanent imprint on American Jewish life by the influence which he exerted through the Seminary, the United Synagogue and its affiliated organizations.

To this day, the Jewish Theological Seminary is frequently referred to as "Schechter's Seminary."

SCHNEOUR, ZALMAN: When one mentions the name Bialik two other names follow by association, Tschernikhowski and Schneour (b. Shklov, Russia, 1887). These three are the triumvirate of "poets laureate" in modern Hebrew. Of the three, only Schneour is still living. He now resides in New York City, to which he fled from Paris when the Nazis invaded France.

Schneour was reared in a Hasidic family which traced its descent from Rabbi Schneour Zalman of Ladi. At the tender age of thirteen he ran away from home. His wanderings led him to Odessa where he was influenced by Mendele and Bialik, thence to Warsaw where he came under the spell of Peretz and Frischman. Later he lived in Vilna which he immortalized in a memorable Hebrew poem; then in Switzerland where he wrote stirring lyrics about the Swiss mountains. From Switzerland he went to Paris where he lived until World War II, and from there to New York.

Schneour was a child prodigy. He began his literary efforts at a very young age. From those early years to the present he has worked continually, producing a rich library which would fill thirty or more volumes. He has written poetry, novels, short stories, children's poems, critical essays and memoirs in both Hebrew and Yiddish. His works have been translated into English, French and other languages. His English translations include *Noah Pandre, Noah Pandre's Village, Rabbi and Emperor* (an heroic novel of the Napoleonic era), and others.

Schneour was once characterized by Bialik as the Samson of Hebrew poetry. Himself virile and strong, he admires power and physical courage. He sings of the brave Jews of old, of discontent and rebellion, of heroic deeds and daring, of revenge and retaliation. He has painstakingly brought to life the picturesque world of Shklov, with its precious Uncle Jama and Uncle Uri, dear Aunt Feiga, earthy Noah Pandre (who is the John Bunyan of Eastern European Jewry), and many other memorable characters.

SCHWARTZ, DELMORE: (b. Brooklyn, 1914) was educated at the Universities of Columbia, Wisconsin, Harvard, etc. He has written verse, fiction, plays and dramatic poetry, and was awarded the Guggenheim Fellowship in 1940. He now teaches English at Harvard.

SCHWARTZ, I. J.: (b. Lithuania, 1885) is the son of a Rabbi and was raised in a very strict, Orthodox, traditional home. A translation of one of Bialik's poems marked his debut in the field of literature. Although he has written several notable original works, he is best known as the translator of Bialik, Yehudah Halevi, Ibn Gabirol and other Hebrew poets, into Yiddish. He has also translated from John Milton, Walt Whitman and Shakespeare. In 1918, while living in Lexington, Kentucky, he began writing "Kentucky," the first American epic poem in Yiddish. The poem unfolds the magnificent chapter of Jewish pioneering in America. It describes the genius of the Jew in adjusting himself to, and striking roots in, his new environment. It gives a splendid insight into the trials, tribulations and ultimate success of many Jewish families whose names now adorn the Main Streets of the far-flung villages and towns of this country. Schwartz has recently translated this poem into Hebrew and has published it through Am Oved, the great Labor Zionist publication house of Eretz.

SENESCH, HANNAH: (b. Budapest, 1921; d. Budapest, 1944) is already an heroic legend in Jewish history. A daughter of a well-to-do Hungarian family, she left kith and kin to become a *halutzah* in Eretz. During the war she volunteered to join the European underground. She was parachuted into Hungary, was caught, tortured and executed by the Nazis. Her life and work have become known to the Jewish people the world over. She has joined the immortal ranks of the revered martyrs of Israel.

SHALOM ALEIKHEM: the pen name of Shalom Rabinowitch (b. Province of Poltava, Russia, 1859; d. New York City, 1916), was the greatest Yiddish humorist of modern times. In America he has often been called the Jewish Mark Twain. With Mendele and Peretz, he is one of the three "Fathers" of Yiddish literature.

Shalom Aleikhem was editor of periodicals and founder of publishing houses, in which capacities he stimulated and encouraged many men of letters. In 1906 he visited America where he was received with universal affection. On returning to Europe, he became ill with tuberculosis. But neither illness nor pain could keep Shalom Aleikhem from his pen. During World War I he settled in New York where he resided until his death shortly afterwards.

Shalom Aleikhem began his literary work both in Hebrew and in Yiddish, but later chose Yiddish as his chief medium. Yiddish was looked upon by many as a jargon but he soon raised it to a high literary level.

No other Yiddish writer has been so fondly regarded as Shalom Aleikhem. If love begets love, Shalom Aleikhem richly deserved the popular affection of his people. For, like Levi Yitzhak of old, he loved his people with a surpassing love. To Jewish children Shalom Aleikhem endeared himself because he was the first to write many delightful juvenile tales. His stories (translated into English and other languages) are as beloved today as they were when they first appeared.

Like Mendele, whose literary "grandchild" he considered himself to be, Shalom Aleikhem recreated the inner world of Eastern European Jewry at the turn of the century. He painted Kasrielevky, the typical town of the Jewish "pale," and Yehupitz and Boyberik, the Jewries of the large metropolitan centers. His Menahem Mendel, day-dreaming and quixotic; Tevyeh, the dairyman, run-of-the-mill Jew; Mottel Peisi's, the cantor's son—all live before our eyes. He even invested the domestic animals with specific Jewish characteristics.

Acclaimed universally by the Jewish world and by great non-Jewish writers like Tolstoy and Gorky, Shalom Aleikhem, in his day, was the most successful of Yiddish writers. His output of novels, short stories, plays and essays was amazing. His Yiddish works have appeared in several editions. And his Yiddish plays—some were filmed for the movies—still attract enthusiastic audiences. His work has been translated into many languages, including Japanese and Esperanto. In the Russian translations alone 3,000,000 copies of Shalom Aleikhem's books were sold in the twenty-five years between 1917 and 1942. It is our good fortune that I. D. Berkowitz, his admiring and devoted son-in-law, himself a Hebrew writer of great prominence, has brought Shalom Aleikhem intact into the treasure house of Hebrew literature by a masterful translation of his father-in-law's works. The love and warm admiration which Shalom Aleikhem has evoked may be seen, in some measure, in Maurice Samuel's captivating, homage-paying book entitled *The World of Sholom Aleichem* (Knopf, 1943).

SHIMONOWITZ, DAVID: (b. Bobruisk, Russia, 1886) is one of the leading poets of Eretz. His early years were spent in Russia where he lived through the first World War and the horrors which followed in its wake. He began to write at the early age of fifteen and has made immortal contributions to Hebrew poetry. Especially is he known for his idylls of Palestinian life such as "In the Woods of Hederah," "The Conflict Between Judah and Galilee," "The Jubilee of the Coach Drivers," "On the Road," "Gleanings," "From the Legends of Safed," etc., in which he portrays masterfully the heroism of the *Yishuv*, the epic of its early pioneering days and the pathos and humor of its life. He has also translated some Russian classics. Like Brenner, Shimonowitz spent his early period as a *shomer* (watchman) and as a laborer in vineyard and farm. Like many of his prominent colleagues, Shimon-owitz earns his living by teaching. He has been serving with distinction on the staff of the Herzliah Secondary School in Tel Aviv.

SINGER, ISRAEL JOSHUA: (b. Poland, 1893; d. New York City, 1944) achieved prominence in Yiddish literature through *The Brothers Ashkenazi* and the drama, *Yoshe Kalb*. The latter was published in English as *The Sinners*. Other books of his in English are *The River Breaks Up*, a volume of short stories, and *East of Eden*, a novel of post-war Poland and the early years of Soviet Russia. His works have been translated into several languages, including Spanish and Swedish.

Fleeing before Hitler, Singer came to America in 1939. He was a regular contributor to the *Jewish Daily Forward*, with which he had been associated for many years as its Warsaw correspondent.

SMILANSKY, MOSHE: Best known as a leader of the Palestinian Jewish agriculturists, Moshe Smilansky (b. near Kiev, Russia, 1874) is the portraitist of the early pioneer settlements of Eretz Yisrael. He is highly qualified to fill this role since he came to Eretz with the first *Aliyah* in 1890 and worked as a farm laborer in the newly founded colonies. During World War I, he was one of the organizers of the Jewish Legion in which he served. He owns vineyards and orange groves at Rehovot, where he now resides.

An authority on Palestine agriculture, Smilansky is famed for his essays, novels, short stories and historical memoirs of the early settlers. But he does not confine himself to Jewish life alone. He paints Arab life as well—its superstitions, its cunning, its poverty and suffering. "Latifa" is one of his first stories of Arab life and was published as early as 1906.

His collected works in Hebrew number twelve volumes. Among his works which have been translated into English are *The Palestine Caravan* and *Hederah*. The universal esteem in which Smilansky is held is attested to by the fact that his colleagues named a new colony in Eretz after him (Kfar Moshe).

SYRKIN, MARIE: (b. Berne, Switzerland, 1900) is the daughter of Nahman Syrkin, one of the founders of the Poale Zion (Labor Zionist) movement. She is a teacher of English in the New York City high schools and active in the Labor Zionist movement. She contributes to the *Jewish Frontier* of which she is associate editor, and to other leading Jewish and general periodicals. She is author of a widely known book on general education entitled *Your Children, Your Schools*, and has translated into English many Hebrew and Yiddish poems.

SZOLD, HENRIETTA: mother in Israel and Zion, founder of Hadassah and of Youth *Aliyah*, Henrietta Szold (b. Baltimore, 1860; d. Eretz, 1945) was the daughter of scholarly Rabbi Benjamin Szold. She began her noble career of service to her people by teaching night classes for the newly arrived immigrants from Russia. From 1892 to 1916 she served as secretary, translator and editor of the Jewish Publication Society. It was during this period that she translated Ginzberg's *Legends of the Jews* and other important works.

But Henrietta Szold will be best remembered for her Zionist work. She founded Hadassah, now one of the largest and most influential Zionist bodies in this country. She directed and influenced its educational and medical program in Eretz and later initiated and guided its Youth *Aliyah* work which rescued over 20,000 Jewish children from the Nazis.

Deep and sincere was the love and regard shown by young and old for this noble woman. In Eretz a colony of her Youth *Aliyah* graduates and a school for nursing were named after her. Honorary degrees and other distinctions were conferred upon her. In 1940 at the Women's Congress she was named one of the 100 outstanding women of the world in the last century. To date her life and work are recorded in two books. One, from which the letters in this book are culled, is by Marvin Lowenthal. The other, intended for young people, is entitled *The Fighting Angel*, and was written by Elma E. Levinger.

TCHERNIKHOWSKY, SAUL: (b. Crimea, Russia, 1875; d. Tel Aviv, 1943) ranked with Hayyim Nahman Bialik and Zalman Schneour as one of the three greatest Hebrew poets of recent times. Tchernikhowsky was a second generation product of the wide, free and windblown steppes of the Crimea. His education was radically different from that of his contemporaries. He knew Russian before he studied Hebrew. He was not brought up in the traditional *heder* and *yeshivah*. While he was not reared in a rigorously observant Jewish environment, Jewish ceremonial life in his home was nevertheless invested with beauty and glamour. He did not study Talmud. But he was deeply rooted in Biblical, Mishnaic and Midrashic Hebrew. All this may explain why Tchernikhowsky was considered the "rebel" in Hebrew literature, why he wrote poems of praise to the Greek god Apollo, the rebel warrior Bar Kokhba, and why he wrote such beautiful idyllic poetry describing the joys of observing *Mitzvot*. It also explains why much of Tchernikhowsky's poetry breathes of the bright outdoors, gay nature and the open world of trees, flowers and birds.

One of the curiosities of Tchernikhowsky's life is that his first poem was printed in a little Hebrew magazine in Baltimore, Maryland. Indeed his associations with America were significant and fruitful. He wrote two truly magnificent translations of Longfellow's "Hiawatha" and "Evangeline." He also translated some of Benjamin Franklin's scientific works into Hebrew.

Tchernikhowsky ended up by becoming a physician. He had studied medicine at Heidelberg, Germany, and Lausanne, Switzerland. Specializing in pediatrics and surgery, he practiced medicine in Finland, Russia (where he served as an army doctor during World War I), and in Palestine where he served as school doctor in the city of Tel Aviv.

Tchernikhowsky loved life and lived zestfully to the full. He wrote stirring poems which inspired the young generation to deeds of heroism and bravery, charming idylls of Jewish home life which conveyed the beauty and meaning of our folkways, poems of wrath on the pogroms against his brothers in the Ukraine during 1919-21, songs on the new life in Zion, etc. Many of his poems were translated into German, Russian, French, Italian, English and other languages.

Tchernikhowsky towered head and shoulders above his contemporaries as a translator of classical Greek, English, German, French and Finnish poetry. Among his most famous works besides those mentioned above, are, *The Odyssey, The Iliad, Twelfth Night, Macbeth.* In addition to Hebrew, he was completely at home in the ancient classical languages as well as French, English, Russian, German and other tongues.

He made a notable contribution to the Hebrew language by coining new words and terms in the fields of anatomy, botany, biology and other sciences. He participated in the creation of Hebrew dictionaries and vocabularies in these fields.

WEINSTEIN, JACOB J.: (b. Poland, 1903) came to America in 1908. He was for a time director of Jewish youth activities on the campuses of the Universities of Texas and Columbia. He is now the Rabbi of the K. A. M. Congregation in Chicago and is a member of the editorial boards of widely read Anglo-Jewish periodicals.

WEIZMANN, CHAIM: (b. near Minsk, Russia, 1874), successor to Herzl's mantle of leadership in world Zionism, is a statesman and a scientist. Side by side with his traditional Hebrew education, he was trained in technical schools in Russia, Germany and Switzerland. A distinguished bio-chemist, he achieved universal fame as a discoverer of important chemical processes. At the age of 30, he was invited to teach at the

University of Manchester. In 1916 he joined the services of the British Admiralty as an expert in chemistry.

Weizmann was a Zionist from birth. He breathed the Zionist atmosphere from childhood. As a student he helped Herzl call the first World Zionist Congress at Basle. At the Congress, he led a group that stressed the importance of the cultural content in Zionism.

During a critical period in World War I, he discovered a chemical formula which was of importance in the manufacture of explosives and greatly aided the war effort of the Allies. When asked what he desired as a reward, he answered, "For myself nothing, but something for my people." The Balfour Declaration was to a large extent a direct result of his efforts.

Weizmann has represented the Jewish cause before the statesmen and the councils of nations. Since 1917 he has been the leader of World Zionism, and from 1921 to 1946 the president of the World Zionist Organization and of the Jewish Agency which he founded. He has traveled on behalf of Zionist causes all over the world. His Zionist addresses reflect a personality that is saturated with Jewish learning, tradition and ideals, and at the same time steeped in the finest liberal democratic tradition of Western civilization. Four volumes of his addresses have been published in Hebrew.

A great laboratory has been established in Weizmann's honor at Rehovot, a laboratory which is the center of chemical research in Eretz. Out of it have come significant discoveries which are revolutionizing the life of the Middle East.

The love and respect of our people for Weizmann was demonstrated when, after the declaration of the State of Israel on May 14, 1948, he was elected unanimously as the first president of the Provisional Government of Israel.

The selection presented in this book contains excerpts of an address delivered on the occasion of the laying of the cornerstone of the Hebrew University in Jerusalem while the Allied and Turkish armies were still locked in battle.

ZANGWILL, ISRAEL: During his lifetime, Israel Zangwill (b. London, 1864; d. Sussex, England, 1926) was the leading figure in Anglo-Jewish literature. His works have earned for him a permanent place in English literature and have endeared him particularly to the Anglo-Jewish world.

He obtained his schooling in the London Jews' Free School and later at London University. At first Zangwill was not a writer of Jewish themes. However, at the invitation of Mayer Sulzberger, then president of the Jewish Publication Society, Zangwill wrote *Children of the Ghetto*, depicting the crowded East End Jewry of London. It was immediately acclaimed as a great success. There followed in succession *Ghetto Tragedies*, *King of the Schnorrers*, *Dreamers of the Ghetto*, *The Melting Pot* and *The Voice of Jerusalem*. He wrote essays, translations (Ibn Gabirol's poems and other sacred poetry which have been included in the *Mahzor*) and lectured far and wide in England and America.

Meeting Herzl in London in 1896, Zangwill threw himself into Zionist activity and became one of the leaders of world Zionism. In 1905, however, he broke with the organization because it refused the British offer of Uganda as a Jewish homeland. He founded and headed the Jewish Territorial Organization which advocated the settlement of Jews in lands other than Palestine.

At least one of Zangwill's plays, *Merely Mary Ann*, was filmed and shown to the American cinema audience. His general works are numerous. They include *Italian Fantasies*, *We Moderns*, *The Mantle of Elijah*, *Blind Children* and others.

NOTES TO PART I

1. In *1881-82* the Russian pogroms broke out and started a huge wave of immigration to the United States.
2. *Rebbi*—Head of Hasidic group. See *Tzadik*, Note 7.
3. *Selihot*—Penitential prayers, popularly known as "The Midnight Penitential Prayers" recited beginning with Saturday midnight before *Rosh Hashanah*.
4. *Mitnaged*—Opponent of the Hasidic movement (which began in the middle of the 18th Century).
5. *Litvak*—One who lived in, or originated from, Lithuania.
6. *Shamash*—Sexton or beadle.
7. *Tzadik*—Literally, righteous one; another title for *Rebbi*; a wonder-worker and intermediary between man and God.
8. Translated by Azriel Eisenberg.
9. *Dayan*—Literally, judge; assistant to the rabbi; officer of the Jewish community in certain countries of Europe.
10. *Hymn of Unity*—A prayer in praise of God recited at the end of the service.
11. *Gass*—Literally, street. The Jewish quarter of a European town.
12. *Musaf*—Additional Service to the regular morning service on Sabbaths and holidays recited because on these days additional sacrifices were brought in the Temple.
13. Frank, Helena, *Yiddish Tales*, Jewish Publication Society, 1938, pp. 270-277.
14. *Pious Sarah*—An anonymous author of prayers for women.
15. *Breaking Plates*—Breaking plates capped the engagement ceremony. Like breaking the glass at the conclusion of the wedding ceremony, it was to remind us of the destruction of the Temple.
16. Mendele Mokher Sefarim, *Fishke the Lame* (trans. by Angelo S. Rappoport), Stanley Paul and Co., London, 1928, pp. 33-35.
17. *Matmid*—Diligent *Yeshivah* student.
18. *Oi, amar Rabba tanu rabbanan*—"Rabbi said, 'Our Rabbis taught' "—a phrase oft repeated in the Talmud.
19. Bialik, Hayim Nahman, "The *Matmid*" (trans. by Maurice Samuel) in *New Palestine*, February, 1926.

20. *Shklov*—Well-known Jewish center situated on the right bank of the River Dnieper. Its population was 80% Jewish.
21. *Kopek*—Russian penny.
22. *Gemara*—Aramaic section of the Talmud which constitutes the explanation of the Mishnah; another name for Talmud.
23. Leftwich, Joseph, *Yisroel* (trans. by Hannah Berman), James Clarke & Co. Ltd., London, Revised 1945, pp. 604-11.
24. *Jews of Morocco*—Like many a Moslem country where anti-Jewish outbreaks occurred frequently, Morocco was often in the Jewish news.
25. Reprinted from *Jewish Children* by Sholom Aleichem (trans. by Hannah Berman), Alfred A. Knopf, Inc., 1922, pp. 79-88.
26. *Balut*—A section of Lodz where the weaving factories were located.
27. Reprinted from *The Brothers Ashkenazi* by I. J. Singer (trans. by Maurice Samuel), Alfred A. Knopf, Inc., 1936.
28. Levin, Shemarya, *Childhood in Exile* (trans. by Maurice Samuel), Harcourt, Brace, 1929, pp. 47-51.
29. *Etape*—A halting place for troops on the march, also a day's march.
30. *Dishes in oven*—It was a custom to put away the Sabbath meal in sealed pots in the communal oven to keep hot over the Sabbath.
31. Sachs, A. S., *Worlds That Passed* (trans. by Harold Berman), Jewish Publication Society, 1928, pp. 95-98.
32. *Tana*—Title of Talmudic rabbis who lived during the first two centuries of the common era between the days of Hillel and Judah Hanasi.
33. *Avot*—A section of the Mishnah popularly known as the *Ethics of the Fathers* which is traditionally recited or studied on Sabbath afternoons during the spring and summer months.
34. Fineman, Irving, *Hear, Ye Sons*, Random House, 1939, pp. 210 ff.

NOTES TO PART II

1. Bentwich, Norman, *Solomon Schechter,* Quoted in East and West Library, London, 1947, pp. 149-150.
2. Kobrin, Leon, *A Lithuanian Village* (trans. by Isaac Goldberg), Brentano, New York, 1920, pp. 168-173.
3. Cahan, Abraham, *The Rise of David Levinsky,* Harper & Bros., New York, 1917, pp. 93-97.
4. Leftwich, Joseph, *The Golden Peacock,* Sci-Art Publishers, Cambridge, Mass., 1939, pp. 141-142.
5. Translated from the Yiddish by Nathaniel Whiteman.
6. Cohen, Hyman & Lester, *Aaron Traum,* Horace Liveright, New York, 1930, pp. 139-141, 158-160.
7. Roth, Henry, *Call It Sleep,* Robert O. Ballou, New York, 1934, Book III, Chap. III.
8. Raskin, Philip M., *Anthology of Modern Jewish Poetry,* Behrman's Jewish Book House, New York, 1927, p. 73.
9. Kreymborg, Alfred, *Poetic Drama,* Modern Age Books, New York, 1941, pp. 846-847.
10. Lewisohn, Ludwig, *The Island Within,* Harper & Bros., New York, 1928, pp. 273 ff.
11. Ferber, Edna, *A Peculiar Treasure,* Doubleday Doran, New York, 1939, pp. 40-44.
12. *Modeh Ani*—"I give thanks to the Lord for bringing back my soul to me." These are the first words of the traditional Hebrew morning prayer for children.
13. Klein, Abraham M., *Hath Not the Jew,* Behrman's Jewish Book House, New York, 1940, pp. 74, 80.
14. Grindell, E., in *The Reconstructionist,* Vol. VII, No. 5 (April 17, 1942), New York.

NOTES TO PART III

1. *Leopold Zunz* (1794-1886)—German Jewish scholar and founder of Jewish Science, a scholarly movement whose aim it was to make known the history and literature of the Jewish people through the medium of critical study.

2. *Dreyfus Case*—A famous case involving a false charge of treason against Alfred Dreyfus (1859-1935), a Jewish officer in the French army.

3. *Warsaw Ghetto*—The historical facts about the magnitude and heroism of the resistance of the Jewish Fighter Organization in the Warsaw Ghetto and their final horrible end, became known after the war. The liquidation of the Ghetto began on July 22, 1942, when the Germans demanded from the Jewish Council 6,000 to 10,000 Jewish souls for deportation to the East Polish murder camps of Treblinka, Maidanick, and others. The revolt in the Ghetto began on April 19, 1943. Although the Germans out-numbered the starved and sick Jews, both in numbers and arms, the Jews at first achieved comparatively brilliant victories. The Germans finally bombed and set fire to the Ghetto. For five weeks the unequal bloody struggle continued. In this battle, the Germans outdid themselves in bestiality and cowardice.

4. For Hannah Senesch see "Biographies." *Enzo Sereni* (1907-1944) was the son of a prominent Italian Jewish family. He settled in Eretz and became an outstanding labor leader. He was killed by the Nazis after parachuting into Italy and joining the Underground.

5. Syrkin, Marie, *Blessed Is the Match*, Jewish Publication Society, 1947, pp. 3-4.

6. Reprinted from *The Brothers Ashkenazi* by I. J. Singer (trans. by Maurice Samuel), Alfred A. Knopf, Inc., 1936.

7. Katz, H. W., *No. 21 Castle Street* (trans. by Norbert Guterman), The Viking Press, 1940, pp. 121-24.

8. *April 1, 1933*—Boycott Day against the Jews in Nazi Germany. The day which marked the beginning of the European Jewish tragedy.

9. Feuchtwanger, Lion, *The Oppermans* (trans. by James Cleugh), The Viking Press, 1934, pp. 258-262.

10. *Beth Jacob*—A system of Orthodox schools for girls in Poland, which attracted an enrollment of tens of thousands before the war.

11. *Neilah*—Closing service on *Yom Kippur*.
12. "Letter of the Ninety-three Maidens" (trans. by Bertha Badt Strauss) in *The Reconstructionist*, March 5, 1943.
13. *Hatzot*—Prayer of mourning for the destruction of the Temple, recited at midnight or early morning hours.
14. *"Life Certificates"*—Yellow cards distributed by the Nazis among those chosen for the Labor Battalions or for other work useful to the Nazis. The holders of such cards believed themselves to be temporarily safe from deportation to the extermination centers and therefore called these cards "Life Certificates."
15. Dworzecki, Mark, "Confessions of a Survivor," in *Jewish Frontier*, October, 1945.
16. *High Holiday Prayer Book* (trans. by Morris Silverman), Hartford, 1939, p. 287.
17. Syrkin, Marie, *Blessed Is the Match*, Jewish Publication Society, 1947, pp. 65-70.
18. *The Reconstructionist*, Oct. 20, 1946 (trans. by Amelia Levy).
19. "Beautiful . . . ground"—Remark made by young Mussolini, who was an aviator, on returning from a bombing expedition in Ethiopia.
20. Mazzini, Guiseppe (1805-1872)—An Italian revolutionary and patriot who rallied his people around the banner of Liberty, Equality and Humanity.
21. "Amos on Times Square" in *The Reconstructionist*, Vol. 8, No. 11.

NOTES TO PART IV

1. *Biluim*—The initials of the Hebrew phrase in Isaiah 2, 5—*Bet Yaakov, Lekhu, Venelkha*—"House of Jacob let us go"; the first Russian Jewish pioneer group to settle in Eretz in the 80's.
2. *Matmid*—A diligent student. One who spent most of his youth studying in the *Yeshivah* or by himself in the *Bet Ha-Midrash*.
3. *Moses Hess* (1812-1875)—A contemporary of Karl Marx, the European Socialist leader; Author of *Rome and Jerusalem*, a Zionist classic; and one of the forerunners of modern Political Zionism.
4. *Peretz Smolenskin* (1842-1885)—Editor of *Ha-Shahar* (The Dawn). Author of *Am Olam* (Eternal People). Pioneer of the modern Hebrew Revival, and forerunner of Political Zionism.
5. *Aliyah*—Literally, "ascension." Used to denote an immigration wave to Eretz Yisrael.
6. *Kishinef Pogrom*—Massacre of Jews in Kishinef, a town near East Roumania, which was inspired by the Russian government on April 19-20, 1903.
7. *Havlagah*—Self-restraint. Symbol of the policy adopted during the Arab undeclared war against the Jews (1936-1939) when the *Yishuv* retaliated only against the guilty and did not shed the blood of the innocent.
8. *Ha'apalah*—The so-called "illegal" or unauthorized immigration to Eretz on boats manned by the Haganah.
9. *Sabbath and Festival Prayer Book* (trans. by Morris Silverman), The Rabbinical Assembly and The United Synagogue of America, 1946, p. 325.
10. *Memento Mori*—Warning to be prepared for death.
11. *Coup-de-grace*—A final stroke of mercy by which the executioner ends the life of the condemned.
12. *Pinsker, Leo, Auto-Emancipation* (trans. by D. S. Blondheim), Zionist Organization of America, 1944.
13. *Baron de Hirsch, Maurice* (1831-1896)—Fabulously wealthy French Jew who organized the Jewish Colonization Association (ICA) and contributed tens of millions of dollars to enable Jews to settle as agriculturists in Argentine and elsewhere, including the United States.

14. *Shnorrer*—One who begs alms.
15. *Leopoldstadt*—Jewish quarter in Vienna.
16. *Basle*—City in Switzerland where the first Zionist Congress was held in 1897, under the leadership of Herzl.
17. "Excerpts from Theodor Herzl's Diaries" (trans. by Maurice Samuel) in *New Palestine,* 1929.
18. Ginzberg, Asher, "Pinsker and His Brochure" (trans. by Henrietta Szold), Federation of American Zionists, New York, 1911.
19. Levensohn, Lotta, *Hashomer, The First Jewish Watch in Palestine,* Vaad Bitachon, Zionist Organization of America, 1939, pp. 24-29.
20. *Lens Polisher of Amsterdam*—Baruch Spinoza (1632-1677), Jewish philosopher of immortal fame; one of the greatest minds the world has known. His profession was polishing lenses.
21. Weizmann, Chaim, "The Hebrew University" in *The Brandeis Avukah Annual* (edited by Joseph Shalom Shubow), New York, 1932, pp. 423-428.
22. Gordon, A. D., "On Labor" in *The Brandeis Avukah Annual* (edited by Joseph Shalom Shubow and trans. by Haim Arlasaroff), New York, 1932, pp. 125-132.
23. *Kishon*—Stream in the Valley of Jezreel. It figures in the story of Deborah (Judges 4, 7) and of Elijah (I Kings 18, 40).
24. Levin, Meyer, *Yehuda,* Jonathan Cape and Harrison Smith, New York, 1931, pp. 343-349.
25. Sampter, Jessie, *The Emek,* Bloch, 1927, pp. 23-26.
26. Smilansky, Moshe, *Palestine Caravan* (trans. by I. M. Lask), Methuen and Co., London, 1943, pp. 265-271.
27. Brenner, Joseph Hayim, "We Are Brothers" in *Hashomer Hatzair,* Dec., 1940, pp. 22-23.
28. Lowenthal, Marvin, *Henrietta Szold, Life and Letters,* The Viking Press, 1942, pp. 265-66.
29. Mosenson, Moshe, *Letters From the Desert* (trans. by Hilda Auerbach), Sharon Books, New York, 1945, pp. 29-32.
30. Syrkin, Marie, *Blessed Is the Match,* Jewish Publication Society, 1947, pp. 345-47.
31. Ibid., p. 348.
32. *Shekhinah*—Glory of God, or presence of God; sometimes used as synonym for God.
33. Lamdan, Itzhak, *"Gevurat Yisrael"* in *Hashomer.Hatzair,* n.d.
34. *Jewish Frontier,* June, 1939.

NOTES TO PART V

1. *Lunel*—Town in Southern France where several famous sages lived, one of whom was Samuel Ibn Tibbon who translated Maimonides' *Guide for the Perplexed* from Arabic to Hebrew.
2. *Noblesse Oblige*—Nobility of birth makes obligatory nobility of conduct.
3. *Brandeis on Zionism, A Collection of Addresses and Statements* by Louis D. Brandeis, Zionist Organization of America, 1942, pp. 40-42.
4. Goldman, Solomon, "The Function of the Rabbi" in *Crisis and Decision*, Harper and Bros., New York, 1938, pp. 95-98.
5. Friedlaender, Israel, *Past and Present*, Ark Publishing Co., Cincinnati, 1919, pp. 274-278.
6. *Reform Synods*—Various meetings called by the early Reform Movement in Germany to make changes and to introduce innovations in the prayerbook, Jewish religious practices and ritual.
7. Friedman, Theodore (ed.), *What Is Conservative Judaism*, National Academy for Adult Jewish Studies, New York, pp. 44-48.
8. Kaplan, Mordecai M., *Judaism in Transition*, Behrman's Jewish Book House, New York, 1941, pp. 301-306.
9. *Carmel*—Mountain on the seacoast of Eretz near Haifa. (See story about Elijah at Carmel in I Kings 18.)
10. *Sharon*—Beautiful and fruitful plain on seacoast of Eretz, running for 40 miles from Mt. Carmel to Jaffa.
11. *Sabbath and Festival Prayer Book* (edited by Morris Silverman), Rabbinical Assembly and United Synagogue of America, 1946, pp. 283-286.
12. Fleg, Edmond, *The Jewish Anthology* (trans. by Maurice Samuel), Behrman's Jewish Book House, New York, 1925, pp. 354-355.

UNITED SYNAGOGUE COMMISSION ON JEWISH EDUCATION

Azriel Eisenberg
Chairman

Arthur H. Neulander
Vice-Chairman

Josiah Derby
Secretary

Max Arzt

Moshe Davis

Judith Eisenstein

Henry R. Goldberg

Morris S. Goodblatt

Simon Greenberg

Jacob B. Grossman

A. Hillel Henkin

Leo L. Honor

Ario S. Hyams

Louis L. Kaplan

Maurice Kliers

Alter F. Landesman

Harry O. H. Levine

Zevi Scharfstein

Samuel Sussman

Albert I. Gordon, *Executive Director*
UNITED SYNAGOGUE OF AMERICA

Abraham E. Millgram, *Educational Director*
UNITED SYNAGOGUE OF AMERICA

—o—

Committee on Textbook Publications
Arthur H. Neulander, *Chairman*

Josiah Derby

Ira Eisenstein

Solomon Grayzel

Eugene Kohn

Leon Lang

Isidore Meyer

Abraham E. Millgram

Simon Noveck

Louis L. Ruffman